ALSO BY ELLEN M. KOZAK

Every Writer's Guide to Copyright and Publishing Law

From Pen to Print

The Secrets of Getting Published Successfully

Ellen M. Kozak

An Owl Book
Henry Holt and Company • *New York*

Henry Holt and Company, Inc.
Publishers since 1866
115 West 18th Street
New York, New York 10011

Henry Holt® is a registered trademark
of Henry Holt and Company, Inc.

Published in Canada by Fitzhenry & Whiteside Ltd.,
195 Allstate Parkway, Markham, Ontario L3R 4T8.

Library of Congress Cataloging-in-Publication Data
Kozak, Ellen M.
From pen to print / Ellen M. Kozak.—1st ed.
     p.   cm.
1. Authorship.   I. Title.
PN153.K68   1990
808'.02—dc20   89-48878
                                                             CIP

ISBN 0-8050-1013-0
ISBN 0-8050-1646-5 (An Owl Book: pbk.)

Henry Holt books are available for special promotions and
premiums. For details contact: Director, Special Markets.

First published in hardcover in 1990 by Henry Holt
and Company, Inc.

First Edition—1992

Designed by Paula R. Szafranski

Printed in the United States of America
All first editions are printed on acid-free paper.∞

10   9   8   7   6   5   4   3   2   1
10   9   8   7   6   5   pbk.

Information contained in this book may not apply to cases
involving specific individuals. Readers are advised that no priv-
ity of contract is created between the author of this work and
any reader or purchaser, and the author makes no representa-
tions as to the applicability of any information contained herein
to the circumstances of any reader or purchaser.

This book is dedicated to the memory of my grandmother

ROSE ALBERT KOZAK

who always believed I would be a writer.

And to the memory of two women writers who were my role models, and who died too young: Dickey Chapelle and Judith Wax.

Acknowledgments

One doesn't produce a book this size and this detailed without a lot of help and moral support. The following people provided encouragement and assistance for which I would like to extend my heartfelt thanks: my parents, Gert and Sid Kozak, progenitors of a verbal clan; my brother, Warren Kozak, and my sister, Carla Kozak; and my sister, June Kozak Kane, who raced neck and neck with me to complete *her* book on teenagers and fad diets almost simultaneously with my completion of this opus.

My secretary, Barbara Riedel, was there when I needed her, despite, among other things, having to deal with sequential bouts of chicken pox at home. I would also like to thank all those people mentioned by name in the text of this book for the inspiration, information, and examples they provided, and I am especially grateful to the Hon. Margaret Dee McGarity, Professor Ramon Klitzke, and Gail Miles for their review of various portions of the manuscript and their helpful suggestions.

Thanks also to my agent, Sharon Jarvis, and to her assistant, Joan Winston, for their encouragement, and to Tracy Bernstein for being one terrific editor (and for laughing at my jokes). Additional thanks for their various contributions go to Karen Case, Marzetta Doss, Alice Kehoe, Diana Rich Segal, Carol Walkowiak, and the Authors Guild— and a special acknowledgment to Gremlin II, for hanging in there.

—*Ellen M. Kozak*

Milwaukee, Wisconsin
October 1989

Contents

From Pen to Print

1

So You Want to Be a Writer

You've been scribbling in the margins of magazines, on odd scraps of paper, in notebooks and in journals since you learned how to write.

Everyone tells you that your writing is wonderful, and should be published.

You've looked at the latest crop of paperbacks and decided, "I can do better than that!"

Maybe you can. But how do the words get from your notebooks into newspapers, magazines, or bookstores?

And, once they do, will that make you a *writer*?

If writing is your dream, will you be able to quit your job and make your living pushing a pencil? And is that an end result you really want?

This book is designed to answer these questions for you, to uncover the secrets of breaking into print while helping you preserve your rights and your sanity. It will reveal some of the joys to be garnered from putting your thoughts into print—and some of the frustrations every writer encounters.

Do you want to be a writer? The first thing to ask yourself is, what kind of writer do you want to be? Do you want to write merely to please yourself, or is it important to you to please others, people like editors, critics, your family, or the public at large? Will you be satisfied to write in your spare time, or do you want to quit your job and earn your living at the (nonmusical) keyboard?

This book is designed to help you answer these questions for yourself by revealing some of the secrets of breaking into print and protecting your rights in your work. It's the book I wish someone had given me when *I* decided to become a writer, so I wouldn't have wasted so much time living up to other people's expectations of what a writer was. A great deal of the *joy* of being a writer is defining the job for yourself.

How did I get to be a writer? The path was a circuitous one. I think I was born to put words down on paper, and I can remember the principal praising a story I wrote back in the third grade. I wrote for my junior high school paper, my high school paper and literary magazine, my college paper and literary magazine, even the law school's monthly paper. Along the way, I won a few prizes (the biggest was $50) and a fair amount of praise. But I didn't have the vaguest idea of how to sell a story or an article to a publication if I wasn't a member of the staff.

That doesn't mean I didn't try. I've kept a journal since I was eleven. I'd started dozens of stories and even a few novels and written about fifty poems. Sometimes I'd even submit a story or poem, only to have them fly back in what had to be some of the fastest round trips ever engineered by the U.S. Postal Service.

But most of the time, what I did was scribble ideas, opening lines, and names for characters on little scraps of paper, stashing them in folders that ultimately found their way into a big box in the basement of my parents' home.

I always meant to be a writer, and would have majored in journalism, but the liberal arts college I attended didn't offer a single journalism course, let alone a major. Indeed, the only creative writing class I could get at the time was taught by an essayist who couldn't understand why anyone would want to write the science fiction and horror stories I produced for his class. He told me that once you'd read one of my little skin-crawlies, you knew the others were going to be in the same vein, so they lost their shock value. (It's a good thing Stephen King never met up with a prof like him!)

Unable to figure out how to get into writing and, by then, too discouraged to try, I went to law school and then into private practice, handling mostly divorce cases. Talk about horror stories! After almost ten years of domestic disillusion, I came to the conclusion that there was no way on earth I could spend the rest of my life beseeching judges to throw the book at men who had brought their children home late after visitation. I packed all those folders of all those writing ideas and fragments into a suitcase (a *large* suitcase) and, in the great American pioneer tradition, headed for California and the first unstructured vacation I'd had in years.

I sat in a beachfront motel in San Diego, in a shabby weekly hotel in Hollywood, in a slightly-less-shabby weekly motel in North Hollywood, and finally in the home of friends of my parents in the northern San Fernando Valley, going through those myriad scraps and notes that I had scribbled or scrawled or typed during all those years—and came home with one short story.

It wasn't much work product, but it *was* the first short story I'd finished since that devastating course in college, and the first story I knew was a whole piece, complete in itself, with no loose threads hanging. And the first time I showed it to anyone—a dozen people at a science fiction convention, who passed each manuscript page along to the next person as they finished it—I watched twelve people, one after another, burst into tears.

It was, I think, one of the most gratifying moments of my life. I had always been able to make people laugh, but never before had I been able to make them cry. I still wasn't sure how to make the transition from manuscript to print, but I knew from that moment that I was a writer.

Believing in yourself as a writer is, I think, a large part of making the transition to *being* a writer. But take a closer look at your dream.

- Do you envision yourself sitting in a Paris bistro, romantically scribbling an occasional line of your novel in a notebook between sips of wine?
- Do you think of yourself as Lois Lane, taking crazy risks to get the story no one else can get?
- Do you picture yourself tamping your pipe and holding forth at a cocktail party with amusing little tales of the rich and famous folk you encountered when you went to pick up your Nobel Prize?

Think again. The jazz age is long dead, Superman won't show up to save you, and to get the Nobel Prize for Literature or the Pulitzer Prize, or any other prize at all, *first you have to write the book.*

On the other hand, if your imagination is rich enough to let you envision yourself in those situations, perhaps you *can* write the book that gets you the prize—if not the Nobel, perhaps an honorable mention from your local writers' society.

Unfortunately, even such small rewards can be few and far between. Are *you* willing to put in the time and effort it takes to reach even the qualifying stage? Do you really want to spend long hours hunched over your typewriter or squinting into the monitor of your word processor for the privilege of receiving yet another preprinted note that reads, "Your work does not meet our present needs"?

If, like me, you're one of those people with a closet full of scraps of paper, you're probably *driven* to write. You don't write by choice any more than you breathe by choice. But you may be in the same position I was when I lit out for California—trying to hit your target with a shotgun. You may manage to hit the bull's-eye, but the scattered shot won't leave a very elegant pattern.

Before you can act on your dream to be a writer, you need to figure out what kind of a writer you want to be.

- Do you want to write as the spirit—or the muse—moves you, or are you willing to write on an assigned topic, even if it bores—or worse, offends—you?
- Do you want to take your time with your work, or are you willing to meet tight deadlines if you have to?
- Are you willing to spend long hours researching your facts and polishing your prose, finding that perfect word, only to have an editor delete the sentence in which it appears?
- And are you willing to accept criticism—fair or otherwise—or does it crush or anger you?

Somewhere in the course of your writing career, you will have to come to terms with all of these questions. In the end, how you answer them will determine the kind of writer you become.

If you have been writing for your own amusement, or for community newspapers and club newsletters when you happen to get an idea, it may seem to you that writing is an ideal way to make a living. As someone who *does* make a large portion of her living writing, *I've* always thought the ideal way to earn my daily bread would be tap dancing in a Broadway show or swimming with the whales at Sea World. When I dream of these jobs, I don't think about the hours of dance practice and the disappointment of failed auditions that dancers endure, or the problems swimmers may face in getting into the water on a cold day, or getting out, *any* day, with red eyes and prune-skinned fingers.

Any occupation has its down side, and writing is no exception. All too often, writing is *not* fun. Oh, it's true that it is:

Sexy	Tell people at a cocktail party that you're a published novelist and then just *try* to peel them away—unless they're published novelists themselves!
Emotionally rewarding	Several times over: when you complete a piece to your own satisfaction, when it gets accepted for publication, when you see it in print, when others tell you they've seen it in print (all the better if they've *liked* it!), and when you get paid for it!
Intellectually stimulating	Finding just the right word or phrase to convey just the nuance you want can be exciting!

But it also requires the direct application of the seat of your pants to a chair in front of your typewriter or word processor, whether you want to be there or not—even when the sun is shining, or the fish are biting, or there's new powder on the slopes. It is work without immediate satisfaction—indeed, when the right words don't come, satisfaction can be the most elusive commodity in the world. And rewards from others, in the form of acceptance, praise, or payment, can be even longer in coming.

Ah, yes—the rewards. Samuel Johnson suggested long ago, "No man but a blockhead ever wrote except for money," but if it's money you're after, you'd better be aware, from the start, that writing seldom pays very well. Just as "there's a broken heart for every light on Broadway," there are probably half a dozen rejection slips for every published article, and, more often than not, those published articles result in payment that doesn't even cover the cost of the typing paper.

It *is* possible to earn a reasonable living from certain types of writing. Staff reporters and editors working for established magazines and daily newspapers are generally situated above the poverty line. People who write advertising copy—whether freelance or for agencies—can also do pretty well.

But I'll bet that isn't what *you* had in mind, is it? *You* want to write the Great American Novel, or reform the world, or win an Oscar for best screenplay, right? Or, at least, see your humorous or nostalgic articles in print in the local weekly.

Easier said than done—which brings us to:

Kozak's Rule #1: *If writing is not to become a chore more dismal than dishwashing, not only must you want to write, you must need to write, and you must love to write.*

If you don't fit that description, if you're just in it for the glamor, try the stage or politics. But if you are the kind of person who lives to write, and you want to see your words in print, you've passed the first test. Read on.

2

Going Back to School

You've seen the ads: someone out there is looking for people who want to write. They'll give you an aptitude test, and if you pass, you get to take their mail-order course.

Americans have an obsession with credentials. We believe in "taking classes," citing the courses as proof that we have learned something. Because we tend to doubt the value of any knowledge that we may have acquired outside of the classroom, and because there are a large number of people who want to be writers, there are a large number of writing classes available.

You can take courses by mail. You can join community self-help groups of would-be writers. You can take classes in writing at your local junior college or night school. But will any of those help? Can anyone teach you to be a writer?

That depends on a number of factors, not the least of which is who is teaching the course you want to take. Remember that college professor of mine, who neither read nor understood science fiction and horror writing? He had little appreciation for popular fiction, and I firmly believe that if I'd shown him my novels, ultimately published twenty years later, about the amorous (and pun-filled) adventures of a woman judge in outer space, he would have strongly encouraged me to burn my typewriter.

But his discouragement may have served a purpose he never intended—delaying my career until I was ready for it. At nineteen, though I wrote fairly well, I didn't have all that much to say.

If not having anything to say is your problem, all the writing classes in the world won't help you become a writer. But learning that *that* is your problem is the kind of peripheral knowledge which—as opposed to what you've been taught—proves most valuable in the long run.

Picking up peripheral, rather than direct, knowledge may be a good thing, because literary criticism is ultimately a subjective exercise. Most writing courses are taught by English teachers whose own works are unpublished, or by writers you've never heard of and whose writing you might not like even if you *had*. Whether what they have to tell you will be really valuable to you is debatable.

Few of these instructors teach for the love of it. Many are earning or supplementing their incomes, which may say something about how (financially) successful they are as writers.

If the money is so tight, are they worried that teaching these classes will create more competition for them? Not really. They're banking on something that everyone who teaches a writing course learns early on: most of the people who take creative writing courses don't know the first thing about the English language. As a result, even if they have something to say, or stories to tell, they probably won't ever sell anything.

Frankly, I do not believe anyone can be taught to be a writer. But there are *some* courses that can be very useful to people who already *are* writers. These include classes in:

- grammar (so that you will be able to use words and punctuation —the tools of your trade—correctly).
- literature (to learn what has already been written, and to be aware of the way the best writers have used the language; courses in literature not only show you what has gone before, but can also teach you about plot, structure, characterization, and literary conventions).
- journalism (to learn the rules of this structured profession and gain practice in using news format).
- marketing your writing (to learn how and where to sell what you write).
- script writing (to understand the technical format required).

How do you determine when a course might be useful to you? How can you tell when you need help, and when your instincts are enough to see you through?

Take a good look in your mental mirror, and assess what you see there.

How good is your grammar? Do you know the basic rules of punctuation? Can you spell? If not, before you spend your money on a writing course, spend it on an English course.

And *read*. Writers are readers, first. Most of us are compulsive about it: as Steve Allen has noted, if there isn't any other suitable reading material around, he'll read the label on a jar of Vick's. *I* read cereal boxes at the breakfast table, timetables in a railroad station, tabloids while I'm waiting in the supermarket checkout line—*anything* I can get my hands on. But I *prefer* a well-written piece, a clever turn of phrase. The more you read, the more facility you develop with words—and that's what makes you a writer. Words are the tools of our trade.

Which brings us to another important tool.

Invest in a dictionary—and use it. Look up words when you are not sure of their meaning or spelling. Like one of my clients who once used the word "rampid" when she meant to use "rampant" (and even "rabid" would have managed to convey her meaning), you may not realize when you are misusing or misspelling a word.

But be of good cheer: help is at hand. Many word processors and memory typewriters now come with built-in spelling checkers. Run the checker through your manuscript and it will stop at every word it questions, giving *you* the opportunity to look up the word and correct it if necessary.

Remember, though, that a spell check program can't tell you if you've used the right word, or whether you've used the word in its proper context. For that, you have to own a *good* dictionary—one that gives you examples of how to use a word—or a book on word usage. (If you're still not sure, after checking out all those sources, resort to the Writer's Easy Escape Clause: find a synonym that's easier to use!)

The goal is to look professional, even on your first try—and nothing makes you look *less* professional than errors in spelling and grammar.

But isn't that what editors are for?

True, that's why there are *copy* editors (see chapter 18 for more about their duties)—but your work won't be seen by a copy editor until it passes the *acquisitions* editor, and to do that, it has to be written in *good* English with proper punctuation. Bad English distracts from, and may even distort, what you're trying to say; an editor who has to divine your meaning by reading between the lines won't buy those lines.

If English is your second language, or if you were asleep or writing notes to your best friend during your English classes in high school, you can buy a good grammatical guide—one of the best is Strunk and White's *The Elements of Style*—to learn where commas go, when to use an apostrophe, and how to use a semicolon.

But I thought, in literature, rules were made to be broken.

It's true that many creative writers, like James Joyce, e. e. cummings, and Donald Barthelme, have broken or even abandoned the rules of grammar and punctuation. But they *knew* them before they broke them. An editor can tell when you are breaking a rule intentionally, and when you are breaking it out of ignorance. Learn the rules first, *then* break them if you feel you must.

Grammar programs for your computer are available, but, while they may be useful for catching errors such as incomplete parentheses and missing periods at the ends of sentences, they do not allow for some of the variations that the English language *does* permit. Some programs seem overly concerned with analyses of active and passive sentence structures, for example; this may be useful to some writers, but may inhibit others (the passive voice *does* have its place, provided its use is intentional, rather than inadvertent).

Again, one of the easiest ways to learn the rules is to read the works of *good* writers. The more you read, the more you develop an ear for the rhythm of the language, for proper usage. You learn how words *should* look on the printed page.

Another reason that widespread reading is better than classes for the aspiring writer is that it will show you what has gone before. While it is true that there is nothing new under the sun, and most plots can be broken down into five, or seven, or twelve (depending on which authority you consult) basic outlines, retelling an already-existing story—unless you do so in a truly innovative way—can run you afoul of copyright and plagiarism laws and an editor's bad temper. Nothing will send a manuscript winging back to you in its self-addressed, stamped envelope (which you must *always* include) faster than a cliché-filled rendition of a trite plot. Reading widely is the best way to know when an idea has been done to death.

This is especially important in genre (special interest) writing. To write in any genre, you simply must read that genre—devour it might be more accurate. Most genre writers—whether they write romances, science fiction sagas, detective tales, or heroic fantasy—are devoted fans of the genre in which they write. They know what has gone before, and they avoid repeating it, unless they are doing a subtle parody or adding a new twist.

Robert Bloch, author of *Psycho* (the novel on which the Alfred Hitchcock movie was based), provides one of the best examples of how reading in a genre can be the first step on the path to breaking into that market.

"I had gotten hooked on *Weird Tales* when I was about ten years old," he confessed when I asked him how he got his start as a writer. "On the day of the month that I knew the new issue would be delivered, I would get up at six-thirty in the morning to go dashing down the alley, pick up my copy," he reminisced, and "read it from cover to cover before I went back to bed."

Bloch finished high school in the depths of the Depression. With jobs hard to come by, he decided to become a writer.

"I got myself a secondhand typewriter for fifteen dollars and a secondhand card table for one dollar, set up the card table in the bedroom, put the typewriter on it, stole some paper somewhere, and started to write. Six weeks later, I had sold my first story."

Where? To *Weird Tales,* of course.

Often, the best place to break into print is determined by what you like to read. If you devour every issue of a particular magazine, you are obviously on its editors' wavelength. Chances are your style already matches theirs, and you know instinctively what might appeal to their readers—because you *are* one. If you find yourself thinking, "They really ought to do an article about . . ." and it's a topic in which you have a particular interest or expertise, have a go at it—but see chapter 8 on queries and assignments for the best way to approach an editor before you submit the piece.

This holds true for fiction as well as articles. Many people who survive by the fruit of their pens will sometimes suggest that the best rule of thumb is to submit to the best-paying markets first. But don't submit a piece of fiction to the *New Yorker* if you've never been able to understand the point of what they publish. They aren't going to revise their editorial policies for you.

Do submit your story to *Ellery Queen's* or *Isaac Asimov's Science Fiction Magazine* if you read those publications regularly, and—based on that familiarity—your story seems to be the kind of thing they publish.

A word of caution: before you send a story in, even to a publication you read regularly, take a look at its length. If a magazine consistently publishes short-shorts (1000 to 2000 words), don't send them your no-vella. If you've never seen verse grace their pages, don't grace their mailbox with yours. The postage you waste will be your own, and rejections are easy enough to come by without *asking* for them!

Writing requires an *ear* for the language. That can't be taught, though it can be learned—mostly through reading and listening, with close attention to the rhythm and flow of the language.

The works of award-winning author Harlan Ellison are wonderful examples of what the rhythm and flow of the English language can be. Ellison attributes his ability to create this kind of magic, at least in part, to the fact that he grew up listening to the old radio dramas: *The Shadow, The Green Hornet,* and others.

Ellison *listened.* He heard the music of the English language. And he has used it to express his own unique voice.

"I get such pleasure out of the pitch and flow of the words," he once told me. He passes that pleasure on to his readers through his writing.

My own ear for the music of the language demands that I write only in silent surroundings, with no background music playing. Language has a rhythm of its own, and the throbbing beat of rock and roll or rap, or even the gentle rhythms of "elevator music," intrude on the music of the language that I hear in my head.

Do you have that ear? If so, the next question to ask yourself before choosing a course is, "What do I want to write?" You can take courses that apply specifically to the kind of writing you want to do, but your choice of course and instructor can be critical to their usefulness.

When choosing a course in journalism or script writing, take one from an instructor who has experience in that field. Someone who has never worked for a paper may be able to teach you journalism theory, but won't be able to tell you how to apply it under the pressure of a deadline or an editor who wants a particular emphasis. And someone who has never sold a script may not be able to explain the various technical terms or tell you how much description *you* should put in and how much should be left to the discretion of the director.

Should you take a journalism course? There *are* certain constraints to writing straight news and features that are probably learned most easily in a classroom setting, but the best journalistic training may come from writing for a good editor and seeing the changes he or she makes in your work. If you can write well, and have something worth writing about, you can usually sell freelance articles to newspapers without much difficulty. However, if you want a full-time job on a newspaper, one or two night school courses won't be of much help, since a degree in journalism is usually a prerequisite.

For screenwriting, you almost certainly need a course. The format and jargon are something you can learn only by working in the business. Indeed, it probably wouldn't hurt to take a film production course or two as well.

What if you aspire to write poetry? My first recommendation, of course, is to take a class in the literature that already exists—or to buy yourself a good, varied anthology and read it, both aloud and to yourself. Then, if you must, find a course small enough so that the instructor can take a personal interest in the works of the students.

Such a course can help you hone your skills and develop your ear— or it can crush your spirit (remember that college professor I mentioned?). So make sure that you are taking a course from someone who has the same vision of poetry you do. Someone who aspires to be poet laureate will not appreciate your greeting card verse, but a greeting card company might!

What about fiction? Again, you must ask yourself, "What kind of fiction do I want to write?" Selling romances can be lucrative, but you have to read them in order to write them (a reader can spot your contempt a mile away). And as for science fiction and fantasy, those who don't know what was written in the past are inevitably doomed to repeat it.

The surest way to a rejection slip is to send an editor—especially a genre editor—a story with a theme that's been done to death, which is why a course in the literature of your chosen genre may serve you better than a writing course ever could.

The best fiction-writing instructors may point out serious flaws in your structure, or awkward phrasing, or confusing references, though you can often get the same kind of assistance from a self-help writers group or a round robin for circulating manuscripts. Nothing points out the flaws in your own writing more quickly than seeing another amateur make the same mistake, in spades!

As for humor, it really can't be taught, and very seldom is classroom criticism of humor pieces anything but subjective.

What is the use, then, of a creative-writing course? There are several:

▲ If you already have a stack of writing that you've completed but haven't been able to sell, a course can help you focus on what's wrong with your writing.

▲ Courses that require you to produce can sometimes force you to put pen to paper (if yours is a muse that *can* be forced).

▲ Your fellow students can provide you with moral support, so that, in the company of these other aspiring writers, you feel encouraged to pursue your goals.

▲ Seeing the flaws in the writings of your classmates can call your attention to similar flaws in your own work.

▲ A good instructor can teach you how to trim away the fat from your writing.

▲ Qualified instructors can provide technical tips in format and marketing to help you sell your work.

But if taking courses is your way of putting off the task of writing, of convincing yourself you *are* pursuing your chosen career even when you really aren't producing at all, forgo the course and apply yourself to the task of writing instead.

3

Putting Pen to Paper

The most difficult part of writing is, undoubtedly, the act of sitting down to write. We writers protect ourselves from it by every means imaginable. Undoubtedly the most popular bar to productivity, however, is procrastination.

Often, procrastination takes the form of ritual. Just as office workers may have to chat with the elevator operator, or sort through the items in their briefcases, or down three cups of coffee and a doughnut before they can start their day, every writer has a set of rituals that must be enacted before he or she can start a task—especially one as onerous as writing.

Onerous, you say? But I love to write.

So do I, except when that labor of love becomes a duty. Sometimes, when I have an article at deadline, even cleaning the basement looks like an attractive alternative.

Being blessed with three separate careers—law, journalism, and fiction writing—as well as two residences, an office, a car, and a dog, I can always find *something* more pressing than writing to take up my time. Usually, it is a legal matter that commands my immediate attention, but sometimes the car is making a funny noise, which means I really ought to stop in at the local garage. Or the kitchen floor, to which I've been oblivious for months, suddenly requires immediate scouring. With so many demands on my time, I have raised procrastination to a fine art, since there is always something else I should be doing besides the task at hand.

I know that not all of these are *real* intrusions, but, rather, the result of some perverse mental quirk, because no matter what task I set myself to accomplishing, my mind is determined to work on something else. Inevitably, the answers to thorny legal problems that I haven't been able to solve for weeks will suddenly occur to me just as I sit down to write an article. A name for a character will occur to me while I am researching a case. And one day, when I meant to sit down to work on this book, a humorous piece on curly hair popped into my head in its entirety, complete from opening sentence through wacky examples to the punch line at the end.

You can't throw away a perfectly good article that has just appeared to you, full-blown, like Athena from the head of Zeus. So, of course, I set it down on paper instead of working on the chapter I had planned to write.

I have been able to fight this problem of avoidance somewhat more effectively since I acquired a computer with a hard disk, which enables me to switch from one piece of work to another with about four keystrokes. When I'm at the computer and unruly ideas rear their impertinent little heads, I dump them from my brain into the appropriate file, store them, and go back to the task at deadline.

Deadlines are the bane of my existence, but they force me into productivity. As a result, they have become a way of life for me. My way of determining priorities seems to be, *whatever crisis comes to the fore comes first.* Let the crisis fade away, and I can take forever sharpening pencils, dusting the windowsills, or rearranging the contents of my desk drawer before I get down to writing.

Sound familiar?

Is your tombstone going to read, "She always meant to write"?

If so, let me share with you several means that I have discovered for defeating my tendency to put off writing. The first is to finish everything you could possibly find to do, including cleaning the closets and calling your great-aunt Sarah. When there's nothing left, you'll simply *have* to write.

Now that we've abandoned that little fantasy, let's talk about strategies that *work.*

For me, the most effective goad is writing on assignment. This means that my writing has deadlines as pressing as those that govern the rest of my life. How does this work? You query an editor (see chapter 8) about an article you'd like to write, and if you get the assignment, it will come with a due date. If you accept the assignment, you'll have to sit down before that day and write the piece.

Actually, even in the face of a deadline, modern science has made it easy to put off the day of reckoning longer than the most ardent procrastinator ever dreamed possible. Writers used to have to allow time for mailing, but the proliferation of overnight delivery services has meant that you can now send an article off the night before it is due and have it in the editor's hands the next morning. With the advent of the facsimile machine, or fax, and the modem, you can actually write the piece the day it's due and transmit it to the editor as quickly as you can make a phone call.

Waiting until the last moment doesn't make any sense, but it seems to be the only way I can write. I've never understood why it is that if I can write an article in one day the day before it is due, I can't write it in one day the day I get the assignment. But I can't—other obligations always intrude, or I can't think of a lead, and somehow it just doesn't get done, until it has moved to the forefront of my crisis list.

I've tried giving myself phony deadlines, but that never works. In my heart of hearts, I know they aren't real. But having a *real* deadline does, at least, produce productivity, even if it does so at the last possible moment.

I can also induce myself to write by having some other obligation. Let me have an appointment to take the car in for a tune-up or the dog to the vet, and a chapter in my latest novel will dance around in my brain, demanding to be let out. If I cancel the appointment or wait till I get home, the idea will be gone. But if I stop at the word processor en route to the door, with my coat on and the dog pulling at her leash, I'll only be a *little* bit late, and the ideas will keep right on flowing until I tear myself away.

Because of this little mental aberration, I have a tendency to overschedule myself—and because of *that,* it is all too easy to avoid writing, especially when there is no assignment. Sometimes avoidance seems legitimate—my sister let a few little things like a cross-country move and two preschoolers delay *her* last book. But, too often, the obstacles we put in our own way aren't really legitimate at all—my mother, who has published a number of articles, often puts off her writing because of an obligation (to herself) to read through a stack of *Time* magazines that she hasn't managed to get to for the past year or so.

Thus I have formulated:

Kozak's Rule #2: There is *always* something else to do, so if you really mean to write, you have to ignore that something.

I have found that it helps to make a list of things that really *do* take priority over writing. My list contains four items:

- ▲ the immediate, pressing interests of my clients,
- ▲ family (or canine) medical emergencies,
- ▲ running *totally* out of clean laundry (being reduced to odd combinations doesn't count),
- ▲ the house catching fire.

Make a similar list for yourself. Then *try* to abide by it. You'll never get the Pulitzer Prize for a clean kitchen floor or by having neatly arranged all the nails and screws in your toolbox by length, width, and metallic composition.

I think that procrastinators, like alcoholics, are never *recovered,* but always *recovering.* Getting at your writing takes lifelong discipline. But I'm learning to do it—and so can you.

Something else that takes discipline is convincing friends and family that your writing is important. I used to write at home in the mornings, but everyone found out that if they called then, they could reach me, and I was constantly interrupted.

Deliverymen and meter readers assumed that if I was home, I couldn't be doing anything important, so of course I could accept a package for a neighbor, or let them in when the building manager wasn't around. (I finally gave up on daytime writing; now I often write in the middle of the night instead. I sometimes go so long without seeing the sun that I feel like Count Dracula.)

Sharing your environment with nonwriters invites disaster. A writer may be carefully balancing a whole thread of a plot line in his head, but to the observer, it looks like he is merely staring off into space, with an occasional hunt-and-peck stroke at the typewriter keys. Surely that can't be as important as "Did you walk the dog?" or "Have you seen my notebook?" or "Would you like to go to a movie tomorrow night?"

Virginia Woolf obviously spoke from experience when she said that a writer needs "a room of one's own." In *my* experience, that room should *not* have a telephone, and should be off-limits to everyone, including the dog.

Even if you barricade yourself in that private room, it is difficult to convince people that what you are doing is *work*. Writing just doesn't *seem* like work to most people—including, sometimes, those of us who do it for a living, and who cannot square the idea that we enjoy what we're doing with the work ethic our consciences have imposed on us.

It may help to rent an office somewhere, but the disadvantage (aside from the expense) is that, if an idea occurs to you in the middle of the night, your equipment and materials are miles away.

I've also heard of writers who dress and leave the house each morning, walk around the block, and return to their work rooms as though to an office. They are officially Not at Home—which also means they don't answer the phone. This is a lot easier in these days of answering machines that can be set to monitor incoming calls, but it doesn't work for me. I am constitutionally unable to ignore a ringing telephone.

What *does* work for me is a mind-set that says, "This is my job. I *am* a writer." Once I've convinced myself of this fact, I seem able to give short shrift to interruptions and interrupters, and get on with the task of writing.

Establishing this mind-set can be difficult. It helps to convince yourself that you're a writer if you have stories or articles in print. It especially helps if you get paid for them—regularly. Unfortunately, it is far too easy to have a crisis of confidence with every rejection slip that arrives in the mail, or to doubt, even after you've sold one book, that you will ever sell another.

This is one of the reasons there are so many articles and books written about how you can make a small fortune by writing full-time, if you devote yourself to writing business brochures and press releases and speeches and—well, you get the picture. Soon enough, what you are doing is, indeed, writing for a living. But it may not be what you had in mind at all when you said you wanted to be a writer.

Americans tend to define themselves by what they do and how much they earn doing it. Because of this, writing an entire novel without an advance contract becomes a complete act of faith in yourself. Often the time must be stolen from other activities. With a long-term project that has no prospect of reward until it is finished—and perhaps not even then—you must retain a burning conviction that you *are* a writer throughout the writing process.

Not everyone can do this. Sometimes it helps to remind yourself that Margaret Mitchell wrote and rewrote *Gone with the Wind* over a ten-year period without an advance contract from a publisher—and, if any book besides *Moby-Dick* comes close to being the Great American Novel, it is hers.

At other times, it may help to intersperse short projects with your long ones. Having a few of your articles see print every so often helps you to maintain the conviction that you are a writer, both in your own mind and in the minds of others.

There are several reasons for churning out shorter pieces while you're working on your magnum opus. The first is, as I've noted, to resolve the crisis of confidence. The second is to establish your credentials so that no one else will rock your belief in yourself.

Sabotage of that belief can come at any time. You are introduced to someone at a party, for example, or you sit next to someone on a train.

"And what do *you* do?" he asks.

"I'm a writer," you reply brightly.

The next question is inevitable. "Oh, really? What have you written?"

I know, from experience, that no one other than a prospective employer ever asks a lawyer what cases he or she has tried. Surely no one doubts a physician enough to ask if he's ever seen any patients. But, whether it is out of envy (because *everyone* seems to want to be a writer), or just out of disbelief that *you* could really be one of *them*, you are always asked, "What have you written?"

"I'm working on a novel," you respond.

Your new acquaintance nods knowingly and begins looking around for other company.

The reason for his reaction is that everyone in the world is "working on a novel," and half of these people are basically illiterate. The rest of the world knows this, and puts you to your proof: You're a writer? What have you written?

This is not to be confused with the antiprocrastination question you should put to yourself at regular intervals: What have you written *lately*?

The novelist who has never published anything is quickly categorized by others into the same class as waiters who have never been cast in a role but call themselves actors, and perpetual office seekers who have never won an election.

If you can do an article even once or twice a year, you can say with confidence, "I do humor pieces for my local paper," or "I'm freelance. I publish all over." *Then* when you say you're working on a novel, they'll believe you.

So will the Internal Revenue Service. According to the tax laws, if you aren't earning money at something, it's a hobby, and you can't deduct your expenses. However, if you *are* earning money, although you have to declare it as income, you *can* generally deduct the legitimate expenses of your work, such as postage, typing paper, and the cost of attending conferences. (See chapter 20 for a more detailed discussion of taxes and the writer.)

Writing articles based on the research you are doing for your book is not only an effective way to make a profit, it is also a time-honored tradition among writers. Alex Haley, when he was writing *Roots,* sold a number of articles on the facts he gleaned from his research. I remember seeing one, in *Writer's Digest,* on the techniques he had used to trace his ancestry.

This article undoubtedly helped keep him in typing paper while he was working on the book—but it also served to whet *my* appetite (and the appetites of most people who read it, I don't doubt) for the forthcoming saga. So it paid him twice: at the time it was written, and in publicity for the book.

Not only can you obtain advance publicity for your novel in the notes about the author that accompany your articles, you can also make valuable contacts within the publishing industry, which you can exploit when the time comes to sell the book. You will also gain a certain professional stature that makes selling your book that much easier.

There is another reason for writing short pieces while working on a major project that won't be done for a long time, and that is to hone your skills. Writing tightly, writing to deadlines, keeping your style consistent—all of these things are improved by practice. The more you write, the more you learn about writing, and the better the writer you become.

When you are working on a major project, it is easy to be seduced by the siren song of short-term gratification found in the publication of shorter articles and stories. Sometimes a book looks like an endless, impossible task, one which can never be accomplished.

I learned a lesson in the completion of novels (and full-length books) from a friend who thought he was encouraging my newfound athleticism.

Around the time I decided I was a writer, I also became a runner. After starting with little jogs around the block, I built up my endurance, and I remember sharing my astonishment and elation with my friend Steve the first time I discovered I could run a steady mile without panting.

"You know, you could work up to a 10K," he told me.

I snickered at the very thought. "Are you kidding? Me? How could I do that?"

"Just the way you built up to the mile," he replied. "Just keep putting one foot in front of the other."

Eight months later, I ran my 10K, just putting one foot ahead of the other.

Writing my first novel was very much like that. I would see a scene in my mind's eye, write it down, and then picture the next scene. One scene after another, an entire adventure formulated itself.

I discovered, then, that big projects—entire books, for example—may seem overwhelming when you think of them in their entirety, but, just like marathons and 10K's, you finish them one step at a time.

A passing word about "writer's block."

I am convinced that there is really no such thing as "writer's block." There *is*—and I am the first to acknowledge it—procrastination. But there is also exhaustion. Both may *appear* to be writer's block, but each should be dealt with in a different way.

The cure for procrastination is often just to bite the bullet and go to work. Start in the middle if you have to—you can go back and put in the opening paragraphs later.

But when you try to write in a state of *exhaustion,* the result is often counterproductive. You work more slowly, and the words you want always seem to elude you. The cure may be to put down your pen and go for a walk or out to dinner or even to bed.

Unless you are procrastinating or exhausted, as long as you have enough irons in the fire, you will never be blocked as a writer. If you can't get a scene in your novel to come out right, you can try working on an article that's nearly due. Write a few query letters. Write a thank-you note.

If you find you are avoiding only *one* out of all your projects, it may be that that project is simply not for you. If you can, bow out gracefully. If there is too much at stake—perhaps an advance that would have to be returned, or a lot of advance publicity, or a large investment in research—put your cards on the table with your agent and/or the editor. Maybe you can restructure the project and manage to salvage it; maybe you can substitute another project that you won't have to do battle with.

While it's true that "when the going gets tough, the tough get going," it is also true that even the tough are sometimes "too pooped to participate." These are the times when your writing just can't be forced. As my friend Alice once observed, producing a writing project is a lot like having a baby: there is conception, there is gestation, and there is delivery. No stage can be skipped or accomplished out of order; each stage is going to take just as long as it needs—and there's nothing you can do about it.

When the words really won't come, it may be that you're pushing too hard. (You're not *always* guilty of slacking off, you know.) Everyone has his own biorhythms, his own periods of energy throughout the day.

When *you* should write is when you are most comfortable writing. So take a break and let the ideas gestate. After all, that's what file folders—and the "save and store" command on your computer—were invented for.

4

The Mechanics of Writing

Where you write and *how* you transfer your ideas onto paper are matters of very personal choice, and you can use, as the saying goes, whatever turns you on. The truth is, very few writers actually *write* anymore. We *type,* or we *keyboard,* our drafts on a computer or word processor, or we *dictate.* There are no rules for the creative process, only for what the final product must look like (which I'll discuss in chapter 7).

So, what turns *you* on? For some writers, a particular pen or notebook becomes a talisman. Others, like me, are more fickle. This year, I happen to be particularly fond of small, hardbound notebooks with very narrow lines and no defined margins; the preferred instrument is a ballpoint pen with a medium point. A couple of years back, I decided I could only write on white (rather than the traditional yellow) legal pads, and only with a number 2 or softer pencil topped by a generous, functional eraser.

Handwriting your first draft is one of the *least* efficient ways to compose a piece of writing, but it does, at times, have its advantages. For example, it allows you to play at being Jo March and pen your text while sitting in an apple tree. If you're inclined to inscribe your thoughts on a notepad while sunning on the beach, or to dash off a few lines while sitting in a bistro on a rainy afternoon, the pen and pencil are still the most portable writing tools around.

Because there is something innately sensuous about the feel of soft lead sliding across smooth paper, writing by hand lends itself well to the composition of love stories—and I can't imagine creating poetry any other way.

Novelist Elaine Bergstrom wrote virtually the entire first draft of her novel *Shattered Glass* in a ringbound notebook while sitting in a restaurant. Another writer of my acquaintance gets up with her husband, whose job starts an hour before hers does. After he leaves, she dons a pair of stereo headphones and spends that extra hour banging away at an old electric typewriter with the theme music from *Star Wars* blasting through her earphones. (Knowing this, I got a particular chuckle out of the opening scenes of the movie *Romancing the Stone*.)

But no matter what method you use, it isn't the *writing* that gets you, it's the *re*-writing. That short story I wrote in California was retyped *fourteen* times, from beginning to end—all 10,000 words of it—before anyone ever saw it.

Until I acquired my first computer, I wrote on legal pads, using alternate lines on only one side of the page so there would be plenty of room for corrections. Ultimately, my manuscripts would be covered with stars and asterisks and arrows leading to circled numbers and letters that matched other circled numbers and letters, somewhere, if only you could find them.

My secretary usually did an admirable job of following this labyrinthine trail, producing fairly coherent typed drafts from the chaos I had given her. Out of deference to her efforts, I became adept at only making changes in a typed manuscript that could be squeezed in without the need to alter the line below. When my corrections *were* lengthier and required reformatting a paragraph or a page, we would cut and paste the manuscript and photocopy it—a process we referred to as "word processing on the copier."

Then I discovered the computer, and my life has never been the same.

Despite the fact that it occasionally gets temperamental and eats a paragraph or even a page of text, the computer has saved vast amounts of time. If I want to add a line in the middle of a page, or a page in the middle of a chapter, or even a chapter in the middle of a book, I can do it without touching the rest of the manuscript. In contrast to the number of times I retyped that first short story, since I've acquired the computer I've seldom had to rekeyboard more than a paragraph.

Granted, computers and word processors have certain disadvantages. Sometimes it takes a while to get the bugs out of a new one, and, even when they're finally on line, they can't be easily toted to the beach or set up in an apple tree. (Oh, yes, I know about laptop versions, but they can be hard to read, especially in bright sunlight, and *no* computer is really designed for the sand and salt spray—not to mention the blistering heat—of a day at the shore.) But when you're trying to meet a deadline, the efficiency of a computer can't be beat.

You don't *need* a computer or word processor to be a writer, but you might *want* one, since computers really help your productivity. Keep in mind, though, if you purchase one, that you don't need a lot of bells and whistles. What you *do* need are:

- A service department that can be reached when *you* need to reach them, even if it's in the middle of the night (if the computer eats the chapter you've just completed at three o'clock in the morning, it's comforting to have someone to talk you through the right procedure for shutting the machine off without destroying all your words that might be hidden somewhere in its innards).
- A word processing program that *you* can understand (and a little training time donated by whoever sold it to you).
- An efficient backup system so that when something does go wrong, *all* is not lost.
- A printer that interfaces (that's computerese for "works in tandem") with *your* computer, and has the clearest print and the fastest speed you can buy for the money you are able to spend.
- The ability to count words (rather than characters) in a document.
- A dictionary/spelling checker and, if possible, a thesaurus.
- A monitor screen (these generally come in amber, green, or black-and-white) that doesn't bother *your* eyes, since you're the one who'll be using it.
- A keyboard that feels comfortable under *your* hands.

Anything else is useful only if you can and will take the time to learn how to use it. Trust me, you probably won't.

Once you acquire a computer, *how* you use it is as personal as was your choice of writing materials before. Some writers do a skeletal outline and expand on the second draft. Others construct mammoth texts far too long to offer to an editor, then use the next trip through to trim the manuscript down to size. My method is to compose what I think is the final form, then print it out and set the printout aside. After a breather, I come back to the printout, sharp pencil in hand. If I've distanced myself enough, even by walking the dog or eating dinner, I can go through it as though I were editing someone else's work. Afterward, I enter my penciled-in changes in my computer file.

When I am writing a piece of a specific length, I do a word count after finishing the first draft. This tells me if what I've constructed is too long, too short, or right on target, and I can adjust the manuscript accordingly.

The computer also improves my efficiency when an editor wants a rewrite, or when I want to update and resell an article I've previously sold. (Yes, you can do this. See the section of chapter 11 on writers' rights.) It's easy to reopen the file and customize the manuscript to meet new and different needs.

I love what the computer can do, but sometimes I don't like what it does to *me*. Working on a computer can give you eyestrain and carpal tunnel syndrome. It can also give you a backache.

Sometimes the cure is as simple as dimming the screen on the monitor, or acquiring a lower table or a higher chair. When I was writing my second novel, I developed back spasms that wouldn't go away. I purchased a kneeling chair, but instead of helping my back, it merely gave me an added pain in my shins. Finally, I replaced the six-foot cord that connected the keyboard to the monitor with a twelve-foot cord, set the keyboard on my lap, and my back problems disappeared.

It is also possible to "crash your disk" (the one in the computer, not one in your back) and lose an entire manuscript. I'm absolutely paranoid about making backup copies and printing out "hard copy" as frequently as I can. I also find it a good idea to hit the "save and continue" key whenever I pause to ponder a word choice for more than a moment, and I've also trained myself to do it whenever I see the page-break indicator. This insures that, even if I lose the file I'm working on, I can bring up the backup copy, and I won't have lost more than a page.

Do I *always* write on the computer now? Hardly. I still write whenever an idea occurs to me, on scraps of paper I've ripped from the margins of magazines, on my check stubs, in notebooks and on notepads, and sometimes even on the inside cover of the telephone book. Once, an entire sonnet occurred to me as I was driving on the freeway, and I scribbled it on the back of a McDonald's bag I grabbed and spread across the steering wheel.

Which only goes to prove, I guess, that even in the computer age, paper and pencil are not obsolete. Writers still *write,* even when they use other tools of the trade as well.

5

Learning to Edit Yourself

You've poured out your heart and spilled your guts onto the printed (or handwritten) page in front of you. It's writing, but is it *publishable* writing? And, more to the point, is it *good* writing?

Sad to say, good writing and published writing are not always synonymous. Banal retellings of hackneyed plots appear in bookstores every day. Newspapers relate the news, but do so ungrammatically. And academic prose raises obfuscation to a fine art.

It has been said that every nation gets the government it deserves. Perhaps this is the case with literature as well. The popular press, like television, merely reflects the educational deficiencies of the public at large. But education itself is obviously no guarantee of graceful or lucid writing, since in academic circles, the murkier the prose, the more profound it is perceived as being.

So there exists the possibility that if you find yourself with a stack of unpublished manuscripts, perhaps you're being rejected because your writing is too good. However, more often than not, your writing *isn't* as good as you think it is, and those rejection slips arriving in your mailbox with more frequency than sweepstakes entries are coming because your material is trite, or obscure, or just plain dull.

Where those adjectives don't apply to your work, it may be that you simply need to modify your style to fit the market—leaving multisyllabic words and semicolons out of newspaper articles, for example, but using them generously when writing for academia. Matching your style to a market isn't as difficult as you might think. It may mean using the second person, rather than the third, to draw the reader in, or inserting humorous examples, or perhaps including footnotes. For the most part, in order to be commercially published, writing must basically be understandable and contain at least a germ of an idea.

Every so often, however, something truly awful makes it into print. How does that stuff get published? In newspapers and magazines, it may be deadline pressure that allows bad writing to slip through the cracks. And a book editor I once asked gave me two interesting reasons for the genuinely bad books that sometimes make it onto bookstore shelves. When a popular author is pressed by his publisher for another book, she told me, he may pull out a "trunk novel"—something he stashed in a trunk years ago because no one wanted to buy it. Now that he has hit the best-seller list, he can sell anything with his name on it.

Another reason some strange books make it into print is that publishers prepare "The List" of books they will bring out in any given month as much as a year in advance, and this list includes books that are contracted for but not yet written. Sometimes a scheduled book comes in and it is not at all what the publisher expected, but it may be easier to publish it and let it die on the vine than to go through the hassle of fighting the author to get the advance back. The alternative, when a scheduled book is terrible or doesn't come in at all, is to grab *any* book of a similar length and genre to fill the gap in The List. If your book floats in over the transom that day, you may find yourself in print. This does not necessarily mean that it is *good*, only that it is *there*.

You don't have to worry about posterity being burdened with all of this literary litter, however. For the past hundred or so years, most books have been printed on acid-based paper, which disintegrates rapidly. Eventually, all that will be left between the dust covers of the books of the twentieth century is dust.

If you want your writing to outlive you, you'll have to produce something that will either stay in print through a number of editions or be worthy of publication by the kind of house that uses acid-free paper, at least in its first editions. But then, if you're writing for posterity, you want your work to be the best it can be, anyway—don't you?

How do you know when your work is publishable, or good, or both? Unless you move in very literary circles, you can't really trust your friends or family to tell you. Either they'll praise you to the heavens, just because they love you, or they'll offer criticism that is not the least bit relevant.

You can join a writers' workshop or round robin, but the comments you receive there will generally be from other amateurs. Often, the only benefits you get from such a group are companionship, an incentive to keep writing so you'll have something to bring to the next meeting, and a vivid awareness of the kind of mistakes other amateurs can make. For example, you may have an occasional tendency to change point of view in your fiction, while one of the other members of your group does it constantly. Sensitized by the bad example of your colleague, you can quickly learn to correct that flaw in your own writing.

However, even though this exposure to the errors committed by others can make you more aware of your own mistakes, the danger exists that reading too much by stumbling writers can ruin your ear.

Remember when I said that a writer has to have an *ear* for the language, and that you develop that ear by reading the works of *good* writers? Reading the works of *bad*—or even just inept—writers can accustom your ear to their errors, until you can't remember how the language is supposed to sound. So be careful of your choice of a writers' group, and be prepared to flee if you find your writer's ear is turning to tin.

The best solution is to learn to edit your own work—and to do so ruthlessly. Hopefully, you haven't given anthropomorphic characteristics to your words, and won't feel as though you are murdering them if you delete them. (I once heard a rabbi teaching a Hebrew School class tell them of a legend that every word that is mispronounced goes up before the throne of God and complains. I imagine that many of the eight-year-olds in that class have paled at the thought of erasing a word ever since!)

Even without anthropomorphizing your words and phrases, it is all too easy to fall in love with a simile that you have created after much pondering and experimentation. It may be a terrific simile—but it may not belong in *this* manuscript. Can you destroy a phrase you love so dearly? And *should* you?

How do you make that decision? One of the best ways is to distance yourself from your manuscript. Put it away for a few weeks or a few months; then pull it out again and take a good, hard look at it as though it were someone else's work. Chances are you'll want to take an ax to it, but butcher it with the nearest blue pencil instead.

If you don't have a week or a month, try setting the manuscript aside overnight. Even that much time will make it easier to edit.

Delaying the editing process has an additional benefit. Too many would-be writers spend their entire careers writing and rewriting their opening paragraphs. If you put off revising your work for a while, you can manage to avoid that trap. Proceeding with the rest of the manuscript after promising yourself you'll fine-tune it later may be the easiest way to engineer an Escape from Page One.

All of this can be summed up in:

Kozak's Rule #3: *Thou shalt not fall in love with thine own words.*

and

Kozak's Rule #4: *Put time between the act of writing and the act of rewriting or editing.*

All right—the time has passed. You pick up your manuscript pages and prepare to wreak havoc upon them. What's the best way to proceed?

The approach you take to editing will vary depending on *what* you are writing. In producing articles, for example, the tighter the writing, the more likely it is to sell.

Taut writing can be a plus in fiction as well, but here, paring away excess verbiage gives you more room for detail and description. Richness and texture do not necessarily mean *more* words, but rather, *more carefully chosen* words.

One technique for effective editing is to read your manuscript aloud, to a friend or to yourself. Always do this with a pencil in hand. You can't skip over words or sentences when you read aloud; you have to pronounce every word. When you read them aloud, awkward rhythms and juxtapositions become particularly obvious—and so do the ways to correct them. You can almost *see* the roughness in your manuscript being smoothed away.

If you work on a computer, you may find it essential, as I do , to edit from hard copy. For some reason, I never seem to notice misplaced punctuation marks on the screen, but become very aware of them on the printed page.

The general idea is to produce as polished a piece as possible, without polishing the piece to death.

One of the best ways to learn to edit your own work is to work for a good editor.

Of course, not all editors are *good* editors. I have known some who inserted grammatical errors that I would never have made, and I've seen others wreck an article by injudicious cutting. On occasion editors have altered my words and, in the process, created awkward phrasing or even factual inaccuracies. While I'll cover dealing with this in chapter 18 on how to work with—or around—a copy editor and its section on moral rights, the best way to deal with people who butcher your work may be to avoid writing any further articles for them.

Sometimes, however, you encounter editors who are terrific. They change a word here and there, and suddenly you look like a better writer than you are and your work looks better than you ever wrote it. When you find one of these editors, cling like glue; write for a pittance if you must. And learn, from what that editor does to your manuscript, to do it for yourself.

I have been blessed by contact with three such editors in my lifetime. The first was my high school journalism teacher, Caroline Gardner. The staff members of the Washington High School *Scroll* used to joke that after Miss Gardner had attacked one of your articles with her red pen, it looked as though it had bled to death. But if you looked carefully at the corrections she had made, you saw that she had tightened up the prose and fixed up the grammar, and made your piece read much better than you'd originally written it. As a cub reporter on the *Scroll,* I decided that before I left the paper, I wanted to turn in an article to Miss Gardner and get it back without a single correction, with the only red mark on it her initials.

By my senior year I'd managed this wondrous feat several times. Writing grammatically had become second nature, and I didn't think much about it until nearly twenty years later, when I was just starting to write professionally. I turned in an article to a local magazine and, a day or two later, received an awed phone call from the editor.

"Yours was the first article ever to pass through the hands of our copy editor without having a single mark put on it," he announced in disbelief. "That's simply never happened before. I never thought it would."

Half an hour later, I got a call from the copy editor, who told me the same thing. Suddenly reminded of my experience on the *Scroll,* I mentioned it to him.

"That explains it," he chuckled. "We were trained by the same red pen."

Miss Gardner perfected my grammar and punctuation, but it was a professional editor who taught me to tighten up my prose. Lennox Samuels edited the weekend magazine of *The Milwaukee Sentinel,* and I began to submit entertainment pieces to him.

I was new enough at the game that when the first one came out, I read it over several times. I recognized most of my original text, but there were a few transitional sentences that looked just too good to be mine. I pulled out my copy of the manuscript and found I was right—like a skilled plastic surgeon, Lennox had tightened up my story with a few simple nips and tucks.

I was impressed with the way he made the story read. I was even more impressed when the next one came out, and I saw that he had once more performed his magic and turned a good story into a great one.

Before I submitted my next story to him, I stopped to consider, "If I were Lennox, what would I do to this piece?"

When I thought about it that way, the changes were obvious. I tightened up the transitions myself before I sent the story out. Lennox made *one* change in that one. In the next one, he never made any changes at all.

Lennox has gone on to the *Dallas Morning News,* and I have gone on to write for publications all over the country. Now, generally, when I look over my manuscripts, I merely tell myself, "Let's clean this up!" But sometimes, when I see loose writing that can be tightened, or a missing transition, I still hear myself asking, "What would Lennox do to this?" The answer to that question never fails to improve the article.

The third editor who cleaned up my act was my friend Fran. She edited a *Star Trek* fanzine (a type of publication I discuss in chapter 16) for which I wrote a number of stories. Generally, she made no corrections in my manuscripts, but I'll never forget the single, most effective change she made, perhaps because it was so simple.

I had started a story with a short descriptive paragraph, followed by a line of dialogue.

Fran reversed the order of those two paragraphs.

Suddenly the story reached out and grabbed you. It was a simple change, but one that never would have occurred to me. And it was a great lesson in self-editing. Apparently, in fiction, just as in newswriting, it is all too easy to "bury your lead."

My friend Joan Winston says she hears the voice of our agent, Sharon Jarvis, in her head as she writes, demanding, "Where are they? What are they wearing?"

I once learned a similar lesson in story construction from a good editor, who I doubt even realized he was teaching. When I was an unpublished but aspiring fiction writer, I ran into David Hartwell, then the director of science fiction at Pocket Books, at a science fiction convention. Over a drink, we discussed submission procedures, and he complained about the great volume of inept submissions he received from amateurs.

"Most of them have never even heard of a dramatic hook," he grumbled.

Until that moment, neither had I. But it was pretty obvious to me what a dramatic hook must be (see chapter 16 if it isn't obvious to *you*), and I began to load them into my fiction. They have never played me false, and neither has the advice David didn't realize he was giving me.

Does all this polishing take time? You bet it does. You'll probably spend a lot more hours honing and editing your work than you will writing it.

Is it worth it? It is if you want to write *well*.

Unfortunately, there may not always be time to edit the way you want to. Even if you aren't prone to procrastination, some works simply must be written in less time than you would like.

This is a universal problem for writers—one that is often alleviated only by possessing sufficient independent income to enable you to write at your own pace, rather than at that set by an editor who will pay you when the work comes in, *if* you can do it under the gun. As the late Frank Herbert put it, "Money to a writer means time to write."

Time to write means time to polish. Most professional writers will tell you that they are never totally happy with their work when they see it in print. Something about the passage of time makes errors and just plain clumsiness much more evident in print than they were when you had the opportunity to correct them.

Sometimes the flaws are invisible to all but the author, but sometimes they are real doozies—and they can even appear as a result of the editing process! I once accidentally put Iago's words into Othello's mouth in the process of redesigning a lead paragraph. I'd credited them correctly when I started out, but the clause that would have saved me disappeared in one of my redrafts.

Whether the flaws in your manuscript are the result of too little self-editing, or too much, as Miss Gardner used to remind the *Scroll* staff every day, "You can't print an alibi." Once your work is published, it is effectively set in stone, and your reputation rides on it. There's no place to say, "I meant to clear up that redundancy" or "This story would have been better if I'd had more time."

So after you have learned to hear an editor's voice in your head, to self-edit, to distance yourself from your work, to put in dramatic hooks and keep a consistent point of view, you will have to learn to do all this *quickly* if you want to meet deadlines, which is usually the case if you think you want to write for a *living*.

But is writing for a living what *you* want to do? I've asked that question before, but I think it bears asking throughout one's writing career. Writing can be a joyous expression of your creativity or a task as burdensome as any other in the workaday world. I'll explore some of the traps that can take the joy out of writing in the next chapter.

6

Writing for Fun and/or Profit

On signing your first book contract, one of the first pieces of advice you will receive from any seasoned writer is "Don't quit your job." Simply put, writing usually does not pay well, often does not pay on time, and sometimes doesn't pay at all. Though you have probably seen books and promotional materials for courses that promise, "You can make (fill in any large dollar figure here) per year writing for a living," I'm convinced that there are only four ways you can make a reasonable living by writing:

- ▴ You can work on the staff of a daily paper in a fairly large city, or on a well-funded magazine.
- ▴ You can write advertising copy.
- ▴ You can write a best-seller or a syndicated column.
- ▴ You can work your typing fingers to the bone as a freelancer. (This category includes journalists, fiction writers, and scriptwriters; even working your fingers to the bone probably won't earn you enough to get by if you want to be a poet.)

The first alternative—working for a paper or magazine—is practical, but it has its drawbacks. First and foremost among these is the fact that you have to be *hired*. This usually means you need a journalism degree, though you can also work your way up the ladder from some job no one else wants (like copy editor), or work your way onto the staff from smaller papers in smaller cities or by freelancing for the publication often enough so that the transition to staff seems logical. But even when you grasp the brass ring and make it to a full-time position, the job may not be what you envisioned.

This is because staff reporters write stories about whatever they are assigned to cover. If you have the City Hall beat, you cover the mayor's office and the city council every day, and you have to turn in a story whether anything noteworthy happens there or not. A regular beat can get pretty dull; for example, after a year on the ethnic beat, the inevitable march of time will bring you round, once again, to writing another story about Cinco de Mayo or Passover or Bastille Day. By the third year, you'll be hard-pressed to find a fresh angle for such stories.

A general assignment writer may garner *some* exciting assignments —but may also be ordered to interview the family of a crime victim ("How do you feel about your daughter being raped and murdered, ma'am?"). This is not always the reporter's idea. I once drew one of these assignments while stringing for *USA Today* and couldn't talk the editor out of it, so—to my everlasting shame—I actually interviewed the family of a young man who had died in a plane crash. I resolved that day that I'd starve before I ever accepted an assignment like that again, and haven't; but such a resolve essentially eliminates the possibility of ever joining the staff of a newspaper or magazine.

Even the plum job of movie critic requires sitting through not only the *good* flicks but also the real dogs. And until you've interviewed a movie star so full of himself that, despite his denture breath, he makes a determined pass at you—but won't give you a single quote on which you can build a story—you don't know what it really is to hate your job.

The chances to break a story like Watergate are few and far between—and even when you find them, wheedling the assignment out of the editor, and then getting him or her to actually print your findings, may be the hardest part of the job.

Being an editor may not be much better. Sure, you've got the power, and even the glory, but think about it—for every issue, you have to come up with enough articles to fill your newspaper or magazine, without repeating a story that you did within the last two years, and with enough variety in each issue to attract readers from all segments of your targeted audience—or if you do theme issues, to manage that with sufficient homogeneity but with minimal redundancy. You also have to fill gaps when writers fail to submit their assignments on time, and rewrite those pieces that do come in but are dreadful.

On daily papers, these problems are compounded by the need to go to press every day and the fact that news breaks unevenly. For weeks, the biggest piece of news you can find may be a fender bender or an alderman's photo opportunity. Then you get a day like June 4, 1989—the government crackdown on the Democracy movement in China, the death of the Ayatollah in Iran, a mammoth train wreck in the U.S.S.R., and the first free elections in Poland since World War II. In the news business, it can be feast or famine, but you have the same number of pages to fill, either way.

As for writing advertising copy, I'll bet that wasn't what you had in mind when you said you wanted to be a writer, was it? It can be lucrative—but jobs in this field are also notoriously unstable. And even when you work for yourself, you really don't have creative control over your work, because the client is your ultimate boss.

The best-seller is, of course, every writer's dream—a dream that rarely sees fruition. Commercial success is, in fact, so elusive that some writers find that the only way to achieve it is through quantity, churning out a book in as little as a month. That kind of productivity is rare. For the rest of us, a book can take six months to a year or even longer, so we try for quality rather than quantity and hope for the best.

Sometimes it works—*Gone with the Wind* took Margaret Mitchell ten years, but it became a smash hit. For the rest of us, devoting that much time to a single work means that until it sells, the wolf is at the door. And if the book dies on the vine, perhaps never selling or, if it does sell, never earning out its advance, its author may never make up those lost earning years.

Even for those few who eventually find success, it can be a long time in coming. Mario Puzo once wrote that until he sold *The Godfather,* his family had resigned themselves to the idea that they would have to supplement his income. Alas, the same is probably true of more writers than you'd guess, and few of them ever garner the kind of success Puzo finally did.

A regular column can be easier to achieve, but it seldom pays much unless you can sell it to a number of publications. This is known as "syndication," and you can do it yourself or through a syndicate.

Before you can "self-syndicate" a column, you usually need to be published somewhere on a regular basis. Then you must target a number of noncompeting markets and convince each of them to buy your work regularly as well. (Yes, you can sell the same piece several places—see chapter 11 regarding rights and copyrights.) But self-syndicating is easier said than done; while selling and reselling individual articles can be difficult, selling and reselling a series of them is often next to impossible.

If you can get one to take you on, a syndicate will sell the piece for you, reaching more markets and bearing the cost of distribution to these markets, then splitting the net proceeds with you. But, again, don't quit your job just because a syndicate is interested in your work. A syndicate once picked up one of my articles, and when they put it out on their wires, *one* newspaper bit. After their costs were deducted, my net was eleven dollars. My guess is that the odds of making real money from a syndicated column are about the same as those of winning a multi-state lottery.

If you do manage to sell a column, you'll discover another negative aspect to this kind of writing: time flies, and next week or next month rolls around sooner than you think. While it may be fun to be funny or wise when the spirit moves you, it's no fun at all when a column is due and you're racking your brain for a topic.

I should have remembered that, because I wrote a biweekly humor column for my high school paper—and sometimes, when the deadline rolled around and I didn't feel the slightest bit funny, my attempts at humor were lame indeed. But twenty years later I forged right ahead and took on a monthly column on publishing law for a newsletter that was then known as *The Inkling.* I suddenly became aware that a commitment to writing regularly can, like a commitment to an installment loan or a lease, make a month rush by with a speed that would put lightning to shame.

Then I took on a quarterly column on writing and the law for the *Bulletin* of the Science Fiction Writers of America. Suddenly, three-month periods were vanishing before I realized they had even begun. Ultimately, both columns grew into the book that is now *Every Writer's Guide to Copyright and Publishing Law,* and writing it was a lot easier because I had already written the columns, but I'm not totally certain of how the last decade disappeared.

This leaves freelancing—which *can* be lucrative, but only if you are willing to work your tail off. To make a living at freelancing, volume is the key, and achieving the necessary volume takes a high degree of salesmanship.

This is because, while there are some markets that pay $1000 and more for an article, they are hard to crack—and even when you do crack them, the sale can be a onetime fluke. Until and unless you can break into those markets on a regular basis, most of your articles will probably garner anywhere between $100 to $500 for 1000 to 2500 words. In order to make even $1000 per month, you may have to write as many as ten articles. And if you want to guarantee you'll be paid, you'll have to sell them before you write them (I'll discuss writing on assignment a little later in this chapter).

If you want to survive by freelancing, you have to be constantly aware of publications to whom you can sell articles, and articles that you can sell to them. Part of this means subscribing to magazines, such as *Writer's Digest* and *The Writer,* that provide market listings—lists of publications that are looking for freelance contributions, generally accompanied by an analysis of the kinds of submissions they want to see.

It also means joining groups that provide market listings, reading business publications that may announce new publishing ventures, perusing the classified ads, and scanning magazine racks for new markets that may have been created by the inauguration of a new publication.

You learn to snatch up never-before-seen magazines from where they have been abandoned in airports, train stations or dentists' offices, to scan them for the kind of articles they publish, and to think, always to think, "What do I have that I might be able to sell them?"

You also become aware, by the frequency of their bylines, of other freelancers who are selling to the markets to which you think you could sell. This awareness begins with a stab of jealousy—for example, when you see a review of your favorite restaurant in the local paper by another freelancer. "I could have written that," you tell yourself, with a swift, figurative kick in the seat of your pants. "Why didn't I?"

Long before we met at a writers' conference, Milwaukee freelancer Carolyn Kott Washburne and I were well aware of each other, having seen each other's bylines on articles we knew we could have written. On being introduced, Carolyn and I both remarked how we'd long wanted to meet each other—obviously, we both recognized real competition when we saw it, and respected it.

It may take a healthy dose of that kind of friendly competition to keep your hand in the markets. It's healthy, because it keeps you alert to sales you could have made, and reminds you that if you put off querying an editor, someone else may get there first with the same idea. And it's friendly because you know you aren't alone in this loneliest of professions, and because, sometimes, after you have finished berating yourself for failing to make a sale another writer has made, you can reply to yourself, "Oh yeah? With what spare time?"

The best way to assure yourself of payment for your work is to write "on assignment" as opposed to "on spec." The latter, short for "on speculation," means that the publication wants to see your article, in full, before they are willing to commit to publishing it. This means that you can put in hours creating an article, only to get it back by return mail with a form rejection—and no money.

While writing on spec is probably an appropriate course for humor pieces or for fiction, both of which are hard to commission, and both of which may have to be seen in their entirety before an editor can commit to them, it is not appropriate for an article that has been researched for and tailored to a particular publication. To put your writing career on a more businesslike footing, you are much better off obtaining an assignment.

You do this by "querying" an editor, suggesting the article you would like to write and explaining why *you* should be the one to write it. I'll discuss the actual query process in more detail in chapter 8, but what is most important about writing on assignment is that the editor makes as much of a commitment to buying your piece as you do to writing it.

In an assignment letter, an editor will usually tell you:

▲ how long the article should be and what slant it should take,
▲ how much the publication is willing to pay, and when,
▲ what rights they are buying,
▲ when the article is due, *and*
▲ how much of a kill fee will be paid if the article turns out not to meet their needs after all.

The "kill fee" may be a flat fee, but it may also be a percentage of the contracted fee. If a publication decides to "kill" the story, it will surrender all rights to you, leaving you free to sell the piece elsewhere, if you can. But it will also pay you the kill fee—which means, from the moment you start to work on the story, you know you will get *at least* that amount, even if the article cannot be reconstructed or rewritten to the ultimate satisfaction of the publication.

In other words, working on assignment means that you are guaranteed *something* for your efforts, even if it is only enough to cover your typing paper and postage. It also means that the publication takes you seriously enough as a writer to be willing to commit to an article, sight unseen. Somehow, it is also easier to take yourself more seriously as a writer when that happens. The down side to this, of course, is that once you have an assignment, you *have* to write the piece—whether you still want to or not.

Writers are generally paid for articles either "on acceptance" or "on publication." For books, an *advance* is often paid in whole or in part "on signing" of the contract, "on acceptance" of the manuscript, or "on publication," and *royalties*—based on a percentage of the sales— are paid either annually or semi-annually, after the advance has been "earned out" (in other words, after the royalties due the author have equaled the advance previously paid). Thus, even if you wind up with a best-seller, if your advance isn't particularly large, you may have to wait as much as a year before you reap any real financial benefits.

As for articles, writers with any clout at all usually hold out for payment on acceptance rather than on publication, and for good reason. Think about it—could you get away with telling your local grocer, "I'll take this can of soup home, and I'll send you the payment for it when I get around to using it"? Our market economy doesn't work that way. So why should a magazine be entitled to hold on to your work product, sometimes for a year or more, without paying you for it?

Unfortunately, even when payment is promised "on acceptance," or when you concede to being paid "on publication," those terms may not mean what they appear to. Many publications have taken it upon themselves to define "acceptance" as "when the payment order works its way through to the editor-in-chief, and then through the Accounting Department—about a month from now." Similar delays occur after publication—and one classic delaying technique is to define "publication" by the date on the magazine, even though you may have a copy in your hands months before that date rolls around.

New magazines appear on the stands—and cease publication— with alarming frequency. A magazine that stops publishing may never pay you; if it goes through bankruptcy, you *may* receive a percentage of what it owes you, but often not until years later. Unless you are merely looking for print credits, this can be painful, especially if your work has already appeared in print and you are waiting for your "on-publication" check that will never come.

Book publishers are not immune from financial woes. Among those whose authors have found themselves pleading with the bankruptcy courts for payment in recent years are Stein and Day, Pinnacle Books, dilithium Press, and Delair Publishing. Writers who had royalties coming from these publishers have had to stand in line with the other unsecured creditors for a pro-rata share of whatever monies were left after salaries and legal fees and printers (with liens on the product) and banks (with secured loans) were paid in full.

Some writers have successfully resorted to small claims courts to collect from delinquent publishers. This is not possible under the law if the publisher has filed for bankruptcy, and may be extremely difficult if the publisher is located in another jurisdiction. Writers tend to find themselves at the end of the line of creditors when it is time for payment to be made.

So if you're writing to get rich, think again—it seldom happens. Writing for a living can be very unpredictable. But even if you're writing just for the satisfaction of it, or simply because you *must,* the following chapters will tell you how to put your career on a businesslike footing so you can maximize your chances of making a profit.

7

Format

Okay, you've taken the courses, learned the rules, and written something: fiction, an article, perhaps even a poem. Now how do you get a publisher to take a look at it?

Even if this is your first attempt at selling your writing, you want your manuscripts to *look* as though you have been doing this for years. Looking professional is one of the first steps to selling.

How do you accomplish this? Let's start out with the basics. In publishing, as in all things, first impressions are important. If you want to be taken seriously, *type* your manuscript. This has been true ever since typewriters became available to the general public, but perhaps even more important than the first impression a typewritten manuscript makes is the fact that, today, more and more publishers who might buy your work are using scanners.

A scanner is an electronic device that enables the publisher's computer to "read" your manuscript without a typist having to keyboard it in. Scanners read uniform text more easily than irregular text.

So do editors, whose tired eyes are more likely to look with favor on a clean manuscript than a messy one. Since *they* make the choice to buy the manuscript, the easier it is on their eyes the better: your manuscript should not only be typed, but typed *neatly*.

A word here about typing. The image of the typist has undergone some radical changes over the years, due in part to sex-role stereotyping and in part to the advent of the computer. Once upon a time, typing was considered a skill with no sex-role stereotyping attached to it; all the old movies about wartime correspondents and hard-bitten big-city newsmen always showed them hunched over their typewriters. As having a secretary came to be a mark of success, however, the secretary's primary task, typing, came to be considered "women's work"—so much so that professional women who could type were loath to admit it, and men who claimed to possess the skill were seldom believed.

I experienced a prime example of this at a real estate closing in the early eighties. Negotiations had kept us in the broker's office until well after five. When we finally settled on a compromise clause to be inserted in the closing statement, the broker's secretary had already left.

The seller's attorney was my friend Joe, who did most of his own typing and was proud of his skill. He volunteered to type the clause, but the broker appeared not to hear him. He turned, instead, to one of my two female clients, who were purchasing the property together, and asked if she could type. She told him she couldn't.

"I can type," said Joe. "I'll do it."

The broker ignored him, and asked my other client if she could type. She also shook her head. Ignoring yet another offer from Joe, the broker then turned to *me*.

"Sorry," I told him. "Why don't we just write it in?"

"*I* can type," Joe fairly screamed. Having exhausted the possibility of female typists, the broker condescended to allow Joe to type in the few words that were preventing us from calling it a day.

While Joe and the broker were out of the room, my clients and I compared notes. We all could type, and quite well. We probably would have been willing to do it, too, if we hadn't been asked so pointedly— and if Joe hadn't obviously wanted to do it so badly.

Happily, the attitude that typing is a menial task beneath the trouble of real men has changed, largely due to the increased use of computers— which require typing skills for programming and data input. As computers have become more and more commonplace, and as it has become more and more apparent that their use is the wave of the future, knowing how to type has become sex neutral, as unremarkable as being able to drive a car (and generally a lot less dangerous).

Typing is one of the simplest skills to learn. Once you know the basic finger positions, practice is the best way to increase your speed—

and nothing gives you as much practice as typing and retyping your manuscripts.

Even "typos"—typographical errors—are less of a problem than they once were. The "correcting" typewriters on the market for the past twenty years or so make it possible to "lift off" errors. Electronic typewriters that have a memory function allow you to correct a line or even alter a paragraph before the keys hit the paper. And computers and other word processing equipment make not only the correction of errors but also revision of text a simple matter.

If you can't type, and if you're serious about being a writer, you may want to include a typing course in your training program. The only alternative is an expensive one: *hire* a typist for your final draft.

How important is it that your manuscript look clean? That may depend on *who* you are. If your last six books soared to the top of *The New York Times* best-seller list and stayed there for a year, and if you have a long-term relationship with your publisher, you could probably submit your next novel written in lipstick on toilet tissue and get it accepted. The publishers wouldn't *like* it, but they'd merely charge the cost of typing it against your royalties and add you to their cocktail party stories about eccentric authors.

However, if you are a stranger trying to make a good impression, the easier your manuscript is on the overworked eyes of the editor to whom you submit it, the more likely it is to be scrutinized carefully. Editors read for a living. They read correspondence, they read solicited manuscripts, they read galleys and page proofs, and—when they get around to it—they read the slush pile.

The slush pile is the name given to the stack of unsolicited manuscripts every editor receives. The slush pile has the last priority, and an editor is likely to be in a state of exhaustion by the time he or she gets around to picking a manuscript from it. When that manuscript tries to sing its siren song, it is far more likely to be heard if it is neatly dressed.

What constitutes dressing neatly for a manuscript? As I've already mentioned, it should be typed—but type it on *white* paper. Another color will get the attention of the editor, all right—and predispose him (or her) to tucking it into its stamped, self-addressed envelope without looking past the title.

And type it *cleanly*. This may be a simple matter of cleaning your typewriter's keys, but it stands to reason that the product of an electric typewriter, which gives even pressure to every keystroke, is preferable to that of an old manual. A new ribbon (or one of single-use carbon film) produces a type that is sharper and thus easier to read. So does a daisy-wheel or a laser printer, rather than a dot matrix printer. And, yes, the ribbon should *always* be *black*.

Bear in mind that the point is to *type* your manuscripts, not to *print* them. The publisher does *that*. So even though your computer may have the ability to create a manuscript that looks as though it has been set in type, use an ordinary typewriter typeface, not a fancy script— and *don't* justify (even off) your right margin. Typing, not printing, remains the form of choice for manuscript submissions, even as we approach the twenty-first century.

Except for scripts (which have their own stylistic requirements) and poems (which may be single-spaced if they are short), manuscripts should always be double-spaced, with reasonable margins—generally an inch to an inch and a half on all four sides. Some publishers will send you a style sheet that indicates they want their stories triple-spaced, or with four-inch margins on one side, but unless you receive such directions, stick to the general format I've described.

If you are writing on a computer, it is simple to print out additional copies of a manuscript, so that you *and* the editor each have an "original." But with plain paper copiers, it is no longer absolutely necessary to submit the original; a photocopy will do—so long as it doesn't *look* like a copy. Whether you keep the original or a duplicate original or a photocopy, remember to *always keep a copy of your manuscript*. If you write on a computer, keep a hard copy in addition to the copy on disk, just in case something happens to your disk. (Those of us who are truly paranoid keep extra copies of our disks and manuscripts in other locations, so that if an earthquake, fire, or tornado should destroy one site, the other copies will survive.)

Even in the computer age, a manuscript should always be submitted on paper first. Once a manuscript is accepted (or if it was assigned), alternative methods for submission may sometimes be warranted. In this era of advanced technology, some publishers even pay premiums for manuscripts submitted on a compatible disk. Others prefer submission by modem or MCI mail. However, *these alternatives are only for manu-*

scripts that have already been accepted or assigned, and should be used *only* after consultation with the editor as to compatible format.

Fail to observe these conventions, and your manuscript or disk will come winging back to you faster than a rubber check—that is, *if* you have provided the customary self-addressed, stamped envelope.

Oh, yes—the *self-addressed, stamped envelope.* Otherwise known as a SASE (it rhymes with "case"), this should accompany every unsolicited manuscript and query you submit. If it does not, the editor is under no obligation to return your submission, or even to respond. Editors receive a lot of unsolicited mail and, depending on the volume and their editorial budget, providing an envelope or postage may be out of the question.

There are some writers who maintain that enclosing a SASE merely encourages an editor to reject your manuscript—but I have often received a contract or a check in the SASE. Sometimes the SASE will disappear entirely when a manuscript is accepted. Although this can result in a waste of postage when a single-page letter of acceptance arrives in an envelope to which you've affixed $2 in stamps (the SASE should bear adequate postage to cover the return of the manuscript), just chalk it up to the cost of doing business and forget about it.

If the waste really rankles you, and if you submit enough manuscripts and queries, it may pay to go down to your local post office and apply for a postal reply permit. This allows you to use those envelopes that say "No postage necessary if mailed in the United States." You pay for the permit and the printing, but you pay no postage unless the envelope is used. If it is, you'll be charged the appropriate amount based on the weight of its contents, plus a small premium. Only you can determine whether that constitutes a saving or a loss in the long run.

If you have a long-term relationship with an editor or a publication, you may be able to eliminate the SASE when submitting an unsolicited manuscript or a query. And you need never enclose a SASE when submitting anything that has been assigned. But when approaching a new market, observe the convention. Your purple prose—whether on purple paper or not—will most likely find its way into the circular file rather than home to you if submitted without a SASE.

One other place to utilize the SASE is when seeking representation by an agent. Once you are represented, the postage becomes the agent's worry; one of the ways agents earn their commission is by submitting manuscripts—at *their* cost. But when making first contact with an agent, treat that agent like a publisher, and always enclose a SASE.

Another convention to observe: the well-dressed manuscript should never wear a staple or any other permanent fastener. A paper clip is permissible for shorter pieces, but very long manuscripts, such as books, are best submitted—without any fastener at all—in the box the paper came in. (Because I also store *my* copies of book-length manuscripts in stationery boxes, I tend to beg boxes from all the other offices in my building, and from my local stationery store as well. As a result, I usually have a shelf filled with empty 8½-by-11-inch boxes in reserve.) You can also buy boxes designed especially for manuscripts— either single boxes or nesting boxes designed so that the inner box can function as a SASE.

If you don't have a suitable box, you *can* place the manuscript between two 8½-by-11-inch sheets of cardboard and secure them with rubber bands inside a sturdy mailing envelope large enough to hold the manuscript without splitting its sides.

I'm assuming that you're using 8½-by-11-inch paper—if not, *buy some.* Your manuscript should stick out of the slush pile because of its quality, not because of its odd size. And make that good-quality paper —sixteen- or twenty-pound bond, or *nonshiny* copier paper. *Never* use erasable paper—it smudges—or specialty papers like those used for fax machines or the old-fashioned two-step or wet copiers. These fade, smudge easily, curl, and sometimes stick together. None of these tendencies is likely to impress an editor.

Of course, if your manuscript is not going to be fastened, it should be obvious that its pages can become separated. For this reason, *you should place your name on every page.* Put it in the upper left-hand corner, and, assuming that you are going to write more than one article, story, or poem in your lifetime, follow it with a slash mark and a "slug." A slug is the identifying word or phrase that lets you know which of your manuscripts a wandering page belongs to.

The page number goes at the top, too, but in the upper *right*-hand corner. Number the entire manuscript in sequence: the first page of chapter 2 should bear the number following that of the last page of chapter 1.

Luckily, most word processing programs are designed to print what are known as "headers"—lines that run across the top of every page. If

Format for First Page of a Manuscript

Pete Moss   One-time serial rights
456 Primrose Path   About 750 words
Garden Grove, WI 53200   © 1989 Pete Moss
telephone: 414-555-1111

              DEALING WITH WHAT'S BUGGING YOUR GARDEN

                             by

                         Pete Moss

     They're back!
     This year's invasion of aphids, strengthened by a mild
wet spring and a milder, wetter summer, threatens to be the
largest in known memory. The beetles are back, too-- in fact,
I've noticed some bugs this year that I've never seen before.
     My neighbor has one of those electronic bug zappers in
his back yard. He says it doesn't really reduce the number of
insects that are dive-bombing his patio, but he plugs it in
because he gets a certain amount of satisfaction out of hearing
them fry. This year, however, there are so many creepy-crawlies
hanging around his yard that his old bug zapper shorted out,
and he had to replace it with a new, heavy-duty model.
     If you're a gardener, you know that, even as you're out to
get those bugs, they're out to get your buds and blossoms.
Aphids consider your roses a gourmet delicacy. Those teas and
grandifloras you've been feeding and mulching and watering so
devotedly are a diet delight to those voracious swarms that

Format for Final Page of a Manuscript

Moss/Bugs   -3-

don't like to use chemical insecticides (which may not work
anyway), there is a natural deterrent for green beetles that
seems to work effectively for most rose gardeners.

Gather up a bunch of these nasty pests and put them
through a household blender (most gardeners who do this like
to keep a separate blender for this, rather than using the one
in which they mix their margaritas). Put the "bug juice"
into a spray bottle and spray it on the roses.

Something in the dead beetles keeps the live beetles
away. No one knows <u>why</u> it works-- perhaps the dying beetles
give off some kind of scent, but it's undetectable to humans,
so it won't interfere with the aroma of your roses.

As the old saying goes, "All's fair in love and war."
If you love roses, you've got to be willing to declare war on
the bugs that have declared war on them. It can be a dirty
job, but somebody's got to do it if you want everything to
come up roses.

-end-your word processing program normally numbers pages at the bottom, it is usually a simple matter to move the page number to the top—although you may need to include a "blank footer" when you do so, or the page number may appear both at the top and the bottom of the page.

The *first* page of your manuscript will need *more* information: not only your name, but also your address and telephone number (or, if you are represented by an agent, your agent's name, address, and telephone number). These usually go in the upper left-hand corner of the manuscript. (In a book-length work, you can include a title page containing the information that might otherwise be on the first page of the manuscript.)

Two other items should also be included on the first page of the manuscript, but these go in the upper right-hand corner. The first is a description of what rights you are offering. I'll discuss this in more detail in chapter 11 regarding rights and copyrights—but let me add here for emphasis that in the absence of any other written evidence of what rights you offered for sale, a limiting indication on the manuscript itself could turn out to be critical.

The second item that should be included in the upper right-hand corner is a word count. The length of a work may determine whether a particular publication can use it and almost always determines what you will be paid for it. It's generally all right to round this off to the nearest twenty-five words or so. Usually, too, a word *means* a word, although some publishers assume a word means five letters, and, when I worked on my high school paper, we were told to count spaces and words of two letters or less as *one-third* of a word. (I have never heard of this system being used anywhere else.)

I often deal with newspaper and magazine editors who tell me they want "about three pages." They mean typewritten pages, of course, but since I use elite (twelve characters to the inch) instead of pica (ten characters to the inch) type, I always have to ask them to translate that into "words" for me. (My choice of a type size is a personal preference; it really doesn't matter, so long as your keys are clean and your ribbon is new and your editor's eyes aren't too bad. I figure it saves me a little bit on extra postage for longer pieces, but I use it just because *I* like what it looks like.)

Because I write so often for magazines, I made sure, when I purchased a word processing program for my computer, that it was capa-

ble of counting the words in a document. When I press the right
sequence of keys, the total number of words in the manuscript comes
up on the screen. I deduct for my name, address, and the title, and in-
stantly know the exact length of the piece.

I generally also include my copyright notice in the upper right-hand
corner of the first page of my manuscript. Strictly speaking, this is not
required, but I feel better about using it because it may offer slightly
better protection than leaving it off. The copyright notice consists of
three elements:

▲ The word "copyright," the symbol © (the letter "c" enclosed in a
   circle—"c" in parentheses will not do), *or* the abbreviation
   "copr."
▲ The name of the copyright holder (generally the creator of the
   work), *and*
▲ The year of first publication.

Obviously, a work that has not been published does not yet have a
year of first publication, but you can use the year in which the work was
completed for the notice. Literary agent Berenice Hoffman once suggested to me that putting such a notice on a work *dates* it, letting potential publishers know that the work has been hanging around, unsold,
for quite a while. I don't know whether that creates a psychological disadvantage. I do know that if you feel it does, it is easy enough to retype
or reprint the title page of an unsold book or the first page of an unsold
article and change the date, since the proper date in the notice is that of
first publication, anyway.

I find that having the notice on a manuscript helps *me* remember
when I wrote it. If it's old enough, I may want to update it before sending it out again.

I also feel that the notice serves as an extra reminder to publishers
that *I* hold the copyright in the work—just in case there is any dispute
over rights later on. And I feel it serves to protect me in one other way
as well. Unless a publisher has a violent objection for stylistic reasons, I
generally ask that my copyright notice be published with my articles.
While this is not strictly necessary, publishing the notice with the piece
can sometimes create increased legal protection, and can make copyright registration—should a writer choose to register the work—less
expensive (see chapter 11 regarding copyrights).

▲ ▲ ▲

One more thing that can be included in the upper right-hand corner of the first page of a manuscript, *when appropriate,* is an indication that the article is keyed to a certain event. This is generally useful only when submitting dated manuscripts to newspapers but may be helpful for *some* submissions to magazines as well.

In uppercase letters and underlined, either just above the offer of rights or just below the copyright notice, type some indication of the date by which the story must run. For example, an interview with a television star might bear the notice, "KEY TO OCTOBER FIRST MINI-SERIES BROADCAST." An interview with a politician might read, "KEY TO JANUARY 7TH LOCAL VISIT." If someone you interviewed has just died, make sure you remind the editor of the timeliness of your article by getting it in as soon as possible after the death and noting on it, "SUBJECT DIED FEB. 6TH. LOCAL PERFORMANCE FEB. 8TH CANCELED."

After you have entered your identifying information on the first page of your manuscript, drop about a third of the way down the page, and center the title of your piece in uppercase letters. Drop down two more lines and center your byline. Drop down another three or four lines and begin your text.

On subsequent pages, start at the top. In longer works, drop down a third of the page whenever you begin a new chapter, just as you would for the first page of a manuscript—but leave all identifying data off, except for your name, slug, and the page number (in other words, the same header you would normally use on any page after the first).

How important is it to have a *title* on the first page of your manuscript? A clever title can sometimes sell the story for you. But even the cleverest title will often be replaced by the editor or headline writer. Title changes are generally the prerogative of the publisher.

If a story is being written on assignment, you needn't rack your brains for a clever title—but do include one if it occurs to you. A lot of writing conventions may go by the boards when a story is being written on assignment, especially if the deadline is tight. I once faxed a story I'd written on a very short deadline to the editor in single-spaced format with *his* name and phone number at the top. This was prearranged with the editor in a short phone call, because we were each being charged per page for the fax.

If you're in a rush, and the editor knows your piece is coming—indeed, if he or she is waiting for it—it is often all right to title it "Aardvark Story" or "February 1991 Column." Of course, if a clever title occurs to you after you put the story in the mail, you can always phone it in.

What goes *on the bottom* of a manuscript page? For most markets, nothing—anything at the bottom of the page will give the typesetter a headache, and may wind up included in the text of your article.

But newspapers have their own traditions, born of their short deadlines and constant need to update breaking news. News stories are specially designed so that any paragraph could be the last paragraph in the story, allowing the editor to merely lop off the end when there isn't enough room. Writing to this kind of specification means it can be difficult to determine just what *is* the end of the story—so at the bottom of pages (except for the final page) of stories submitted to newspapers, it is often a good idea to write the word "more." Skip three lines before you do, so it is clear the word is not part of the story. Setting it off with hyphens ("-more-") or repeating it with slash marks ("more/more/more/more/more") are also acceptable ways to indicate that a story continues on the next page.

Whether a piece is submitted to a newspaper or to any other publication, you should *always* indicate when it ends. You can do this with the words "the end" or "end" or with a number of marks that have come to mean "the end" in the publishing world: "–30–" or "#" or "000." Skip two or three lines after you finish the text; then center the end indicator on the next line to show that your story has been told.

One last item to help your manuscript put its best foot forward: unless it is less than four pages long, *don't fold it*. You can fold the SASE, but the manuscript should be sent along its way in a flat envelope large enough to hold it comfortably (if you have to jam it in, buy the next-larger-size envelope).

Because the Post Office may assume that a 9-by-12-inch flat envelope contains junk mail, invest in a small stamp (I prefer the self-inking kind) that says "First Class" in bright red ink. Stamp this on both the front and the back of the envelope. Don't even consider sending a manuscript at any rate other than first class unless you don't have enough money for dinner. It looks tacky, and it seems to stand a far greater chance of being lost in the mail. It also takes much longer and

—given the pace at which most publishers respond—will slow your career down considerably.

Conversely, so will using overnight mail or special delivery unless an editor is *expecting* your manuscript. Overnight mail is useful for getting a piece on deadline to your editor, and for a multi-page manuscript, it may not be much more expensive than first-class postage. But sending a piece by overnight mail to an editor who is *not* eagerly awaiting it—who, indeed, has never *heard* of you—will appear to be an attention-getting device, and it will get you precisely the kind of attention you *don't* want to garner.

There are a lot of arguments, pro and con, for submitting a cover letter with your manuscript. I've heard some editors complain that cover letters are redundant—it's obvious, at least to them, that this is a manuscript and it has been submitted for publication. However, as a lawyer, I believe in creating a paper trail; your carbon copy of the cover letter proves you sent it out, and when.

And if you are writing on assignment for a magazine with more than one staff member, it can't hurt to write "Requested material" or "Assigned material" on the outside of the envelope in addition to attaching a cover letter. It is also a good business practice to recap the assignment, just in case the editor who assigned the article is not there when it comes in (you wouldn't want it buried in the slush pile by accident, now, would you?).

The recap should read something like this:

Dear Jack:

Here's the piece on water buffalo that you wanted to see by next week. It ran about 3200 words; I know that's 200 words long, but I figured the part on obedience courses could come out of the main article and make a nice sidebar. And I can get more detailed information on it if you want to expand that part. Let me know what you think—and how soon you can send the $300.

Reading this, there's no way a secretary could mistake your manuscript for a slush-pile piece, the editor knows what can be trimmed and what can be expanded, and you've reminded him that you're not chasing around after water buffalo for your health.

If you're not writing on assignment, and the editor doesn't know you, a cover letter is often a good selling point. Your letter, like your manuscript, is the foot that you are putting forward, so, again, it ought to be your best. Type it neatly on good-quality paper (or dignified sta-

Looking Professional

USE	DO NOT USE
White bond paper (preferably twenty pound, although sixteen pound *may* be acceptable). Good-quality copier paper—*not* the shiny stuff—may also be acceptable.	Colored paper (although cream or pale gray are all right for your stationery, especially if it is imprinted with your letterhead) or erasable paper.
A typewriter (preferably electric) or a daisy-wheel or laser printer (avoid dot matrix submissions).	A pen (except for your signature) or pencil (ever).
A black typewriter ribbon (preferably a new one or a single-strike black carbon ribbon).	A colored typewriter ribbon, or a worn one that produces faded, hard-to-read characters.
Standard typescript.	Fancy fonts or formats.
One- to $1\frac{1}{2}$-inch margins, never justified.	Justified margins; margins wider than $1\frac{1}{2}$ inches; no margins at all.
A flat 9-by-12-inch envelope for more than four sheets, or a standard (number 10) envelope for fewer than four sheets.	A standard business envelope for more than four sheets, or any envelope smaller than a number 10, *ever.*
Paper clips.	Staples or brass fasteners.

tionery, if you have it), make sure you use proper business-letter format, and double-check your spelling and grammar. Above all, spell the names of the editor and the publication correctly.

A word about your stationery—*don't* illustrate it, not even with a sketch of books or of an inkpot. *Don't* list yourself on your letterhead as a "freelance writer" or "professional writer"—the professional tenor of your prose should do that for you. If you have a degree that is relevant to your proposal, it's all right to use it (when I offer to write articles on legal subjects, I use my law office letterhead). But does the fact that you

---

Ten Basic Rules for Submitting Manuscripts

1. Type your manuscript.
2. Never submit your only copy of a manuscript, photo, or illustration; always keep a copy of anything you send out.
3. Put your name, address, and telephone number on the first page of your manuscript.
4. Put your name on the top of each page of your manuscript.
5. Number pages (except for the first page) sequentially in the upper right-hand corner of each page.
6. Always enclose a SASE with your submissions.
7. Never fold a manuscript that's four pages or more in length; use a 9-by-12-inch envelope or a stationery box for substantial manuscripts.
8. Never staple or bind a manuscript. Use a paper clip for shorter pieces, and submit longer pieces with no fastener at all, in a box of the appropriate size.
9. Check manuscripts for spelling and typing errors. Spell the name of the editor and the name of the publication correctly.
10. When a manuscript begins to look shabby, put another *clean* copy into circulation.

---

have an M.A. or Ph.D. have any bearing on the article you're submitting about your grandmother's attic? If not, plain stationery with just your name on it might make you seem less pompous—remember, the only impression of you an editor will get is from the letter you write.

Your article will ultimately stand or fall on its own merits, but it doesn't hurt to explain in your cover letter why the publisher should take an article on this subject from *you* and why they should take it *now.* You can also open up more potential sales—including the possibility of an assignment on a related subject if they can't use the article you're submitting—by indicating your availability and flexibility in the cover letter. For example:

Dear Mr. Smith:
    The changes in U.S. copyright law that went into effect on March 1, 1989, have caused great confusion among members of the work-

ing press. As a working journalist as well as an attorney, I am aware of this confusion and have tried to shed some light on it with the enclosed article. I have attempted to tailor it to your readership, but if you would prefer a shortened piece or something exploring the subject in more depth—on these changes or any particular aspect of them—I'd be happy to revise the piece to order.

My articles on the legal aspects of writing have appeared in publications like *Writer's Digest* and *Editors Only,* and I am also the author of a book entitled *Every Writer's Guide to Copyright and Publishing Law* (Henry Holt, 1990). The usual SASE is enclosed for your response.

Very truly yours,
Ellen M. Kozak

I've heard a lot of arguments for submitting a manuscript as you would an advertising package—in a printed folder, with full-color illustrations and three-color printing. Unless you're writing a book *about* hype, don't hype your manuscript. It should be able to speak for itself —though you may have to add a word or two about yourself in your cover letter.

Fiction and humor submissions, especially, stand on their own. It may be a good idea to identify the kind of fiction you're submitting—a mystery or a western, for example. And, since editors do like to know a little about you if they like a piece, a short letter introducing yourself is not really out of place. But if you have to retell the story in your cover letter in order to sell it, you probably didn't tell it very well in the first place.

No matter how well you've told your tale, if it isn't professional looking, it is unlikely that it will be read at all. So always make sure to dress your manuscripts for success if you want them to sell.

In the next chapters, we'll look at how to sell manuscripts *before* you've written them.

8

Selling Your Writing Before You Write It

Although short fiction and certain articles, such as humor pieces and trivia tests, do best when submitted in completed form to an editor, most magazine sales and many book sales are made before the text is actually written. In the periodical world, this is known as "writing on assignment." In the world of book publishing, the reference is, instead, to "having a book under contract."

The alternative method is "submitting over the transom." This is a curious expression, because I can't imagine that mail ever arrived via the transom, even in those days before air conditioning when transoms —those small windows located above the doors in older buildings— were open all summer long. Perhaps publishers barred their doors to unsolicited manuscripts, and eager writers became adept at catapulting their works through the openings above them, but they still would have been delivered *through* rather than *over,* the transom. Nevertheless, the expression persists.

The disadvantage to submitting completed works over the transom is that they may never find a home. Editors assign articles (or books) so that they can plan their issues (or their lists) in advance. Even though yours may be the best article ever written on how to cook a turkey, if an editor has space for only one such article in the November issue and has already assigned someone else to write it, your manuscript will be returned to you.

The only real advantage to submitting works over the transom is that *you* have the freedom to control the shape and form the work will take. If you feel the proper length is 800 words, you will not have to search high and low for the material to fill another 400 because the assigned length is 1200 words. Nor will you be forced to cut the piece to its bare bones because the editor only wants 500 words. And, if you have no deadline, it won't matter if you let the piece sit until *next* Thanksgiving because you aren't quite happy with it and want to give it some time to percolate.

There are, of course, some markets that *prefer* receiving completed works. Newspapers, because they function on immediacy, will often purchase feature stories in this way, especially if they receive them at the appropriate time. When is the appropriate time? That will vary from paper to paper. Sometimes all the feature stories for the Easter edition are chosen by February; sometimes extra ad sales create extra space at the last moment, and a story received only a week or so before the holiday will be purchased to fill that space.

If your work is geared to a particular holiday issue—Thanksgiving, Easter, or perhaps the Fourth of July—there is nothing wrong in asking an editor what the "lead time" normally runs. And if you have been writing for a publication with considerable regularity, it might be useful to you and the paper if you inquired about "special issues" in the planning stages. You just might have—or be able to create—a feature the paper could use for the cruise issue, the Florida or European vacation issue, the automotive issue, or the adult education issue. (But be warned: newspapers are not always willing to divulge that kind of information in advance except to writers who are *known* to them.)

Newspapers usually purchase articles in the 500- to 1000-word range. Pieces longer than 1500 words are likely to be cut or rejected outright. And newspapers usually pay comparatively low prices. Sometimes they do not pay at all—opinion pieces, for example, may not earn you anything but a print credit. And newspapers seldom send courtesy copies (although they may give you several if you stop in), so if you are not a regular subscriber, you may not even know your article has seen print.

Short deadlines and the sheer volume of verbiage that a paper must produce every day govern the etiquette at most newspapers. However, magazine articles that do not fall into the humor category are more likely to sell if you *query* first.

Basically, the purpose of a query is to pitch an idea for a story, but generally you have to pitch not only the story, but why *that* publication should buy it, and why they should buy it from *you*. A good query letter tells an editor what kind of article you want to write for the publication, convinces him or her that your article would interest the publication's readers, and establishes your credentials to write the piece—while showing off both your professionalism and your style.

Is this a tall order? You bet it is. Sending query letters is an art in itself, for a query letter must catch the editor's attention (with its content, *not* with purple ink or illustrated margins!), and then convince the editor that *his* readers would be interested in *your* article, written from *your* proposed slant, and in *your* style.

How do you do this? It is easiest to query a magazine that you read frequently, for you will be familiar with its style, and you will also know if your proposed subject has been covered in a recent issue.

If you're serious about writing for the magazine, you have to learn to *read it like a writer*. Pick up the last three issues and go over them with care. First, check the bylines against the masthead (the masthead is the column in the beginning of the publication that lists the staff). Are all the contributors members of the editorial staff? If so, the publication may not purchase freelance materials. Submitting to a publication that doesn't purchase from outsiders is a waste of postage.

Next, check out the length of the articles. Do they vary, or do they all fall into a certain range—say, 1500 to 2000 words? Can you keep to that length for your article? If not, perhaps you should query another publication.

Now go over the articles to determine whether they are written in the first, second, or third person. You can't sell a first-person reminiscence to a publication that only uses third-person references. Don't even try.

Go back and read over the articles again. Do they use humor? Specific names and addresses? Footnotes? Are some of them the *kind* of article you want to write (for example, a how-to piece or a travelogue)? And is the kind of article you propose to write normally accompanied by a sidebar (a separate, related box or column) providing specific references or statistics? Could you provide such a sidebar with your article?

Chances are, the kind of material a publication has bought in the past is the kind of material it will buy in the future. It's highly unlikely any publication will change its editorial policies for you. On the other hand, a publication is also unlikely to repeat a subject it has recently covered, although if there is breaking news on the subject—a new law or a new discovery—a sale on that subject is a possibility.

In the ordinary course of events, however, articles repeat only on the basis of a readership cycle. You can find out the length of this by researching back issues. A household magazine may do an article on gardens every spring, on picnic foods every summer, and on Christmas gifts every December. But other articles—such as how to make sure your homeowner's insurance is adequate—will show up only once every two or three years. Find enough of these articles, and you will know what the cycle for that publication is, and when it will be ready to look at another article on the subject you want to write about.

In addition to carefully studying back issues, the best way to get to know about markets for your material is to check out some of the books and periodicals specially designed for this purpose.

One of the best places to discover the purchasing policies of a publication is in the current issue of *Writer's Market*. This book is published every fall and lists hundreds of markets that buy materials from freelancers. Unfortunately, because *Writer's Market* is an *annual* publication, with a lead time of several months between submission of final copy and actual publication, some of the listings may be out-of-date. Also, although it probably provides the most comprehensive one-volume listing of freelance markets available, it does not list *every* market—not by a long shot.

Most newspapers, for example, are not listed in *Writer's Market*. You can find a fairly comprehensive listing of newspapers, both daily and weekly, in *Working Press of the Nation,* but this is a multi-volume set and quite expensive—and, because of the mobility of members of the working press, it, too, is often out-of-date by the time it sees print. *Working Press of the Nation* may be available at your local library, or your local newspaper or television station may have a copy and may be willing to let you look at it.

Literary Marketplace is another annual publication, but one more geared toward book publishing than articles. LMP, as it is known to those in the business, costs about five times as much as *Writer's Market*. Both books are usually available in your public library.

There are also several books that list all the publishers in a specific region (which may or may not include national publications located in that region). Cassell Communications of Fort Lauderdale, Florida, publishes directories of Florida, Georgia, and Texas markets. Writers Connection of California (Cupertino, California) publishes *California Publishing Marketplace.* All of these are annual volumes and may be at least partially out-of-date by the end of the year in which they are published.

For more up-to-date market information, you may want to look at *Writer's Digest,* a monthly magazine geared toward helping freelance writers sell their work. It's available at most newsstands and is usually among the magazines you can order through those sweepstakes that "you may already have won." *The Writer* is another monthly containing market information, but I find *Writer's Market* more helpful in keeping abreast of market conditions.

Even more current is *Freelance Writer's Report,* a monthly newsletter from Cassell Communications (Post Office Box 9844, Ft. Lauderdale, Fla. 33310), one of the best sources of information on new markets. Monthly market reports are also issued by the National Writer's Club (located in Aurora, Colorado). This is not really a club at all; it does not elect officers, and the "members" have no say in organization policies. However, it does provide fairly comprehensive market listings, although *Freelance Writer's Report* is, in my opinion, a better bargain.

Other good sources of market listings—particularly listings for specialized markets—are specialty publications (such as *Romantic Times*) or legitimate writers' organizations (such as the Science Fiction Writers of America and the Mystery Writers of America). I've provided a partial list of writers' associations at the end of this book.

Many times these publications will provide the names and addresses of *new* markets. A word of caution here: writing for such markets has both an up side and a down side. Some announced new markets never manage to get off the ground; others never get beyond the first issue. New publications are often more open to freelance submissions than markets that have already built up a "stable" of writers from whom they normally purchase materials. But if you've never seen the publication, you can't always tell what its editors are looking for, so you are more likely to wind up having them "kill" your story. And because many new publications are undercapitalized, they may run out of money before they can pay you, or may cease publication before your piece sees print. Approach all start-up markets with cautious optimism—and never count your money from them before the check clears the bank.

▲   ▲   ▲

A small codicil to the foregoing—when I began my law practice, an older attorney conveyed this pearl of wisdom to me: "The good lawyer knows the law; the smart lawyer knows the judge." From which I would extrapolate for writers, "Know your market—but it never hurts to know the editor."

Conventional wisdom in the writing field tells you never to *telephone* an editor, but this is not necessarily the case for a local newspaper. If you don't catch the editor there on deadline, he or she may even be willing to sit down with you and discuss the paper's needs and purchasing policies. And *any* editor may be willing to discuss a truly relevant, truly newsworthy piece whose subject matter might be out-of-date by the time a written submission went through channels. An example of this might be a lengthy interview you had done with a nuclear scientist regarding the inherent danger in U.S. nuclear reactors. Such an interview would have acquired a sudden timeliness the day after the news of Three Mile Island or Chernobyl broke.

One place to meet editors is at your local press club. As a published freelancer, you may qualify for membership. Another place to meet editors—especially those from other parts of the country—is at writers' conferences. But more often than not, as a freelancer, you will have to submit your material to an editor you've never met.

To whom do you direct the query letter if this is the case? The market listing may suggest a specific editor, but if it doesn't, when submitting to magazines I favor the "managing editor"; this is premised on a trickle-down theory that presumes that if the managing editor passes the material on at all, it will arrive on the desk of the appropriate underling with a certain imprimatur that enhances the likelihood of its purchase. There are, however, other theorists who maintain that a minor editor will be less deluged and more likely to pay attention to your query, championing it before any higher authority (a "trickle *up*" theory, I presume).

In any case, beware of writing to a "contributing editor." These folks are actually freelancers whose material is published frequently in a magazine, or who are experts in one category or another and so are consulted before the magazine buys articles in that category. They may have a corner on *all* articles in that category, or they may review submissions in that category—or they may have been given a title in lieu of a higher pay rate for their frequent articles. A simple rule of thumb: *never* query a contributing editor.

▲   ▲   ▲

Writing a query letter can be as difficult as writing the actual article about which you are inquiring. You can't just send off a letter saying, "I'm fascinated by the purple trees in Los Angeles and no one seems to know what they are. Wouldn't you like me to investigate and do a story?" You might *never* find the answer; why should the publication take the risk?

On the other hand, I sold a story to *Travel & Leisure* about the jacaranda trees of Los Angeles precisely because no one I met out there in the City of Angels could tell me what they were called. I made it my business to find out—by phoning actress Jane Wyatt, whom I had previously interviewed, and who, I remembered, was an avid gardener and on the board of a group that oversaw street plantings in L.A. She not only identified the trees, but also gave me the name of a contact at the Los Angeles Street Trees Department. *He* gave me statistics on the number of jacarandas in Los Angeles, problems involving their plantings, and the areas where most of them could be found. A quick trip to our local museum's botanical library, and I knew I had plenty of material on jacaranda trees that would appeal to the general public— enough, in fact, for a 500-word article. That's what I sold them, that's what they got, and that's what they printed.

You don't necessarily have to do *all* of the research in order to write a query. Basic research will tell you how much material is available, and how much is likely to be relevant. You can do the rest of the research after you get the assignment, but the basics have to be done *before*.

How long should a query letter be? Generally, one typed page is best, but no one will shoot you for using two pages if you absolutely must. Remember, though, that the query is a sample of your writing style—the first sample that the editor will see. Tight, concise, but expressive writing will help you to obtain the assignment.

Some people favor starting the query with the same lead they will use in the story. This sometimes works—and sometimes makes you sound like an idiot. A letter that begins "Dear Ms. Brown: Out of the more than 200 million people in the United States, 2 million will go to bed hungry tonight . . ." sounds like a solicitation for a charitable contribution, not an offer to write a piece on dieting.

You could clearly mark the letter (where most business letters would have an "attention" or "re" line) "ARTICLE QUERY," to keep it out of the box filled with solicitations for starving third-world chil-

Prequery Checklist

▲ Will this article appeal to the typical readership of this publication?

▲ Has this publication published this *kind* of article (e.g., a "how-to" article, a travel piece, or an account of a personal experience) in the past?

▲ Have any articles appeared in this publication on *this subject* in the past three years?

▲ If so, how is mine different? What service will it provide to the readers that the previous article(s) didn't?

▲ What approach will I take to appeal to this specific readership?

▲ How long do articles of this sort in this publication usually run? How much detail do they provide? Can I provide that kind of detail or authority?

▲ How long will this article have to be to say what I think should be said? Can I make it longer or shorter by adding or eliminating details?

▲ Have I ever met or written for anyone at the publication? Would that person be an appropriate person to query? If not, who *is* the appropriate person?

Once you answer these questions, you are finally in a position to write your query. Always accompany a query with a SASE to guarantee response. Address a specific editor, and *spell his or her name correctly.* Get the address of the publication right—the editorial offices may be different from the advertising or sales offices.

And be sure that your letter is neatly typed in business-letter form, on one side of the page, with no mistakes in spelling or punctuation. Again, this is *not* the time to use the italic or Germanic script on your word processor—a plain typeface will serve you much better.

dren and mistreated pets. Or instead of trying to be clever, you could use a style that maintains a normal business footing, as this letter to the editor of an imaginary holistic diet magazine illustrates:

Dear Mr. Smythe:

After spending most of my life gaining and losing the same 25 pounds, two years ago I embarked on a new and different diet with the help of a nutritionist. In an attempt to keep my cholesterol and blood pressure down as well, I ate sensibly, but was careful to include in my diet whole oats and oat bran, raw apples, and raw carrots. I called this, "Eating like a horse."

Spell that name right!
Why you should write this article.

Cite authority—you are not a kook!

The substance of the diet plan.
Clever title—selling point.

I found I was seldom hungry, and my weight came off slowly and steadily—and has stayed off for 18 months, without any real effort on my part to keep dieting.

It worked—another selling point.

Having written professionally for many years (my articles have appeared in national publications like *Modern Food* and *Kitchen Kings*—samples are enclosed), I would like to write about this diet for you. I envision a piece of approximately 1500 words, in which I would cite my nutritionist, F. Atchance, Ph.D., R.D., and would provide up to half a dozen kitchen-tested recipes, such as Oat-Bran Meat Balls and Apple-Oat Snacks. I could also provide before and after photos of *me*. (They were taken by my husband, so rights are not a problem.)

Again, why you are qualified to write this.

What the piece would be like, how long, etc.

What authority you could cite.

Extras you could provide.

Photos are often a plus.
Clear any problems before they arise.

Let me know if you'd like to see this article, and when you'd need final copy.

Remind him that this is a query.

Cordially,

Let's be friends.

Enclose appropriate copies of your published work—other how-to pieces if you're querying a how-to article, other travel pieces if you're querying a travel article (see chapter 19 for the best way to keep these on hand). Put all this, *paper-clipped* together, into a large flat envelope, along with your SASE. Log the query six weeks ahead in your calendar

---

Query Content Checklist

- ▲ Have you spelled the editor's and publication's names correctly? Is the address of the publication accurate?
- ▲ Have you worded the query to catch the editor's interest?
- ▲ Have you told the editor why this article (or the approach you have chosen) would appeal to this publication's readership?
- ▲ Have you established your expertise in the subject area or explained why you should be the one to write this article (already obtained interviews, etc.)?
- ▲ Have you included your credentials as a writer, including appropriate tear sheets? (Note: a tear sheet is a copy of a published article. The name originated when writers had to tear out the pages containing their articles from the publications in which they had appeared. With the prevalence of copiers, it is now possible to photocopy your published manuscripts—see chapter 19 —but the term remains.) Are your name and address on each tear sheet?
- ▲ Have you suggested available photographs or illustrations, or suggested any graphs or sidebars that should accompany the article?
- ▲ Have you enclosed your SASE?

---

to make sure you've had a response by then, attach appropriate postage, and drop it in the mail. You've queried an editor, and you're on your way to your first assignment.

A word of caution here about multiple submissions. Sending the same article or query to more than one publication used to be an absolute taboo. *Some* of the barriers in this regard have fallen—but not all.

One of the best ways to determine whether submitting a story to more than one publication will get you into trouble is to check the market listing. Magazines that say "multiple submissions accepted" or "buys first, onetime, or reprint rights" obviously don't mind if you send your work to other, noncompeting markets. Other publications will never deal with you again if they discover that you've been doing this.

I think a multiple query may be more legitimate than a multiple submission, for several reasons. First among these is the fact that the article is not yet written. Different publications may respond with different assignments—one may want a short piece, another a long one. One magazine may have a long lead time; another may want to bring out the article within the month. And one may want the article slanted for a select group (e.g., parents or employers), while the other wants it slanted for an entirely different group (teachers or employees).

Since you may be producing totally different stories for totally different readers, and since you always retain the option of declining a proffered assignment, the submission of multiple query letters should not offend the editor; but be forewarned that editors are human, and some of them will take offense at what seem to be the most innocuous things. Others are simply quirky or arrogant or unbusinesslike themselves, and will "lose" your query letter or respond with sarcasm. If you have been polite and businesslike in your approach, and have observed the conventions I have been outlining here, you can chalk this up to a personality conflict and avoid that market—at least, until that editor moves on to another publication.

Multiple queries are better than multiple submissions of fully written articles for another important reason: not only do complete articles offer less flexibility, they can get you into trouble if an editor decides to accept your submission and has it set in type or printed before you learn of the acceptance. The first inkling you get may be the arrival of your check and contributor's copy in the mail. This can create an embarrassing situation if you are submitting to more than one market at the same time. To avoid overlapping sales, it is common courtesy to inform the editor in your cover letter that you are making a multiple submission. However, you had better have a legitimate excuse for doing so.

What constitutes a legitimate excuse? The best, I think, is time pressure due to a breaking story to which you have exclusive access. A reclusive actor wins this year's Best Actor oscar; no one can get an interview with him—but *you* went to school with his brother, who gives you his unlisted number. Or a new kind of cancer treatment is developed at the hospital where you work.

Given the pace at which much of the publishing world responds to correspondence, if you wait for a response from the first publication to which you have sent your story or query, your news may be "old hat"—so of course you're going to multiply submit. I'd still suggest querying first, and seeing which markets bite. But if you've written up the story and want to send it out to a number of places, *tell them that's what you're doing.*

Try something like this: "Because of the timely nature of this article, I am submitting it to several markets; I will, of course, keep you informed of any other sales that might preclude a sale to you. However, as I would be happy to revise the article to order, let me know if a version specially tailored to your needs might be of interest to you.''

Another multiple submission that is generally acceptable is self-syndication—submitting a manuscript to noncompeting publications. What constitutes a noncompeting market? Location is one of the principal distinctions; readership is another. If you have not submitted the piece to a national publication (whose readership would, of course, overlap on local or regional markets), you *can* submit it to newspapers or magazines in different regions, states, or localities. General features are often circulated in this manner.

For example, a nostalgic story about foods your grandmother used to serve could be sold to newspapers in Omaha, Denver, Milwaukee, Chicago, Miami, Pittsburgh, Columbus, and Providence—but don't offer it to two papers in the same town or to a local magazine and a regional magazine whose circulations overlap.

Audience rather than location sometimes distinguishes the readership of one publication from another. It would, for example, be possible to submit the same Christmas story with "universal appeal" to a Baptist magazine, a Catholic magazine, and a Lutheran magazine—since their readership doesn't overlap—but *never* to *two* Catholic magazines at the same time. You can also sell a story on coping with stress to publications catering to every professional group in the country—doctors, lawyers, engineers, clergymen, auto mechanics, cement contractors, loggers—you name it. But *never* submit the same story to *two* national engineering magazines simultaneously.

As I've noted, you really should never submit the same material to competing publications, unless it contains news so timely that you have no choice. Once it is published, you should never accept an assignment to write up the same material for a second, competing publication unless considerable time has passed or unless you have cleared it with both editors involved. And because this can mean revealing information about the makeup of a future issue to the competition, the first editor you should clear it with is the first editor who published the work.

9

Selling Books Before They're Written

All that information for selling articles is fine, you say—but you're writing a *book*. Are the rules for books the same as the rules for articles? Can you get an "assignment" from a publisher? Can you make multiple submissions?

Let's take that last question first. Agents almost *always* make multiple submissions of books, but many editors complain when unrepresented authors do so. (No one ever said life was fair.)

Compounding this unfairness is the fact that if you have an agent, your work arrives on the editor's desk with a kind of imprimatur; most editors will read agented works—even from unknown agents—before they read unagented ones. Thus the response time for agented submissions is usually shorter than that for unagented works, which means multiple submissions really make more sense if you *don't* have an agent; but if an editor is offended by your tactics, they won't gain you a sale.

As with periodicals, the only reason to submit to more than one market at a time is that your topic is timely, not merely that you are anxious to see your work in print (*everyone* is in a hurry for *that!*). Choose your markets carefully (you have a better chance of hitting a bull's-eye with a rifle than with a shotgun), and tailor your cover letter to each publisher; if you've taken the time to write a book, why skimp on a letter?

As you would when submitting articles, spell the editor's name—

and the name of the publishing house—correctly. Spell the street name and the city correctly, too—the first impression your book is going to make is the label on its package.

Manuscripts that are addressed to a specific editor usually get more attention than those merely addressed to the "Editors," but there is a lot of movement in the publishing industry, and a manuscript addressed to an editor who is no longer at a publishing house may languish for some time before it lands on another editor's slush pile—a good reason to make sure your market information is up-to-date.

But how do you choose which publishing house to submit your work to, or find the name of an appropriate editor there? Two of the best sources of market information are *Literary Marketplace* and *Writer's Market,* but these annual publications may be out-of-date by the time you check them. Reading *Publishers Weekly* is one way to keep abreast of which editors have moved to different houses and what they are buying. (PW, as it is known in the trade, also reports on interesting sales made by agents; if you read about an agent who seems to handle your kind of material, you might want to query him or her about representing you.)

A great place to meet editors and agents is at a writers' conference. Conferences that are geared to publishing-related interests, like the American Library Association and American Booksellers Association annual conventions, also draw publishers' representatives and agents. So do book fairs and—in their special areas of interest—mystery, romance, and science fiction conventions.

There's also nothing wrong with exploiting a connection if you have one—contacting a second cousin once removed or a friend of a friend —as long as you're not obnoxious about it. Take your lead from the willingness of the editor or agent to talk to you, and don't push, since antagonizing a contact won't sell your work for you.

However, if someone *is* willing to meet with you, seize the opportunity. I met my agent when she was an editor; she edited the books of two of my friends who spoke of her so often I felt I knew her. On a trip to New York, I called her and introduced myself, and she invited me to drop by her office.

Not all editors are that friendly. Some might be downright indignant if you were to phone them. Unless you're sure an editor is the kind of person who welcomes phone calls, use the mails for your first contact.

Just knowing an editor won't do you any good, of course, if that editor handles history and you've written a romance novel—although he or she might be willing to give you the name of another editor who does handle the kind of book you have written. Rejection slips are easy enough to garner without courting them by submitting to an inappropriate publisher. Even if you don't have any contacts, a little research can go a long way toward helping you find the appropriate place to submit your manuscript.

What kind of research? Go to the library or your local bookstore and see who has recently published books *of the kind* you are writing. (But beware a company that has already published a book on your topic— unless *all* their books are on that topic!) Then call the publishing house and ask who edited the books you think are similar to yours. Ask if that person still works there, and verify the spelling of the editor's name. (Do *not* ask to speak to that editor!) If you address your manuscript specifically to that person, you might stand a better chance of its getting a good reception. Then again, the editor might be sick of that kind of book. In publishing, success is often based on the luck of the draw and what the editor had for breakfast the day your materials came in.

There is one important rule when approaching publishers and agents —so important that I'm going to list it here as:

Kozak's Rule #5: *They pay you, you don't pay them.*

There are minor exceptions to this rule. If you are an unpublished author, an agent may charge a reading or handling fee. If this fee is nominal—say $50 or so for a book or sample chapters—the agent is probably legitimate. But beware of agents who charge hundreds of dollars; agents normally receive a percentage of what you are paid for a book, and should never be paid out of your pocket except for extraordinary expenses, such as legal fees, the reasonable cost of photocopying, and overnight (but not ordinary) mail service.

Publishers who ask you to pay are known as "vanity" or "subsidy" presses. They will usually publish anything by anyone willing to pay them. Reviewers know this and generally will not review the products of a vanity or subsidy house.

As far as I'm concerned, there are only three valid reasons for *paying* to have your work published, and in all three cases you may do better with a local printer and binder than with any vanity press. These reasons are:

- ▲ The work is of limited interest, like a family genealogy or a guide to local restaurants,
- ▲ The work can be sold or given away to your business clients (for example, if you conduct seminars, it can serve as a handbook or be sold in conjunction with presentations), *or*
- ▲ You have tried every legitimate source and no one wants to publish your work, and you refuse to accept this consensus judgment as accurate (in which case, as they say, it's your nickel).

You can submit your manuscript—and your money—to a vanity press in almost any format, although the more professional your materials, the more professional your book is likely to be. For professional submissions to legitimate publishing houses, however, the rules of format discussed in chapter 7 apply.

The procedure for obtaining an agent is pretty much the same as the procedure for obtaining a publisher: you submit your work, biographical information, and a cover letter, along with return packaging (an envelope or a box) and sufficient postage. The only difference is, with agents, it is often a good idea to inquire first if they are willing to read material from nonclients; an agent who is not accepting new clients will return your manuscript unread, and, as I mentioned, some agents will refuse to read it unless you tender a reading fee first.

In this respect, publishers and agents differ. Legitimate publishers *never* charge a reading fee. This is because it is their business to be on the lookout for manuscripts to fill their publishing quotas each month, while agents who know their own limitations try not to represent more writers than their time and expertise allow. Indeed, it is sometimes actually easier to interest a publisher in your work than it is to interest an agent.

Contrary to what you may hear on the publishing grapevine, it *is* possible to sell a book to a publisher even if you don't have an agent—and even if you've never sold a book before. I am called on, all the time, to negotiate contracts for first-time authors who have sold their work unrepresented. The most important consideration is not whether you are represented by an agent, but whether your writing is of a professional caliber and content, your manuscript looks professional, you have chosen your market carefully, and you have approached the editor as one professional to another.

This means no whining, no boasting, no insults, and no threats. A cover letter that reads "You have to buy this manuscript because I need the money for a kidney transplant" or "My relatives and friends think this is the best novel they've ever read" or "This will be a best-seller, if only you have the sense to realize it" is guaranteed to turn off the recipient. If you're not sure how much to say in a cover letter, say less rather than more. A letter that reads:

> Enclosed please find the manuscript [for my mystery novel, or my children's history of the Kennedy administration, or whatever you have written] for your consideration, along with postage and a mailing label for its return if it should not meet your needs.

doesn't exactly set off fireworks, but it won't antagonize anyone either. It will at least allow the manuscript to speak for itself.

You can submit your entire manuscript to an agent or publisher if you've completed it, but you don't always have to do so. Nonfiction books can be submitted as "proposals" before they are written, fiction books as "partials."

There is an art to writing proposals and partials, just as there is an art to writing a query letter. Indeed, in many ways the techniques are similar—only the book proposal is longer.

The form of a proposal for a nonfiction book may vary, but generally it should be made up of five elements:

- ▲ A *cover letter* pitching the marketability of the book.
- ▲ The basic *proposal* itself: a description of the book, what you intend to accomplish with it, what angle you will take, what kinds of material (including illustrations and supplements) you will include, and the estimated length.
- ▲ A *biographical statement* about you as the author, written in the third person (much like a cover blurb would be), explaining why you are the right person—indeed, the *only* person—who should write this book.
- ▲ A *chapter-by-chapter outline*, with a description (anywhere from a paragraph to a page in length) of the contents of each chapter.

▲ At least one *sample chapter* that is indicative of the type of material you will be including *and* of your writing style. Three chapters (one of these should be the *first* chapter) or at least fifty pages of material are usually better than one chapter.

The cover letter for your proposal should be carefully researched. If you are capitalizing on a trend, use facts and statistics to prove that the trend exists. Remember that the lead time in book publishing is normally at least a year, so it may help to anticipate a trend rather than to catch it at its crest.

The cover letter is a good place to note your basic credentials for writing the book (including your prior publications). It is also the appropriate place to discuss your ability to market the book—do you, for example, travel frequently, and are you willing to do so in support of the book? Do you have a national network of friends and relatives who can help you set up book signings and obtain local press coverage when you come to town? Do you host a show on your local radio station (an indication that you are comfortable on the air and may have some connections in the broadcast industry)? If so, mention these things.

The cover letter should not run more than two pages—save the "meat" for the actual proposal.

Because it should offer potential publishers an idea of your writing style and the way you intend to approach your topic, the proposal itself should begin much the same way you intend to begin the book. Here's your chance to show off your fancy footwork, hooking the reader with amusing anecdotes and enlightening examples.

The proposal should be a synopsis of the book, describing its thrust and its slant. The text of the proposal is also a good place to contrast your book with other books on the market that address the same facts or issues, explaining why *your* book will be different. And somewhere in your proposal you should note the estimated length of the book and detail any special features, such as charts, graphs, or photos, that it will contain.

This summary of what you hope to accomplish with your book can run anywhere from one page to twenty, whatever is necessary to indicate what the book can do—and what it can't. Don't promise anything you can't deliver; remember, if you sell your proposal, you'll have to write the book.

▲ ▲ ▲

Your biographical statement should be an exercise in public relations —interesting and comprehensive without being too detailed. Give personal facts that are relevant and that help your cause. If you are proposing a self-help medical tome, do mention that you graduated from Harvard Medical School; if you got your degree from a school no one has ever heard of, you might consider leaving out that fact and merely referring to yourself as a physician in private practice who is board certified in a specialty appropriate to your topic.

If the book you are proposing is a guide to amusement parks throughout the country, the fact that you are a doctor is only useful for its novelty value. Your bio might read something like this:

> Ever since he first rode the Cyclone at the age of ten, Sturmond Drang has been a devotee of amusement park rides. Throughout his years of premed at U.C. Berkeley, medical school at Harvard, internship in New York, and surgical residency in Texas, he has sought out local amusement parks as respite from the strain of his studies and his work.
>
> Dr. Drang thinks amusement parks may be the best way to prepare ourselves for a future in space—but for those who can't wait for their seat on the shuttle, he offers this guide to the best rides here on earth (with a little bit of professional insight into how to keep the contents of your stomach in place while hanging upside down, and which rides to eschew if you want to avoid whiplash).

A history of your political activism has no place in a bio for a guidebook on amusement parks, but it might if you were writing a book on welfare and amusement parks as the equivalent of the old Roman "bread and circuses," or one about under-the-table licensing of such parks. For topics like those, editors will want to know that you served as deputy director of the Department of Health and Social Services or on the OSHA board.

In other words, if your experience is relevant, include it. If it isn't, leave it out.

One thing that is always relevant is the fact that your work has been published elsewhere. As seems to be the case for any type of employment, you get a job by proving you have already had one. However, since a bio is not a résumé, you don't have to list *everything* you've ever published. My bios usually say something like this: "She has over 250 articles in print in publications ranging from *Savvy* to *Australian Video and Communications,* and is also the author of two pseudonymous science fiction novels.''

For nonfiction works, a chapter-by-chapter outline is very useful. Generally, a prose description of the contents of each chapter is better than the formal outline format you learned in grade school. Summarize each chapter in a paragraph or two—whatever it takes to show what you will cover.

What you want to do is whet the editor's appetite for the material you're going to provide. You also want to show that you have enough material for a book-length work and that you've thought through the order in which you'll present it.

Do you need sample chapters? Generally, if you're an unpublished writer, the answer is yes. The publisher will want to see if you can actually write the kind of prose needed for the book.

You can submit your introductory chapters as your samples, but if you have a particular chapter that is illustrative of some of the real meat of the book, you might want to include that as well. ("I am enclosing chapters 1 and 2, and also chapter 7, which deals with the incidence of heart attacks and whiplash occurring on roller coasters, and which I thought might be indicative of some of the particular expertise that I, as a medical doctor, can bring to this subject.")

As an alternative, if you have written a lot of articles, some of which might be expanded for the book, you might want to enclose copies of those articles in lieu of sample chapters. They can serve as samples of your writing (and obvious proof of the fact that you have been published elsewhere).

You can also submit *fiction* to an editor before it is finished. While an author without a track record may find it difficult to sell an incomplete novel, it is not impossible. This is where having an agent can be particularly helpful; agents are more likely than authors to sell first novels before they are written—or where you *could* sell it yourself, to get more money or better terms in the book contract.

Instead of a "proposal," what you submit for works of fiction is a "partial" and outline.

The partial should consist of approximately three chapters or about fifty pages of text—but they must be the *first* three chapters or fifty pages, and they had better possess a dramatic hook to grab the reader —in this case, the editor who might want to buy your book.

The partial should be accompanied by a 10-to-12-page *narrative* outline. This outline tells your story in summarized form. You might begin something like this:

> Rosemary is unsure whether to reenlist and remain in the safe world of the military, where choices are made for her, or to use the leverage of her executive rank and all the training she has had to move into a position of authority in civilian life—where she will have to make decisions not only for herself but also for others. She has less than a month left in her current enlistment to make the choice.

If you have some particularly good scenes planned for later in the book, you can include outtakes from those scenes in the outline—for example:

> Rosemary is in her room, chastising herself for not having the courage to live up to her potential, when there is a knock at the door. She opens it to find her close friend and coworker, the ship's chief medical officer, Dr. Basil Sage, obviously drunk. Concerned that someone will see him, she pulls him inside and shuts the door. He proceeds, with the courage he has found in the bottle he has brought along, to berate her for using the military as an excuse to hide from herself.
>
> Though this is precisely what she has just been thinking, she is not pleased to hear it put into words by someone else, even a friend as close as Basil. "I don't see that it's any concern of yours," she tells him stiffly.
>
> "Maybe it isn't, but I just don't like to see a good mind going to waste." He takes a drink from the nearly empty bottle, then, re-membering his manners, extends it toward her. "Sorry—you wan' a drink?"
>
> "The pot is calling the kettle black," she sneers. "Talk about a good mind going to waste—at least I haven't pickled my brain to, as you so aptly put it, escape reality."
>
> "No," he replies. "No, you haven't. You don't need liquor. You block out reality by hiding behind your fantasies."
>
> "And just what do you mean by that?" she demands.

The doctor sits down heavily. He levels his gaze at her, and there is a clarity in his eyes that belies his drunken state. "You think I don't know that you enlisted in the first place so you could pretend that being stationed at opposite ends of the earth was what broke up your marriage? So you wouldn't have to face what was *really* going wrong?"

Her response is a sharp intake of breath. She draws herself up to her full height and tells him, very slowly, "I think you ought to leave now."

Having shown, rather than told, how you will develop the characters, you can return to your summary—"Rosemary pushes Basil out the door, convinced she never wants to see him again, but hours later, they are forced to work side by side after the starboard engine explodes and sickbay is suddenly filled with dead and dying sailors." The summary becomes stronger for the insertion of the essence of a dramatic scene.

In the cover letter accompanying your partial and outline, it helps to say what *kind* of novel it is—thriller, romance, or mystery, for example. As a selling tool, you should also provide information that adds to your credibility for writing this novel. As an example, you might want to note that it is drawn in part from your experiences as a nurse in Vietnam. Don't go into detail about your background, however; the place for that is in the bio—the same kind of third-person bio that would accompany a nonfiction proposal.

Submitting a partial or a proposal may enable you to obtain a book contract (and an advance) before the book is finished. This gives you several advantages: you know that there is a market for your book, you can work with your editor as you write the story and benefit by suggestions the editor may make—and you can make use of the advance to keep yourself financially afloat while you work at your book instead of some mundane job. It was that kind of independence from other obligations to which the late Frank Herbert was referring when he observed that, to a writer, money means time to write.

But having your novel under contract has certain disadvantages as well. If the characters suddenly take over and want to go in a different direction, you may be committed by the contract (and the editor's wishes) to the original plot. If you become bored with the book, you still have to write it. And having a deadline means you have a finite amount of time—perhaps less time than you want to devote to the task—in which to fine-tune the manuscript. (On the other hand, if you are crisis-oriented, having a deadline may serve as a goad to production.)

The partial and proposal are useful selling tools even *after* you have finished a book, as a way of saving on mailing costs or of inducing some editors and agents, who don't want to see the entire novel unless they ask for it, to read your opus. Summarize your plot or your chapters as described above, but use your cover letter to tell the recipient, "This work is essentially complete. It runs 285 pages. Feel free to contact me if you want to see the rest, or return the submission in the enclosed stamped, self-addressed envelope."

10

Putting Your Soul on Sale

Writing is only half the job of being a writer. With very few exceptions, the other half of the job is sales. This is one of life's little ironies, since writers are very often by nature contemplative and reclusive; unfortunately, to get your work into print, you must develop the gregarious personality of a huckster.

Think about it. The query letter, the book proposal, the partial and outline, even the cover letter—all are sales techniques. You are selling yourself and your writing ability to an editor. If you write articles, poetry, or short fiction, you will soon discover that you are devoting almost as much time to selling your work as you are to producing it.

What? You thought your *agent* was supposed to do the selling? Think again. Not all writers have agents, and even those who do soon discover that agents—who are, after all, only human—may not have the time or the awareness to take advantage of *every* opportunity to sell their clients' works. Besides, most agents handle only book-length works, since the average freelance article, according to a 1985 survey by *Editors Only*, brings in only $255. This is the *average;* many markets pay considerably less. An agent's 10 or 15 percent of this would seldom earn back the cost of sending out the article.

Even if you write only books and have a crackerjack agent who does a phenomenal job of placing them with publishers, half the selling job begins *after* the books are published. That's when *you* begin selling your book and yourself to the public, through interviews, signing parties, and appearances. Until your name becomes a household word and your books start to sell themselves without any promotion on your part, you're going to be out there pitching with the rest of us.

Perhaps this is not what you had in mind when you said you wanted to be a writer. Perhaps you pictured yourself, like Thoreau, doing your thing beside your version of Walden Pond, or, like Emily Dickinson, stuffing your scribbled poems through the cracks between the floorboards for others to find or not to find. The truth is that if you want to see your works in print in your lifetime, you have to pitch them—at the very least by shipping them off accompanied by the famous SASE.

Sensitive though the poetic side of you may be, you'll find you have to develop a hide of steel for the sales aspects of your job. If you feel, as many writers do, that your creations are little pieces of your soul, their rejection is your rejection. You can't indulge those feelings if you want to submit your work for publication *and* maintain your sanity. But there are a number of techniques for dealing with the sales aspect of writing that I have discovered work for me; they might work for you as well.

First of all, listen to your own internal clock. Each of us has one—it's the reason we have energy at certain times and no energy at others. I noted, in chapter 3, that I don't believe there *is* such a thing as "writer's block"; I believe it is the result of forcing yourself to do one kind of work when your internal clock is telling you it is time to do something else.

Admittedly, when you are working against a deadline, you may be forced to ignore that clock—and the final product may suffer for it. But I have discovered that I have fiction moods and nonfiction moods and marketing moods, and if I try to do one when I am in the mood for the other, whatever I'm trying to accomplish takes me twice as long.

Luckily, the sales aspect of writing has two phases: research and follow-through. When you are not in the mood for research, you can plow through tons of market listings, and none will seem to match up with the ideas you have for articles or fiction. Then, some morning when you couldn't write if your life depended on it, you discover you can pick up your copy of *Writer's Market,* open it to any random page, and fifteen articles that are a perfect match for the publications listed there will occur to you.

Go with the flow. The best times to write your query and submission letters are those mornings that you wake up feeling that you can take on the whole world and best it. Whatever you write those days will brim with the confidence you're feeling.

As for those days when you awaken with the main characters in your novel finally resolving their differences by staging a dramatic battle just inside your head, for heaven's sake, call in sick and *write it down.* (Unless you do, you won't be any good at work that day anyway!)

This may be easier said than done, and if your job requires your presence, coupled with punctuality and attention to detail, your writing may seriously conflict with your obligations. Though we all have days, sometimes even *weeks,* when we know we shouldn't be operating heavy machinery (like a stapler or a fork), if those periods go on too long—if your writing begins to interfere with your job performance— you will need either to abandon your writing or to switch to a different line of income-producing work.

Sometimes you can take control of your internal clock by writing at se- lect times—early in the morning, before the pressures of the day dis- tort your perspective, or perhaps late at night, after your work and obligations are behind you. I find, for example, that I tackle fiction best on Sunday nights or Monday mornings, after I have had a day away from the office (I tend, as most lawyers do, to do catch-up work on Sat- urdays, but I *try* not to go in to the office on Sundays).

Sometimes you can alter your mood by writing in a different loca- tion, playing music, exercising—or even by completing some mind- less but necessary task like scrubbing the kitchen floor.

You can control incoming telephone calls by monitoring them through an answering machine, and you can control the effects of the mail on your life by refusing to open it until you're strong enough to deal with it. (*My* writing-related mail goes to a post office box, an in- convenience when I don't want to drive downtown to pick it up, but a godsend when its arrival would break my stride on a work project!)

Eventually, all of those marketing exercises of yours are going to re- sult in phone calls and mail. And what they bring you will be, as so many jokes have it, good news and bad news.

First the good news—acceptance.

A century ago, if Louisa May Alcott's semi-autobiographical account of Jo March's writing career is to be believed, acceptances came in the form of a check in the mail, and the writer was forced to run out and buy a copy of the publication to see his or her work in print.

This still may hold true for completed stories submitted to newsletters or newspapers. If you don't read a publication regularly, you may miss the issue with your article, and your first inkling that you've been published may be phone calls from friends who've read your piece or —if no one you know has seen it—the payment you receive.

Since the check *may* come in your SASE (sometimes accompanied by a contributor's copy of the issue in which your story appeared), you shouldn't automatically assume that the arrival of your SASE always means a rejection. I have, on occasion, received my 9-by-12-inch SASE, bearing perhaps a dollar's worth of postage, with nothing but a single page inside—but what a nice page and worth the wasted postage:

> We'd like to purchase your article for publication in our March issue. We can pay $300 for first serial rights, as soon as you let us know if these terms are acceptable to you.

Most of the time, though, acceptances come in the printed envelopes of the publication to which I've submitted them. These letters often—though not always—outline the rights the publication wants to buy, as well as stating the compensation offered. Sometimes they are accompanied by a contract. Sometimes the contract isn't forwarded until I've accepted their acceptance or made the changes they've requested. And sometimes a contract doesn't appear at all.

In the absence of a contract, the publication acquires no exclusivity —although you may antagonize a good market if they assume they have it and the work appears elsewhere. Thus, *some* discussion of rights is probably advisable, just to get everyone's expectations out in the open. And if you don't open the topic of rights or at least ask whether a contract will be forthcoming, you may be in for some nasty surprises yourself. For example, you may be told after you've done lengthy revisions that signing an unacceptable contract is a condition of payment. Additionally, in the absence of a contract, the copyright law gives a magazine or newspaper the right to reprint the article in subsequent issues or reprints of the same publication (though not in a "best-of" anthology).

I'll discuss terms and rights in greater detail in chapter 11, but for now, let us just note:

Kozak's Rule #6: *Where a contract doesn't appear, or where its terms are unacceptable to you, you can and should always negotiate for terms you can live with. If you don't get them, pass up the sale.*

More often than not, I've found that an acceptance comes in the form of a phone call (one of the main reasons you should put your phone number on the first page of all manuscripts and on your stationery). An editor will call, tell you that he or she likes your query or your story, and discuss changes, deadlines, and how much you'll be paid. Unfortunately, other details of the contract, like rights, are seldom mentioned.

Mention them yourself. Take this opportunity to ask questions about the terms of the sale, the timing of your payment, when and whether a contract will arrive, and whether any of your research expenses will be covered. Ask about their policy regarding kill fees (the amount they'll pay if they don't like the finished work). And don't forget your marketing hat: if the editor is really enthusiastic about your submission or query, it may be appropriate to mention similar pieces that you have outlined or completed.

Make sure you ask any editor who is offering you an assignment by phone when you can expect a letter of assignment. Log your calendar for that date, and drop the editor a reminder if the letter hasn't come. Bear in mind that until you have an assignment letter, you have no proof that an offer has been made to purchase your materials. The editor who spoke with you may leave, and his or her successor may have (or pretend to have) no knowledge of the assignment.

If you want to get started before the assignment letter arrives—or if it never does—you can protect yourself by confirming the call in writing yourself, with a memo like this:

> This is to confirm that you called on March 8th and offered $500 for first serial rights in a 2000-word piece on raising elephants in your back yard for fun and profit. You said you needed the finished piece by April 4th, would pay documented expenses for telephone and research materials up to a total of $50, and would pay the expenses plus a 25 percent kill fee if it turned out you couldn't use the piece after all.
>
> Because of the short deadline, I want to start work on the article and shall do so based on the terms of your phone call as outlined above. You can expect the piece by the April 4th deadline, and I will expect the payment within two weeks after that, as we discussed on the phone.

You have put the ball back into the editor's court with this letter. If there is some confusion as to the terms—perhaps they pay only a 20 percent kill fee or want additional rights or won't pay until a month after publication—it is up to the editor to correct your misconceptions. If he or she fails to do so, you generally have a right to rely on the terms offered, and your letter gives you proof in writing of what you understood those terms to be when you undertook the work.

Now you're in trouble. You've got an assignment—and you've got a deadline. You are as bound by the acceptance of an assignment to write the piece as the editor is to pay you for it.

I've discussed procrastination in chapter 3 and format in chapter 7. I'd also like to make mention here of the benefits of honesty as the best policy if you hit a snag.

If you *can't* complete the work by deadline; or if your research leads you to a conclusion opposite that proposed in your query letter (for example, if elephants can be raised in your back yard for fun, but seldom for profit); or if there is no way the material can be covered satisfactorily in less than 5000 words or more than 500, *let your editor know in time to accommodate the changes.*

If you need an extra month, or if you need more room or less for the piece, perhaps the schedule can be rearranged. However, if your article is scheduled as part of a specific theme issue, this may not be possible, and the editor may need the warning to substitute or add a piece on eagles in order to fill in the gap, or to kill the piece on aardvarks to make more room for your story. Letting the editor know in good time may preserve your relationship, making it possible for you to continue to sell to that publication.

When a book or book proposal is accepted, either you or your agent will generally receive a call or a letter saying so and outlining the basic terms of the offer to publish. At this point, let me reiterate Rule #5: *They pay you, you don't pay them.* If the offer to publish asks for money from you, forget it.

If the publisher offers to pay you, you have another quandary. Are you going to be paid enough? What rights does the publisher want for the payment you are being offered? These terms will be outlined in the book contract, which will usually be sent to you within a few weeks of the initial offer. Until you've seen the contract, you are under no obligation to accept the publisher's offer, and even then, remember Rule 6 and always negotiate. Never sign anything that makes you uncomfortable or anything you do not understand.

I'll discuss book contracts in more detail in chapter 13, but at this juncture, what you should know is that if you get one, *run, do not walk, to a literary lawyer or legitimate literary agent or both.*

Both? Yes. Just as you can employ both a real estate agent and an attorney to assist you in the sale or purchase of a house, you can retain both a literary attorney and an agent. Is it overkill? Sometimes yes, sometimes no. Indeed, sometimes your agent will even *suggest* retaining a literary attorney for a rather thorny legal problem.

The difference between literary agents and attorneys lies in their training and licensing and the way they get paid. Very few literary agents are attorneys. Even those who have attended law school may not be admitted to practice law. Lawyers must be licensed before they can practice, and generally must abide by certain standards of practice —including, in many jurisdictions, obtaining annual continuing-education credits—in order to maintain their licenses.

Literary agents are not required to be licensed (although *script* agents are, at least in California). Two self-policing associations (the Society of Authors' Representatives and the Independent Literary Agents Association) recently merged to form the Association of Authors' Representatives (AAR), which attempts to hold members to certain standards, and the Writers Guild of America (WGA) requires agents representing its members to abide by its basic agency agreement. Nevertheless, it is legal for agents to operate outside these groups, so losing their sanction does not drive an agent out of business. *Anyone* can hold himself or herself out as a literary agent.

As I mentioned, some agents *are* attorneys. And some of the largest agencies *employ* staff counsel. But more often than not, agents obtain their legal knowledge of the meaning of a book contract from experience and from the publishing grapevine. Even if agents have previously worked as editors or rights administrators in the publishing industry, if *your* contract provides the experience from which they learn about the workings of the law, or if the information they've picked up on the publishing grapevine is incorrect or out-of-date, you may be better served by retaining an attorney instead or in addition.

Unfortunately, literary attorneys are hard to find. This is so for a number of reasons. First of all, those of us who concentrate on publishing are very few in number. It may be hard to find a literary attorney in your area, or even in your state, since most literary attorneys practice in New York (because that's where most publishing houses are). This doesn't mean that if you can't find one locally, you can't consult with an attorney in another state, only that it will be less convenient than being able to drop in at his or her offices.

It also doesn't mean that there aren't attorneys with experience in publishing law and custom in your area, but they may be hard to find because in many states attorneys are not allowed to refer to themselves as "specialists" except in admiralty—law of the sea—and patent, both of which require special bar examinations.

The number of literary attorneys available for consultation with the general public is also small because it is not the most lucrative area of practice, and because most people interested in the field receive their training in publishing houses or the copyright office—and stay there.

There is, of course, no guarantee of the degree of experience any attorney has, just as there is no guarantee of the degree of experience an agent has. The primary distinction is that an attorney cannot practice without a license, which subjects him or her to a certain level of regulatory standards, whereas agents generally require no licensing at all.

The other difference between an agent and an attorney is that an attorney is normally paid by the hour for his or her services. However, while the time devoted to negotiating your contract or registering your copyright may be considerable and therefore costly, it is a onetime fee, and once it is paid, you need never consult with the attorney again—unless you encounter other legal problems.

Agents normally do not receive money up front from you except for initial reading fees discussed earlier, and they seldom charge you more than the agreed-upon percentage except when they incur extraordinary expenses for activities such as converting your check into ringgits and messengering it to you in Kuala Lumpur. However, agents collect their percentage not only on the advance, but on all the sales derived from the book, in perpetuity. Every royalty check is sent to the agent, who deducts his or her percentage before forwarding the balance on to you. If, as is generally the case, a book sale includes other rights—such as translation, motion picture, or T-shirt rights—the agent takes his cut from these sales too.

This is not to say that the agent's job is over after the book is sold and the contract is negotiated. The agent may be called upon—for no additional consideration—to hound the publisher for late royalty payments, to review foreign-rights sales, and to act as a buffer between you and your editor if you don't get along. Agents also allow you to cry on their shoulders when the book isn't going well, where attorneys or psychiatrists would charge by the hour—and, once retained, most reputable agents do not charge a fee for reviewing your subsequent proposals and manuscripts.

Since the agent's job is not only to negotiate your contract for you, but also, of course, to sell the book to a publisher (something attorneys do *not* normally do), if you have already obtained a legitimate offer from a publisher, a large part of the agent's job has already been done. It is therefore not really difficult to get an agent to take you on at this juncture—and probably without a reading fee.

However, just because you have an offer on a book, it does not follow that you should accept that offer.

The agent may know of another publisher who might be interested and may—despite the snail's pace at which publishers normally respond—be able to obtain speedy consideration of the manuscript from that publisher in view of the existing offer. You, as someone less familiar with the publishing world, generally do not possess the savvy to locate such markets, although if the book has already been submitted several places, it is not inappropriate to call the other recipients and tell them that you have an offer but will also consider one from them if it is forthcoming quickly.

If more than one publisher makes an offer, you have entered into the world of bidding wars and auctions. This is no place for an amateur —retain an experienced agent or a literary attorney or both as soon as possible. Among other reasons, this is because comparing book contracts is sometimes like comparing items as disparate as apples and skateboards—the money being offered in the advance can mean very little compared to the royalty rate, the rights acquired, and—given the volatility of the publishing world—the stability of the publishing house.

But what if they *don't* want your work? Remember when I mentioned good news and bad news arriving at your door? Rejections are the bad news side of the coin, and rejections are always painful, whether you receive them in the mail, over the phone, or forwarded by your agent.

If you receive too many rejections on a day when you're feeling vulnerable, you may take them too much to heart and decide to abandon writing as a career. Agent Sharon Jarvis suggests that you should never pay any attention to rejection slips unless they all say the same thing. (In that case, you are either doing something wrong or submitting to the wrong markets; pay attention and *learn!*)

What you *should* do with rejection slips is *save them.* If they are standard form letters, make a note, somewhere on them, of the date you received them and the manuscript they concerned. File them with the copy of your original submission letter or, if they contain an editor's name and personal comments, in an alphabetical file where you'll be able to relocate them—someday, you may want to lay your hands on the name of that editor so you can submit something else. In either case, a stack of systematically filed and dated rejection slips can be used to substantiate for the Internal Revenue Service that you are, indeed, attempting to run a business and have, indeed, been attempting to sell your wares. (See chapters 19 and 20 on office procedure and taxes.)

How do you cope with being rejected? First of all, consider that it is the *manuscript* that has been rejected, not *you.* No matter that you consider the manuscript a little piece of your soul—to the editor who received it, it is just a piece of paper. Remember, even an all-powerful editor is—usually—a human being. And never forget that what one editor hates, another may love—indeed, what any editor hates today, he or she may love tomorrow (or vice versa).

Bear in mind, too, that a form rejection slip that says "Your manuscript doesn't meet our present needs" may mean that they just bought another manuscript on the same subject yesterday—bad timing, but not a condemnation of your right to life, liberty, and the pursuit of happiness.

And what if you *should* get a rejection slip that says something like, "You scum, how dare you think you have the right to crawl the earth, let alone submit a manuscript to me?" (I know of one editor who actually sends rejection letters along those lines!) Do what your mother told you to do when kids on the playground gave you a hard time: consider the source. Figure the poor jerk can't possibly have any friends and make a charitable donation to the local mental health society in his name.

As you may have gathered from what I have just told you, there is an art to reading a rejection slip. Anything that is not an anonymous form letter should be read as encouraging (unless it tells you that you're slime, in which case—if you have been polite and professional in your submission—it should be read as an indication that the slush pile has driven the editor off the deep end!).

Try to look at the letter objectively. What does it *really* say? "We liked your story, but the ending doesn't work for us"? Maybe someone else will *like* that ending. (In the alternative, you could always write back and ask, "Would you buy the story if I reworked the ending?" But never rework it unless they answer that one in the affirmative.)

An editor from a publishing house who requests specific marketing information—regarding other books like yours already on the market, or who you think your target audience might be, for example—has sent you anything *but* a rejection. This kind of letter means the editor may want to bring the book up before the editorial committee and may want extra ammunition with which to sell it to them. *Get the information to that editor with all due haste!*

Perhaps the letter says, "Not this time, but try us again." *Do so*—as quickly as possible—with another piece that seems to fit that publisher's needs, accompanied by a note that says something like this: "When you returned my story, 'It's a Dog's Life,' you suggested that I try you again, so here is 'Duck Soup and Ducktails,' which I think might be suited to your readership. Let me know what you think."

Or maybe the letter says, "We're overstocked right now—try us in six months." Put a note on your calendar, six months from now, to do just that.

Even an unsigned personal scribble reading "Sorry—try again" on a form rejection slip should be regarded as an incentive to do so if you have appropriate materials.

Remember, there are a lot of reasons why manuscripts get rejected, and not all of them correspond to the quality of your work. There may be hints or even blatant suggestions of these reasons in the rejection letter. Among them might be:

- ▲ Yours is a Thanksgiving story, and the November issue closed in August. Find out what their lead time is, and submit the piece again—early enough to be considered for the appropriate issue next year.
- ▲ You stuffed a form letter addressed to a competing magazine into the envelope. Return to square one, and don't send these guys anything for at least a year, or until you're sure they've forgotten you.
- ▲ They just bought a story on a similar topic.

▲ They never buy stories on this topic or in this style (go back and look at sample copies of the magazine again).

▲ All their stories on this subject are written in-house, by a member of the magazine's staff. It probably says this in the market listing; go back and reread it.

▲ You're ahead of the times; they don't know about this trend yet. You may have to redraft your cover letter to explain why this subject is about to take off, even providing some statistics, if you want to sell the article. Consider resubmitting after an appropriate interval, lest someone else's proposal lands on the editor's desk once the light has dawned. (This once happened to me, and the editor felt so guilty that she had rejected my earlier proposal and then assigned the topic to someone else that she came up with an alternative assignment for me, as a consolation prize!)

▲ You're behind the times; they've done this one to death, and the fad is over, anyway. Remember, it's always a good idea to read back issues of the magazine before you submit something.

▲ The style in which you wrote your story isn't right for *this* publication—but it might be right for another one.

▲ The format you've used simply doesn't *look* professional and has prejudiced the editor before he or she read a single word. Go back and review chapter 7 to be sure you've designed your pages appropriately.

▲ This publication only buys stories that are accompanied by photos, and you don't have any photos.

▲ You have the same first name as the editor's ex-wife, and he hates all women with that name.

Sometimes there's no good or bad reason; your submission simply failed to grab *this* editor. When this happens, keep in mind what Joanie, my agent's assistant, often scribbles on the copies of rejection slips she forwards from editors who *should have* accepted a manuscript: "What do *they* know, anyway?"

Of course, some rejections *are* based on the work's quality—or lack thereof. Do all your paragraphs begin with the same word? Do you ramble pointlessly? Is the story preachy or trite? Take a good, hard, objective look at the manuscript now that it has been out of your hands for a while. You just might be horrified at what you see.

In dealing with rejection slips, perhaps the best philosophy is to let Reinhold Niebuhr's prayer—adopted as the motto of Alcoholics Anonymous—be your guide: "Lord, give me the serenity to accept what cannot be changed, the courage to change what should be changed, and the wisdom to distinguish the one from the other."

Repair any flaws that are apparent to you in your manuscript or your submissions procedure, then pick yourself up, dust yourself off, and get back in the race. Draft another cover letter to another publication, attach it to the manuscript, stuff both—along with a fresh SASE—into an envelope, and drop them into the nearest mailbox before you allow yourself even the smallest wallow in your misery.

After you send the manuscript out again, you can go on your consoling chocolate binge, but not before.

11 /

Rights and Copyrights

Unlike most other vendors of goods and services, writers seem to have no idea of what it is they are offering for sale. Perhaps this is a problem based in semantics: we speak of "selling a book" or "selling an article," when actually, we are licensing the right to *use* our material—to reproduce copies of it and distribute them. Booksellers sell books; writers sell rights. That's what the copyright law is all about.

Writers are not alone in failing to understand copyright law. Few lawyers have even the vaguest idea of what a copyright is, probably because, in most law schools, copyright is lumped together with patent and trademark law and given at most a week or two of classroom time. Copyright is also given short shrift in journalism schools—possibly because the instructors were never taught anything about it when *they* were in school.

But understanding how the copyright law works enables you to get a lot of mileage out of a single article—to sell and resell it to different publications. Knowing your rights, and retaining as many of them as possible, means no one will be able to stop you from using the characters in your novel in subsequent stories. Even if you are writing part-time, with no intention of making a *living* at this game, with article sales averaging in the $250 range and book advances averaging around $5000, the only way you will ever be able to make the hours you spend at the typewriter earn back what they cost you is by exploiting your creations as many times and in as many ways as possible. You can't do that unless you recognize and exercise the rights the copyright law gives you.

Just what *is* a copyright, anyway? The traditional definition is "the bundle of rights that exists in a work."

And just what is in that bundle? Current U.S. law delineates five basic rights that belong exclusively to the copyright owner:

- ▲ The right to reproduce copies of the work,
- ▲ The right to distribute copies of the work to the public by sale, gift, or loan,
- ▲ The right to prepare derivative works based on the work,
- ▲ The right to perform the work in public, *and*
- ▲ The right to display the work to the public.

These five rights are subject to virtually limitless subdivision, which is one of the most cogent reasons I can think of for refusing to sell "all rights" to anything—you never know just what that word "all" might encompass. If your novel is made into a movie that spawns a television series that gives rise to a spin-off series, the right to sell T-shirts and lunch boxes bearing the face of a character from that second series can be among the merchandising rights that derive from the original work.

The rights to "reproduce" and "distribute " your work are inherent in its being published, but they can be broken down several ways. For example, there are different types of print rights. The two most important are book rights and serial (periodical) rights. *Book rights can be broken down by the form in which they will appear*: the four most common being hardcover, paperback, trade paperback, and the right to publish book club editions. *Serial rights can be broken down by the order in which they will appear*—for example, into first serial rights (the appearance of the piece for the first time in a serial publication) and second serial rights (variously, either the second appearance in a serial publication or the first serial appearance after publication in book form), onetime rights (any time, but no guarantee that it won't appear somewhere else first), or simultaneous rights (appearing in other noncompeting publications at approximately the same time). *Both can be broken down even further by territory*—first North American serial rights, British book rights, South American paperback rights—*and by language*—English language rights, German language rights.

The right to "prepare derivative works" can also be broken down into type (motion picture, television, sequel, merchandising, translation, and condensation, to name just a few) and territory (United States, North America, or Fiji), and can be limited by time (for instance, a one-year license to develop the work as a motion picture, renewable at six-month intervals). The right to "display" the work is generally more applicable to artwork, but can also apply to reading a book aloud on television while the camera focuses on each page—or the right of someone else to frame and display a piece of your personal correspondence. The right to "perform" the work would cover sales of audiotapes of authors (and others) reading books aloud—a newly developing and booming business. Or, if your work is a script, it would cover actual performance.

Having become aware of the many ways you can exploit your work, are you starting to see visions of dollar signs? Now that I've got your attention, let me emphasize once more that anyone who wants to be a writer should make it his or her first order of business to understand at least the basics of the copyright law.

The founding fathers of the United States thought the rights of writers were important enough to merit mention in Article I of the Constitution. They gave Congress the power "To promote the Progress of Science and useful Arts, by securing for limited Times to Authors and Inventors the exclusive Right to their respective Writings and Discoveries."

Congress created the first Copyright Act in 1790; the current version, a complete revision generally referred to as "the new law" or "the 1976 law" (for the year it was passed), went into effect on January 1, 1978. There have been several minor amendments since that date, and one major set of amendments incorporated as a result of the Berne Convention Implementation Act (the "BCIA"), which became effective on March 1, 1989.

It is important to be aware of the January 1, 1978, and March 1, 1989, dates, because *copyrights are generally governed by the law in effect at the time of a work's first publication.* While this may be somewhat confusing, the 1976 law actually cleared up a lot of conflicts in the law that had existed before it went into effect by preempting all state laws concerning copyright. All U.S. copyright matters are now the subject of the federal law, and state laws regarding copyright no longer apply. A working knowledge of this federal copyright law (Title 17 of the United States Code) can be the writer's best protection against getting ripped off or getting into trouble for infringing someone else's copyrights.

The U.S. Copyright Law provides copyright protection for "original works of authorship fixed in any tangible medium of expression." It then lists a number of categories of works that may be copyrighted. These *include, but are not limited to,* literary, dramatic, musical, audiovisual, pictorial, graphic, sculptural, and choreographic works. The classifications mentioned in the law also include pantomimes, motion pictures, sound recordings, and—since the BCIA went into effect—architectural plans. But if you can come up with a way to "fix" your work in some other "tangible medium of expression," the work can be copyrighted—so long as it qualifies as an "original work of authorship."

Originality is an interesting term. Unlike inventions, which, according to patent law, must be *novel* (never before created or discovered), copyrighted material need only be *original*. This means, in essence, that you must come up with an idea for a work all by yourself, without having been exposed, either consciously or—as the case involving George Harrison's song "My Sweet Lord" suggests—subconsciously, to someone else's work. Thus, the copyrights in two virtually identical stories or poems can each be held by the creators of those works, and neither copyright will infringe upon the other—*if those works are created independently of each other without their authors having had access to each other's work.*

The law states quite specifically that there is no copyright in facts or ideas, so it is the *form* of your expression—your words—that you copyright. If you come up with that form spontaneously without having had access to the work yours resembles, you aren't infringing. A writer typing away in his basement in Michigan and another scribbling away in her attic in Maine can produce virtually identical stories, and if they haven't had access to each other's work, they'll be innocent of infringement, and each will be entitled to the copyright in the work he or she created.

Just as there is no copyright in facts or ideas, there is also no *copyright* protection for titles or short phrases. These, however, *may* be covered by trademarks, another area of the law which I will discuss in chapter 12.

At the heart of the writer-publisher relationship are the rights to *reproduce* a work and *distribute* it. When you "sell" your story for publication, you are really licensing its reproduction in copies and the distribution of those copies. But, as I mentioned earlier, the copyright includes not only *print* rights but also derivative, display, and performance rights. These include things as far removed from publishing as the right to make a movie or a T-shirt based on the work, and the right to use characters from the work in a subsequent story. Lest you think this concerns only fiction writers, not journalists, remember that the movies *Saturday Night Fever* and *King of the Gypsies* both originated with life-style articles in *New York* magazine. *Saturday Night Fever* not only became a hit movie but also spawned a sequel, *Stayin' Alive.* Since you never know when something like this will grow out of *your* work, can you think of a better reason for refusing to sell your copyright or "all rights"?

Assigning a copyright and assigning all rights are essentially the same thing, but there are a lot of people in the publishing world who don't seem to realize that. I once encountered a publishing house contract that specified the copyright would be registered in the name of the author-illustrator but required him to license each of the rights to the publisher for the entire term of copyright. The author-illustrator obviously held the copyright in name only, since virtually all of the rights contained in the copyright had been assigned to the publisher.

I'd like to suggest that no one *ever* sell all rights or assign a copyright or sign a work-made-for-hire contract (more about these later), but sometimes financial need may make it necessary. Before you sign such a contract, however, stop and think: *if you assign all rights—or the copyright—you don't own any part of the work any longer.* You could, conceivably, be sued for infringement if you reuse your own work in any way—even photocopying it to send to relatives. When you sign this kind of contract, try at least to include a provision allowing you to reproduce the work for restricted distribution or to quote from it. This keeps you safe from infringing if, for example, you want to photocopy and distribute "tear sheets" as part of your portfolio.

Needless to say, the greater the grant of rights you give away, the more money you should get for them. Only *you* can decide whether a contract is reasonable for you, but you should only make that decision after weighing all the facts and with an understanding of what your rights are.

How do you acquire a copyright in the first place? Under the copyright law that went into effect on January 1, 1978, *copyright in an original work of authorship exists from the moment the work is created*—that is, fixed in any tangible medium of expression. Copyright, even in a note to the milkman (provided that note is *original* enough), belongs to you, as the author, from the moment you set the words down on paper. Indeed, when you leave a recorded message on an answering machine, you technically hold the copyright in your performance as soon as it has been "fixed" by recording it.

This applies to manuscripts and even something as pedestrian as a letter to the editor of your local paper. *Custom,* rather than law, decrees that the act of sending such letters implies the right to publish them; as far as the copyright law is concerned, letters fall into the same class as any other written work. This means that the copyrights in them remain with their authors, and they may not be reprinted other than on the magazine's own pages without the permission of the letter writer.

Similarly, you can't publish *both sides* of your correspondence with someone unless you obtain your correspondent's permission. You own the copyright in the letters you have written, and your correspondent owns the copyright in the letters he or she has sent you. However, because copyright is distinct from ownership of a material object, you could probably sell the letters themselves to an autograph collector. That sale doesn't infringe on a copyright, but reproduction *does*.

This is also true of graphic and sculptural works. Selling an original painting does not prevent the artist from making copies of it, and buying the painting does not give the purchaser the right to reproduce it while its copyright endures.

A radical change in the way the rights to works are transferred took place when the 1976 copyright law went into effect. Before January 1, 1978, in the absence of any agreement to the contrary, it was *assumed* that "all rights" were transferred by a writer to the publisher. Where a periodical publisher was not interested in reusing or reselling the work, it would often "reassign" the rights back to the author.

Under the new law, any transfer of copyright must be made by its owner in writing. Absent an assignment or "the operation of law" (for example, a bankruptcy judgment or other decree), the author retains all rights in his or her work. The only exception is found in the case of contributions to collective works.

A collective work is a publication—such as a magazine, anthology, or encyclopedia—in which individual contributions can be distinguished from each other (as opposed to a "joint work," in which it is impossible to separate the work of one contributor from the work as a whole).

In the absence of a contract, the law states that the owner of the copyright in the collective work is presumed to have acquired only the right to reproduce your piece as part of that collective work, any revision of that collective work, or any collective work in the same series. This section of the law is actually geared toward encyclopedias or anthologies, which might revise a work from year to year or print a new, updated issue of it in a subsequent year. But it has an interesting effect on contributions to magazines and newspapers—absent an agreement, the magazine or newspaper *could* reproduce your story in every subsequent issue. This is unlikely, but it would be legal!

What constitutes an agreement is something I will go into in more depth in chapter 13, but you should be aware that a contract can be inferred from an exchange of letters outlining what rights will be purchased, and subsequent actions—such as reading the galleys and cashing the check tendered in payment for the article—that indicate agreement with the terms outlined in those letters.

As far as "all rights" assignments go, my own experience is that few magazines actually want to "buy all rights and reassign them," no matter what their market listings say. That was the system that took the least paperwork under the old law, but it would take two formal documents under the new law. Many magazines that claim to buy all rights actually operate without any contracts at all and don't want to be bothered with a bunch of documents. In fact, "buying all rights" may be their way of simplifying the acquisition process—making sure they are covered for everything they might ever need, without having to think it through at the time of sale.

If you write for a magazine and have no contract, your work falls into that contributions-to-collective-works category I've already mentioned. The magazine or newspaper could technically reuse your article a second time without paying you for it, but it couldn't reprint it in a "best-of" anthology or grant anyone else any reprint rights. By the same token, *you* couldn't really grant another publisher any *exclusive* periodical rights in it, because the piece could show up again, at any time, on the original magazine's pages. However, since publishing etiquette and basic honesty would have required you to level with the second publisher anyway, explaining that this was a reprint, it is highly unlikely that the second publisher expected any exclusivity, so long as the piece didn't appear simultaneously in a competing publication.

▲   ▲   ▲

What if an editor sends you a contract to sign, and it gives away more rights than you want to release? In my experience, the best approach is to phone or write the editor to discuss the contract. Try asking, "*Why do you really want all rights?*" Often, the editor really wants first serial rights and perhaps an exclusive publication privilege for a specific period of time. The magazine may have bought "all rights" under the old law and continues to do so because they think it's simpler that way. It isn't.

When I have one of these discussions, I always follow it up with a letter granting whatever rights we've agreed will be sold, and retaining all the rest. I am then free to resell the material or excerpt it in another article, after any conditions of exclusivity are met.

But what if you have already given away more rights than you feel you should have? Sometimes you can negotiate with a publisher, who probably doesn't even realize he or she has them, to give them back. If that isn't possible, there is a special escape clause provided by the new copyright law.

To keep some future Edgar Allan Poe or Charles Dickens from coughing out his lungs in debtors' prison while his publisher grows fat on the fruits of his genius, Congress stuck a special termination provision into the copyright law. When you have made an all-rights assignment or assigned the copyright—or even just assigned more rights than you should have—you or your heirs can, after thirty-five years, take back the rights you've given away.

This procedure is *not* automatic. It requires specific action on your part, following the somewhat rigorous rules for notice and reclamation laid out in the copyright law. If you are no longer alive, this right of termination vests with your surviving spouse, children, or grandchildren. The termination right cannot be assigned in advance—and your spouse and children inherit it even if you disinherit them in your will (although it isn't valid against grants you make by that will).

If your work is of ephemeral value, terminating a grant may not be worth the effort. But if you've given away all rights—or even just serial rights or movie rights—to the Great American Novel, it's nice to know that you or your heirs can get them back before the copyright runs out.

Before the copyright runs out? Just how long does a copyright last, anyway?

Remember, the Constitution mandates securing copyrights "for limited times." Once those limited times are up—or if certain conditions have not been met—the copyright lapses, and the work enters the public domain, to be reproduced, distributed, displayed, performed, or derived from by the public at will.

Before 1978, copyright in a published work could be secured for twenty-eight years, *if* the work was published with proper copyright notice. (I've discussed the form of that notice in chapter 7.) In the twenty-eighth year after publication, it could be renewed for an additional twenty-eight years, making copyright protection possible for a total of fifty-six years from the date of first publication. Copyrights expired precisely twenty-eight years from the date of publication, so the actual month and date of publication, as well as the year, were important.

This changed for works first published after January 1, 1978. They generally receive copyright protection for the life of the author plus fifty years; in the case of a joint work, most copyrights expire fifty years after the death of the last surviving author. Until March 1, 1989, proper copyright notice was required on all works published in the United States to keep them from falling into the public domain. However, copyright in works published without notice between January 1, 1978, and March 1, 1989, can be salvaged if one of the following three conditions is met:

- ▲ If the notice was omitted from no more than a relatively small number of copies distributed to the public; *or*
- ▲ If the notice was omitted in violation of an express requirement in writing that, as a condition of publication, the notice would be placed on all copies of the work (in this case, the publication would be considered an unauthorized publication, and the work therefore unpublished); *or*
- ▲ If the work is registered with the Copyright Office within five years after the publication without notice, and a "reasonable effort" has been made to place the notice on all copies or phonorecords distributed to the public after the discovery of the omission.

The single notice on a collective work protects the copyright in all of the individual contributions to that collective work (except advertisements), even though the person named in that single notice may be the publisher of the paper, magazine, or anthology, not the owner of the copyright in the contribution.

Works that were still in their first term of copyright on January 1, 1978, continue to require renewal in their twenty-eighth year, but since all copyrights now expire on December 31 of their final year of protection, the month no longer matters. And the renewal period has been extended from twenty-eight to forty-seven years, making a total of seventy-five years of protection for renewed works. Works that were already in their second renewal term had that term extended to forty-seven years, so that they, too, enjoy protection for a total of seventy-five years from the date of first publication.

On March 1, 1989, the United States joined the group of nations that are signatories to the Berne Convention for the Protection of Literary and Artistic Works. That international convention stipulates there must be no formalities required to establish copyright protection. As a result, works published in the United States since that date need no longer bear copyright notice in order to preserve their copyrights.

However, works published before that date are still subject to the law in effect at the time they were published. Thus, if a work was published without notice before 1978, it is in the public domain and its copyright cannot be salvaged. The same is true of works published since January 1, 1978, but before March 1, 1989, if the conditions for curing lack of notice were not met in a timely manner.

Because of the changes in the law, it can be impossible to ascertain the copyright status of a work merely by looking at it; unless you know the publication date, you cannot be sure which law applies. And you can never be certain whether what you have is an unauthorized copy of a work, or one of the "relatively small number" of copies published without notice, or—unless you check its status with the copyright office—a work whose lack of notice was cured by registration.

Registration is not required to establish copyright protection, but it *is* necessary before you can renew a copyright, and before you can bring a suit for infringement, although the nationals of other Berne member nations need not register a work before they can bring such a suit in the United States.

Registration within three months of the first publication of a work affords the best protection for that work, making it possible to recover attorneys' fees and statutory damages (which are easier to prove than lost profits) even if the work was infringed before you registered it. If you wait more than three months after publication, these special remedies may be lost, even if you prevail in an infringement suit. Registration of unpublished literary works is *generally* not necessary; most legitimate publishers are not going to steal your work. It's simply easier for them to purchase an already-completed work than to pay another writer to duplicate an effort you have already made.

Registration currently costs $20 and generally requires the deposit of two copies of each published work (one copy of collective or unpublished works). This means the entire publication (or, in the case of newspapers, the entire section), not a tear sheet. If you intend to register your pieces that have appeared in collective works, make sure you have at least two copies of each publication in which they appear so you can keep one for your own archives. All of your contributions published in periodicals within any twelve-month period can be registered for a single fee.

Should you register a work? It may pay you to register short works if you think they are of any lasting value—in other words, if you think you can resell them somewhere or incorporate them into a book someday. And, of course, registration can be used to cure notice deficiencies. Though you will generally have to register articles or short stories yourself, your publisher normally registers your book-length works for you. To make sure this has been done, and done correctly, it never hurts to ask to see a copy of the registration document.

Earlier in this chapter, I mentioned a kind of contract that I consider particularly heinous—the work-made-for-hire agreement. The term has a somewhat Dickensian ring to it, and many writers and editors have sometimes assumed it was just another term for writing on assignment.

It isn't. Where a work is truly "made for hire," the commissioning party is deemed to be its author, and the party that does the actual writing has no rights in it whatsoever.

True works made for hire fall into two categories, the first of which, works created by employees within the scope of their employment, seems a reasonable allocation of copyright ownership. Copyrights in works produced by newspaper reporters, advertising copywriters, and company publicists, when those works are created within the scope of their normal duties as employees, belong to the employer.

Copyright in works that employee-writers create *outside* the scope of their employment generally belongs to *them*. Thus, if you are a newspaper reporter and write a novel in your spare time, the novel's copyright is *not* the property of the newspaper—nor, unless you have a special contract that says so, is a book you write based on information you have gathered in the course of your job.

This is because, since there is no copyright in facts, *copyright* law will not prevent you from using facts gathered in the course of regular employment in a book based on those facts. However, other areas of the law, such as unfair competition or employment contracts, may prevent you from doing so.

You don't have to be a formal salaried employee for the purposes of this section of the law. Freelancers can be included based on a multi-faceted test which includes such elements as where the work is done, who provides the materials, and who sets the working hours. Thus volunteers can fall into the category of employees if their regular duties include preparing works under the supervision of the organization for which they are donating their efforts.

Where you are not an employee, your efforts can only be categorized as a work made for hire if three specific conditions are met:

▲ *The work must be "specially ordered and commissioned."* This means that a completed work that comes in over the transom can never be considered a work made for hire.
▲ *The parties must "expressly agree in a written instrument signed by both of them that the work shall be considered a work made for hire."* The law is quite clear on the requirement of an express agreement signed by *both* parties that must contain the words "made for hire."
▲ *The work must be "for use as a contribution to a collective work, as part of a motion picture or other audiovisual work, as a translation, as a supplementary work, as a compilation, as an instructional text, as a test, as answer material for a test, or as an atlas."* If a freelancer's work doesn't fit into one of these nine categories, it isn't a work made for hire.

Representatives of the Copyright Office have suggested that a work-made-for-hire contract that doesn't meet all three criteria will be interpreted as an all-rights assignment. The only real differences between the two are the term of copyright (for a work for hire, it's one hundred years from the creation of the work or seventy-five years from the first publication, whichever is sooner) and the fact that you can terminate the all-rights assignment after thirty-five years (with a work made for hire, you can't take back the rights, because you never had them in the first place).

I have the same objection to works made for hire that I do to all-rights assignments: the rights in your work are no longer your own. Even though you wrote the piece, you may not resell it, read it aloud in public, even run off copies of it and send them out. You have no control over adaptations or resales. Indeed, if you are foolish enough to write fiction under such a contract, you may be barred from writing any other stories about the characters you invented, because those stories will be considered derivative works, and the right to prepare derivative works belongs exclusively to the copyright owner. And a special variation on Murphy's Law designed just for writers guarantees that the piece to which you give up all rights will turn out to have the most lasting value.

Obviously, one can't cover the entire copyright law in a single chapter. Indeed, I've devoted most of another entire book to it—*Every Writer's Guide to Copyright and Publishing Law,* also published by Henry Holt. And I'll be touching on related areas in other chapters of *this* book.

You can obtain free copies of registration forms by writing to the Copyright Office, Library of Congress, Washington, D.C. 20559. Other copyright materials that may prove useful to writers can also be obtained from the Copyright Office; ask for the Copyright Information Kits 109 (books), 119 (drama), and 104 (contributions to collective works).

The Copyright Office is located in the Madison Building of the Library of Congress, in Washington, D.C. Its halls and lobby contain some fascinating exhibits of copyrighted material and are open to the public.

12

More Legal Matters

I think it helps for any nonlawyer to regard the law much the same way you would the plumbing in your home. If you understand certain basic principles, you can usually unstop a drain, replace a showerhead, or stop a dripping faucet. The trick is to know when you're over your head before the water is over your head—when to call the guy with the knowledge and the right tools.

Like your plumbing, your legal rights and responsibilities are something you live with every day, never taking much notice of them unless something goes wrong. As with plumbing, knowing the general principles of the law can help you handle the small problems that come up, but when it comes to something complex or subtle that doesn't quite fit into one category or another, it may be time to call in an expert.

Of course, even an expert may not be able to give you a precise answer—that's what court cases are all about. Nevertheless, understanding the basic principles of the laws that apply to writers and writing can at least alert you to potential dangers. And once you know where the dangers may lie, you will have a better idea of when to call for help.

Probably the most important areas of law about which writers need to be concerned are copyrights and contracts. I've already discussed copyrights, and I'll discuss how contracts work in more detail in the next chapter. This chapter will be devoted to a lot of little legal loose ends that should be tied down if you really want to write professionally.

First, I want to discuss using a contract to define the terms of a couple of relationships for which you may not have thought you needed one.

The poet Robert Frost suggested that "good fences make good neighbors." Contracts make good fences—and your closest neighbors, as a writer, are your agent and any collaborators or writing partners you may have. Do you need a contract with these people, who are supposed to be on your side? You bet you do. Do most writers *have* contracts with their agents and collaborators? Too many of them don't even bother with the traditional handshake!

Just what can you expect of the relationship with your literary agent? Though such affiliations are the subject of a large and complex body of law (known, appropriately enough, as the Law of Agency), the legal essence of the relationship is that *an agent acts for a principal.*

Who is that principal? *You* are. That means the agent acts *for* you, presumably with your consent. When your agent messes up, your ability to distance yourself may depend on how much authority you have given him or her. In the absence of a contract, the scope of that authority may ultimately be defined by evidence of the normal "course of conduct" between you.

What is "normal" in an association between writer and literary agent? Certainly, an agent should be able to offer your work for sale, but seldom is it advisable for an agent to have the power to sign a contract on your behalf. However, most literary agency relationships only *begin* with the sale of a writer's work.

In addition to their formal duties—selling works and negotiating contracts—many literary agents take on a vast array of informal duties (shrink, loan institution, provider of a place to crash, etc.). The broader the normal course of conduct (Does your agent walk your dog? Pay your child's tuition or your car loan out of monies received? *Advance* those payments for you when the money hasn't come in yet?), the more power the agent acquires by it.

If your agent acts for you in a way that is contrary to your wishes (hiring third parties to "doctor" your work, for example) and you don't have an agency contract, you may nevertheless find yourself responsible for the consequences of the agent's actions (e.g., payment to those people or an agreement to share the copyright). The test, in the absence of a contract limiting or granting the agent's authority, is whether the general history of your relationship indicates that such hiring—perhaps of typists, indexers, or proofreaders, for example—has been sanctioned by you in the past. Indeed, if the apparent authority that you've given your agent is broad enough, it might even be possible for someone to commence a lawsuit against you by serving the papers on your agent.

The problem is similar to that of a marriage. Two people never really become one, and they may have conflicting interests. Although your agent usually acts *for* you, there may be times when his interests —or those of others he represents—are decidedly antagonistic to yours. Consider, for example, what happens if he has established a good working relationship with a publishing house that manages to totally distort your manuscript in the process of copyediting it. Will he be willing to rock the boat for you, at the risk of jeopardizing his future sales to that house?

And what happens when one of his other clients comes in with a book on the same timely topic as yours—say, a biography of the darkhorse vice presidential nominee—and it's clear that only one of those books is going to make it into print? Will he pitch them both, and let the editors choose, or pitch the one from the other guy who has the more established reputation, because the agent knows he can get more money for it?

Of course, if his acts turn downright criminal, you may have recourse to the courts. Literary agents who make off with your royalties are subject to civil suit and even criminal penalties, just as any embezzler would be, though collecting the lost funds may be impractical —or even impossible. But what if he attempts to bribe someone for you or to doctor your receipts so that your tax returns show less than you've earned? Your agent's acts can become *your* acts when he appears to be acting with your consent—an excellent reason for defining the parameters of his actions by contract.

There are also times when an agent acting in good faith can cause you as many problems as an out-and-out crook. For example, if your agent does not maintain a separate account for funds received on behalf of clients, instead commingling those funds with his own, his ex-wife (or any other creditor) may be able to attach his account and seize *your* money. However unintentional such acts may be, the damage is still done.

You can also find your works and your funds tied up when your agent ceases to act at all; what, for example, do you do when your agent has a mental breakdown—or dies? You may adore his widow, who knits you bookmarks every Christmas and mails you cookies on your birthday, but if your agent has died without leaving a will, his widow (and perhaps his children, too, depending on the applicable probate laws) inherits his assets. One of his assets is his business—and part of that business is the interest you have granted him in your works.

Suddenly, your advance and royalty checks are coming to your agent's widow (or his Great-Aunt Charlene, if she is his next of kin under the law), who stuffs them into her knitting basket instead of depositing them in the bank. She doesn't act for you, because she doesn't know how—so when your publisher fails to pay your royalties on time, or holds back 99 percent of them in case all shipped books are returned, that sweet old lady brings him cookies instead of writing threatening letters. (Come to think of it, maybe cookies would be just as effective!) What's worse, she hasn't the vaguest idea of how to sell your next work, let alone negotiate the contract.

There must be fifty ways to leave your agent (or his widow), but unless these are spelled out in writing, you may find yourself unable to sell subsidiary rights to the novels your agent sold before his death without bringing a suit to terminate your relationship with the agency. Even if you can wrest control of future sales from the agency, you may never be able to get the royalty checks for your past works out of the widow's knitting basket. And even if she wants to deposit them for you —or turn the rights back to you—she may be prohibited from or delayed in doing so by probate laws.

Many of these problems can be prevented, or at least mitigated, by having a comprehensive contract with your agent. The contract should spell out the *kind of works* your agent will represent, the *percentage* he or she will take for this representation, the *duration* of the contract, and *how it can be terminated.* It should also spell out the *rights that may continue after termination* (such as the continuing right to receive a percentage of all monies from books the agent sold), and what happens in the event that *either of you dies* while the contract is still in force.

A contract is also your best protection if a dispute develops with any collaborators or writing partners you may have. As an example, consider the fact that in the absence of a contract, it is usually assumed that all participants will have an equal share in a project. This is certainly the case under the U.S. Copyright Law, which makes no distinction between degrees of joint ownership. The law gives the copyright in a work jointly to all the joint authors of a work. If your respective interests are unequal, it is important to spell this out in the contract.

You say the interests are equal, so there is no problem? Let me pose certain scenarios, and then tell me if you *still* believe that.

- ▲ You and your best friend create a series of books and stories which becomes immensely popular. Then you have a falling-out. Which of you gets to continue the series? Under the copyright law, either of you could do so without the consent of the other.
- ▲ Your collaborator drops dead, and his will leaves his entire estate to his seven children in equal shares. (Under the law, a copyright is property and can be willed.) Before you can sell exclusive rights to the next book in the series, you must have the consent of all of the copyright holders. This can become even more complex if some of them are minors and must have a guardian act for them.
- ▲ You are writing an "as told to" book, and the subject decides midway through the project to tell it to another writer.
- ▲ You spend six months ghostwriting an autobiography for a business executive. No publisher wants to buy it. Should you still get paid?

Other disputes may arise between collaborators over what should be included in a work, what should be left out, the order of the authors' names, and even whether to sell a book on the terms offered by the first publisher who wants to buy it.

Something else you may want to consider is that in the absence of a contract, certain courses of conduct can be construed as creating a legal partnership. Collaboration *might* be one of these. All partners can be held individually liable for debts of a partnership, which include any debts the other partner contracts in the name of the partnership, whether you've approved them or not. And in some community-property jurisdictions, the spouse of a partner may have an interest in the assets or a liability for the debts of the partnership.

Even if the collaboration is not construed to be a partnership and you are not deemed responsible for your collaborator's debts, you can be left at a financial disadvantage by his or her actions. Consider the following scenario:

- ▲ You both sign a contract with the publisher to produce six books this year, intending that each of you will write three of them. You do your three, but your collaborator does only one. The publisher cancels the contract and pays for only four books—but the book contract specifies that monies paid by the publisher are to be paid in equal shares to the two of you.

There are problems in any business association, but the ones I have just mentioned are specific to writing. They are among the reasons for having contracts drawn up—or at least reviewed—by an attorney who knows the publishing business.

What kinds of issues should be covered in contracts with collaborators? Among them are:

- ▲ Ownership of the copyright in the work.
- ▲ Responsibility for payment of the expenses of writing the work.
- ▲ Control of derivative works, such as sequels or films based on the work.
- ▲ The right to use information garnered in creating the primary work in other works, such as articles, whether related or not to the original work being produced. (There is no copyright in facts, but a contract can include agreements not to compete, which can operate both ways: you may not be able to write about your famous subject once the contract is terminated, but he may not be able to give his story to another writer either.)
- ▲ Responsibility in the event of lawsuits for libel or copyright infringement, or for failure to meet the terms of a book contract.
- ▲ Division of the proceeds (including any guarantees made to a ghostwriter to pay whether the work is ever sold or not).
- ▲ Any financial settlement in the event of termination of the agreement.

Bear in mind that a contract need not be a formal document. The courts might construe a contract from a body of correspondence (including correspondence confirming telephone discussions)—or even from a single letter that is not refuted and upon which a course of action appears to be predicated. This is a good reason to be careful about *anything* that you put in writing.

But what, you ask, of trust? If I can't trust my agent, or my writing partner, whom *can* I trust? I once saw a sign in a small-town grocery store that read, "In God we trust—all others pay cash." That just might be one of the best guidelines around.

▲   ▲   ▲

I've talked about the process of selling your work, but what about its content? For example, when are you liable for libel? (For the record, "libel" is defamation in print, whereas "slander" is spoken defamation. The term "defamation" covers both and may clear up a semantics problem where broadcasts and tapes—which can be reproduced and replayed—are involved in injuring a person's reputation.)

There are no easy answers to the question of when defamation exists, because libel law in the United States is inextricably interwoven with our First Amendment right to freedom of the press.

Complicating the laws that deal with defamation are a number of factors ranging from the standards of care you exercise in verifying your facts to the social status of the subject of your story. Perhaps the most troublesome element is the fact that libel is subjective. Something that may seem perfectly innocent on its face may be disturbing enough to your subject to cause him or her to bring suit.

This could include attributing a quotation to a person that might cause him to lose a job or potential clients. When we think of libel, we tend to think more in terms of detrimental accusations: "A is a liar," "B is a thief," or "C is consorting with enemy agents." But *anything* that might lower the subject in the opinion of the average reader is potentially libelous.

Whether it *is* actually defamatory depends, first of all, on whether it is *conveyed to third parties*. Calling up your subject to verify a rumor will not create a case—but leaving a detailed message containing the accusation with his secretary *might*.

Second—for the most part—the old saw that "truth is a complete defense" to a charge of libel still holds. Your statements must be substantially untrue, or must create a false impression due to the context in which they appear, before a question of libel will arise. But actual statements are not the only sources of libel; altering a direct quotation can also give rise to such "untruth," as can a less than precise paraphrase.

Even more complex are the questions of *identity* that enter into any question of libel. A dead person (or an institution that no longer exists) can't be libeled. And the subject must be identifiable—either by name or by reference—before libel will hold (remember, a person need not be *named*, but only identifiable, to be libeled).

The standards of libel vary depending on *who* is libeled. The law distinguishes between "public figures" and private persons. In this respect, the law of libel becomes closely interwoven with "right of privacy." Generally, you have no right to invade the privacy of a private person, including telling his or her life story in a barely fictionalized manner. This is why merely changing a name in a story about an otherwise identifiable person may not suffice to protect you from charges of libel (where you've stretched the truth) or invasion of privacy (where you haven't).

The highest standard of care should be used to make certain that you never say anything about a private person that might cast him or her in a bad light. This includes making up a pseudonym (for example, for a grocer who has been accepting food stamps for beer) that turns out to be the name of a real person (some real-life grocer or liquor store owner) who might be reasonably assumed to be the subject of your story.

"Public persons" are assumed to have more access to the media to refute your charges than a private citizen would have. Case law generally divides public persons further, distinguishing between "public figures" and "public officials."

Generally, where "public figures" (celebrities) are concerned, normally there must be some showing of intent to defame or, at least, total disregard of fact-checking procedures on the part of the publisher before damages will be awarded. Unfortunately, that requirement may not prevent the defamed party from bringing a lawsuit, the defense of which may prove lengthy and costly.

Where "public officials" (officeholders and government officials) are concerned, there is a strong First Amendment argument that preserves the right to criticize—so even if the subject is identifiable and the statement false, there must generally be a showing of *actual malice* on the part of a newswriter before damages will be awarded.

Every potential libel case turns on its individual merits. Certainly, all facts should be verified before you include them. The best rule of thumb may well be, if in doubt, don't publish the information. If you feel you must publish, check with your lawyer *before* you submit the article—there may be ways of modifying the language that will ward off suit or, at least, prevent money damages.

One such modification may be to couch a statement in terms of opinion rather than fact. Unfortunately, this does not always afford protection, so even statements of opinion should be checked out with counsel if you have any concern about what the consequences of publishing them might be.

What about quoting from the works of others? When can you do it, and how much can you quote?

Basically, you can quote from anything that is in the public domain without getting anyone's permission. But defining works that are in the public domain is the difficult part.

A work enters the public domain when its term of copyright protection expires. Among the works that can generally be assumed to be in the public domain are:

- ▲ Works that were first published in the United States more than seventy-five years ago.
- ▲ Works that were published in the United States with insufficient or erroneous notice before 1978 (or between January 1, 1978, and March 1, 1989, *if* it has been more than five years since the last day of the year in which they were published, *and* the proper steps to cure the omission were not taken).
- ▲ Works that were first published more than twenty-eight years ago and did not have their copyrights renewed.
- ▲ Works first published in other countries whose copyright laws the United States recognizes, if their copyright protection in those countries has expired.
- ▲ Works of the U.S. government (though copyright may extend to some of the material contained in such works).

Every other copyrightable work can currently be assumed to be protected by copyright in the United States, including all unpublished works—even those created well before 1978, protection for which expires after the turn of the century.

If a work is protected by copyright, the only way you can legally reproduce it without permission, in whole or in part, is if your use falls within the exceptions found in various parts of the copyright law.

The most common exception is the "fair use" rule, which allows anyone to transgress the five exclusive rights of a copyright holder without permission, *if the use meets a subjective test based on four guidelines, all of which must be considered.* As set forth in section 107 of the copyright law, these are:

1. The purpose and character of the use, including whether such use is of a commercial nature or is for nonprofit educational purposes;
2. The nature of the copyrighted work;
3. The amount and substantiality of the portion used in relation to the copyrighted work as a whole; *and*
4. The effect of the use upon the potential market for or value of the copyrighted work.

As I mentioned, these criteria are subjective. There are no set rules, such as the old myth that you can use 500 words, because where, for example, a 1000-word article is concerned, 500 words would clearly be too substantial. And if the 500 words you quote from a long work go to its essence, destroying its market potential, you may be infringing the copyright even though the proportional size of your quote is small.

I suggest that the best way to test whether your use is infringing is to ask first, whether the work is being used, as the applicable section of the law suggests, "for purposes such as criticism, comment, news reporting, teaching . . . scholarship, or research," and then to apply the golden rule: if it was *your* work, considering the four guidelines contained in the law, would you feel that someone else using it as you have in mind would be infringing?

If you think so, avoid doing with the work of someone else whatever you would feel infringes on *yours*.

There are other exceptions to the exclusive rights of a copyright holder besides "fair use." Most of these apply to schools and libraries, or to churches, veterans' or fraternal organizations, to governmental or nonprofit institutions performing a work "in the course of agricultural or horticultural exhibitions," or to performances for the handicapped. Even for these uses, certain conditions must be met for the use to qualify.

So how do you get around the restrictions? You ask permission—and get it in writing.

Suppose you want to quote poetry at the beginning of each chapter of your novel. The first thing you have to do is ascertain which poems are in the public domain. These may be quoted with impunity (but give credit where credit is due, or you may be guilty of plagiarism, or "passing off" someone else's work as your own). For a small fee the Copyright Office will conduct a search for you to determine whether a work has been registered or its ownership transferred; but if you're on deadline, this won't help, because the results seldom come back in less than six weeks and may take as long as three months.

If the poem *is* protected by copyright, locate the copyright owner or his or her heirs. The notice on the work is your best source for the name of the original copyright owner, and a Copyright Office search can provide you with information regarding registrations, transfers of ownership, and the addresses of persons named in such documents, at least at the time of registration or transfer.

Very often the publisher has the rights to the material you want to quote, and if not, may be able to tell you who does, so it's probably worth your while to write to their Permissions Department, which will forward your request to the author or his heirs if that is who holds the rights. If the publisher has gone out of business, you can sometimes find an author's current address in a reference like *Who's Who*.

When writing for permission to quote in print, always identify the work you want to quote, the exact quote from it you intend to use, the nature of the work you intend to quote it in, and how many copies of that work are likely to be printed. Permission will usually be forthcoming, but it may be conditioned on payment of a fee. Whether you are required to pay or not, *always get the permission in writing* so that you can prove you obtained it.

Make sure, too, when you obtain written permission, that it includes some reference to the fact that the person granting the permission *has the authority* to do so. If it turns out that he or she doesn't, this statement can put you in the position of an innocent infringer, and you can pass the buck for infringing use back to the granting party.

While, as a rule, newspaper reporters do not get the permission of interviewees, if you are writing a book—especially if it is an exposé, or if you want a certain amount of exclusivity—it makes sense to obtain releases and exclusivity agreements.

Remember, too, if you are supplying photographs with your article or book, that you need to get releases from anyone in your photos who is neither a public figure nor a participant in a public or news event, since it is possible to libel a person—or invade his or her privacy—with a photograph as well as with an article. A photograph of an ordinary passerby in a non-newsworthy situation may be an invasion of privacy —perhaps your subject didn't want anyone to know he was in town that day. Unless he is a political candidate, a suspected ax murderer, or a television star, he is generally entitled to keep his activities private.

Although a model release will generally enable you to use a photo in any way, the position of a photograph in print can give rise to defamation, either of the subject or, in some instances, even of someone else. For example, if your photo of an innocent child holding a flower is juxtaposed to an article about incest, it can create the impression that *that* child was the victim of incest. A disclaimer in the caption ("Professional model used in this illustration") may be a wise and necessary precaution in such a case.

The first day of my senior year in college, all of those in my major assembled in a senior thesis seminar, and the first thing our thesis adviser said to us was, "The only thing a scholar has is his integrity."

When you get down to it, that's the only thing a writer has, too.

Back in chapter 11, I mentioned that there is no copyright in ideas. When you publish the ideas of others, it is usually called reporting—unless you claim credit for someone else's ideas or research without attribution, in which case it is called plagiarism. That's what my adviser was talking about when he mentioned integrity. Plagiarizing can get you sued, but even if it doesn't, allegations that you have plagiarized can damage your reputation.

You avoid plagiarism by giving credit for ideas where it is due. If you are not an expert in a field, do not pretend to be one. Quote experts if you must, and use those quotes to document your arguments—but don't pretend your writing is based on your own knowledge if it isn't.

Asserting expertise you don't possess is a mistake many writers make because the "how-to" article or book is such a temptation. The how-to is one of the easiest kinds of articles to sell—especially if it's on a popular subject. But too many writers confuse the two ways of writing this kind of article, which is what gets them into hot water.

The first is the kind of article that distills the advice of experts in a field. You yourself don't need expertise to write this kind of how-to article, just access to those who do. But when you interview those people, give them credit for their knowledge—acknowledge them in your story. Don't pretend you are the expert just because you've interviewed them.

Of course, if you do possess the expertise, you can write the other kind of how-to piece, based on your own authority. If you are a nutritionist, as is my sister, you can write a book on fad diets (as she has done). If you are an attorney, you can write an article about some particular area of the law with which you are familiar. But if you are an ordinary freelance writer who happens to have lost twelve pounds over the summer by eating a lot of raw vegetables, you should *not* write a book advising others to lose weight the same way unless you back it up with lots of quotes from doctors and nutritionists who agree that this is an appropriate diet. Nor should you write an article on copyrights based on what an editor once casually told you about them over the phone.

I've seen writers do just that—share their "wisdom," which may, in fact, prove ill-advised. Fools rush in where angels fear to tread, as Alexander Pope once noted.

This doesn't mean that you can't put together an article that expounds a new theory, as long as you can back up that theory with verifiable statistics or with quotes from people who have the expertise you lack. But never claim their expertise as your own.

Note that the how-*to* article is distinguished from the *how* or experience article (which can be serious—"How I survived a tornado"—or humorous—"How I lost twelve pounds without eating the wallpaper") by its thrust. In the experience article, you talk about how *you* decided to go on a diet that fit your life-style and food preferences, ate nothing but carrots and tomatoes for two weeks. You lost weight all right, but your skin turned yellow.

You might sell that as a humorous vignette, though you can get even more mileage out of it by interviewing a doctor and a dietitian about how and why this happened. If they conclude that you're lucky you merely turned slightly yellow, that you could have become ill from vitamin A poisoning or malnutrition on a diet like that, you have the makings of a serious piece with how-to (or how-*not*-to) overtones. But if you choose to write that kind of article, *quote the experts;* don't imply that you're an expert yourself.

One good reason for attributing expertise to the experts is to avoid products liability exposure.

Products liability is an area of the law that usually deals with things like defective brakes on a car or flammable children's wear. But such cases *have* been known to arise in the world of publishing—and if you give people bad or dangerous advice which they follow to their detriment, you could find yourself in court defending such a suit.

This is less likely if you are merely reporting on what a bunch of experts have said. But make sure those experts are quoted accurately—this is one instance in which it pays to run the story past your source again, just to be sure your quotes and your thrust are accurate.

As with any interviews, you should always make sure that words within quotation marks are indeed those of the person you are quoting. Misquote your expert, and you open up yet another legal can of worms: you may damage his or her professional reputation, setting yourself up for a libel suit!

Even when a lawsuit doesn't result, publishing anything you later have to retract damages your credibility as a writer. The best you can do in such an instance is print a retraction, but no one will ever let you print an excuse. Remember the dictum of my high school journalism teacher, Miss Gardner: "You can't print an alibi."

There are a number of other things you may not be able to print—expletives, for example. Censorship depends on your publisher and the market for which you are writing. Newspapers generally refrain from using an actual word they deem improper:

> As he was being arrested, the suspect grew violent, shouting obscenities at the arresting officers and the crowd that had gathered. A priest attempted to intervene.
> "I don't want none of your interfering s——," the suspect shouted at him.

Sometimes, this kind of allusion detracts from the story. The ending of *Gone With the Wind* just wouldn't have the same impact if Rhett Butler had told Scarlett, "I don't give a d——." Nowadays, unless you are writing for children or the religious market, it is usually considered all right to include decidedly blue phrasing within quotation marks when such language is appropriate to a character.

Outside of a direct quote, obscenities will, at minimum, raise eyebrows. They are more permissible when a character is telling a story in the first person (as in *The Catcher in the Rye*), or when you are revealing his thoughts in a segment written from his point of view. Use words that offend community standards at your own risk, however—those standards change from day to day, and enforcement of obscenity laws waxes and wanes. (And even if a case is ultimately dismissed on First Amendment grounds, defending it can cost you a considerable sum!)

Just what *is* obscenity? The Supreme Court has never really defined it but has judged it, over the years, by such criteria as whether the material had any "redeeming social value," whether it "offended community standards," or whether it "pandered to purely prurient interests."

Justice Potter Stewart once opined that he couldn't define it, but knew what it was when he saw it.

All of our words and expressions of obscenity seem to fall into four main categories: sacred oaths made common, calling upon a deity to witness, implications about someone's ancestry, or the casual mention of sexual acts (particularly those that are generally regarded as taboo).

The definition of obscenity varies as societal norms change. If you have any doubt about that, think about the Victorians who covered the legs of their pianos and referred to them as "limbs," and imagine getting turned on by a glimpse of the underside of a baby grand!

A century obviously makes a great deal of difference in what we hold sacred and profane—which is why there are books in circulation today that would probably have garnered their authors or even the people who sold them a jail sentence fifty years ago, why seemingly innocent books have been the subject of school board banning in some parts of this country, and why the publication of others has resulted in death sentences in absentia for their authors from religious leaders in some parts of the world. The best you can hope for is to abide by current law and hope that law doesn't change too drastically too soon.

One more area of law that applies to literary works is trademark law. There is no copyright protection for a name, title, or short phrase, but *trademark* rights may protect some of these things. For example, it is possible to obtain trademark registration for the name of a magazine or periodical, though not for the name of a book or a motion picture. This is why you may see several novels with the same title. So long as there is no attempt to pass off the novel of one author as the work of another, using the same title generally does not present a legal problem. Cover photos and subtitles are often used to distinguish between one book and another to avoid any problems that might arise. Thus *Gone With the Wind: The Definitive Guide to Kite Flying* would not be confused with Margaret Mitchell's Civil War saga, and *War and Peace: The Presidency of Dwight D. Eisenhower* would never be confused with Tolstoy's novel.

But "passing off" or "palming off," while not strictly the same as a trademark infringement, is part of the related law of unfair competition. The victims of passing off may be the general public in addition to the authors or publishers of the original book (which may even have lapsed into the public domain), so passing off may even be punishable as a form of consumer fraud.

Because the Constitution grants Congress the right to make laws governing patents and copyrights, but is silent on the subject of trademarks, federal jurisdiction in trademark cases is limited to those dealing with interstate or international commerce. This means that laws and decisions that apply only to trademarks in use within a single state may differ from laws and decisions in other states.

The diversity of laws covering the use of trademarks makes it advisable to check for the laws applicable in your state. But for the careful writer, the use of a previously used title or of a product name should always raise a flag of caution.

Bear in mind that a product can be libeled just as a person can, and the loss of "good will" can be as devastating to a manufacturer as the loss of good opinion regarding a person. Use brand names and trademarks with care. (Proper use of a trademark is as an adjective, as in "Xerox copiers," "Kodak cameras," "Kleenex tissues," and "Q-tips cotton swabs.") Remember, a manufacturer who feels he has been libeled may be just as angry as a private citizen—but is far more likely to have the resources to take the matter to court.

13

Before You Sign on the Dotted Line

Most people assume that a contract has to be a long document written in that foreign language known as legalese, printed in tiny type that no one can read, and intentionally incomprehensible. However, as I have suggested previously, a contract need not be an official-looking document, or even a *single* document—in fact, a contract doesn't need to be in writing to be valid.

Of course, a written document signed by both parties will take precedence over a series of letters, and if a contract dispute goes to court, the existence of anything in writing will usually rule out the admission of any testimony in support of an oral understanding. But any time two or more persons agree on a promise or promises which the law will enforce, a contract exists.

The written document that most people think of when they hear the word "contract" is merely a reflection of all the terms of an agreement —and elemental to any *agree*ment is the idea that the parties to it must *understand* and *agree* on its terms. When you put your signature on it, you are affirming that you understand it and agree with what it says.

It follows, then, that you should never sign anything you haven't read or don't understand. This is such basic wisdom that I can't take credit for it as one of my rules, but I can't repeat it often enough: *Sign any document without reading the fine print at your own risk, and never sign anything you don't understand or which doesn't reflect the terms you've agreed to abide by.*

This seems like simple common sense, yet you'd be surprised how often I am consulted in my law practice by people who want to get out of a contract they've signed—a process that's usually unsuccessful and always costly. Any attempt to rescind the contract usually costs some multiple of what it would have cost to review it *before* it was signed. Yet people persist in signing all manner of documents without thinking about the consequences.

Sigh. Sign in haste, repent at leisure. But *you* would never do that, would you?

Okay, you'd never sign a contract without knowing what was in it. But remember that I mentioned that a contract doesn't need to be reduced to writing? Be careful of what you promise verbally as well, because an oral contract is legal—the only problem is proving it.

How do you prove the existence of an oral contract? One way is by establishing a course of conduct. If you have been sending a column in to your local weekly the first week of every month and getting paid $20 for it on the fifteenth of the next month, it could be construed that a contract exists. Its terms and conditions, defined by the course of conduct upon which both parties have come to rely, are that you will turn in a column by the first week of the month and that the publication will pay you $20 by the fifteenth of the next month. If it tries to pay you less or pay you later, you could validly assert that you had relied on its prior conduct and want your full $20 on the normal payment date.

In addition to a course of conduct, you can prove the existence of an oral contract if there are witnesses to it or if it is confirmed later in writing. This is why sending a letter-memo to "confirm our understanding" can be very helpful in establishing the terms of an agreement.

And precisely because the terms of a contract can be construed from correspondence, it is *always* very important to refute a letter that reflects an error ("Yes, I did agree to write a 500-word article for you, but the agreed-upon payment was $150 on acceptance, not $100 on publication as your letter seems to indicate. Can we clear up this misunderstanding?").

There are really only two reasons it has become customary to reduce a contract to writing. The first is to lay all the cards on the table so that no one will be surprised by the conduct of the other party in a working relationship. The second is to make sure that no one has a convenient memory lapse before fulfilling his or her end of the bargain—in other words, to make sure that the agreement will be kept because everyone knows what it is and what is expected, and you can prove it, if you have to, by producing the document.

If the contract accomplishes those ends, you don't need a lawyer to draw it up for you, but bear in mind that we lawyers have spent three years of law school getting our heads bent so that we won't look at the world—or the English language—the same way nonlawyers do. Our phrasing may seem stiff and redundant, but it is less likely to result in a dispute over what the terms of the contract mean and whether the parties are abiding by them than a "cut-and-paste job" created by a nonlawyer.

Obviously, for minor matters—like articles that earn that average fee of $255 or even less—it is seldom cost-effective to retain a lawyer. The magazines themselves often operate without legal counsel, and, indeed, so often do magazines operate without written contracts that there is a special section in the copyright law that deals with this problem.

Magazines and newspapers fall into the category of collective works—works "in which a number of contributions, constituting separate and independent works in themselves, are assembled into a collective whole." For such works, the law specifies that "copyright in each separate contribution is distinct from copyright in the collective work as a whole"—even if there is only one notice on the collective work as a whole.

As I mentioned in chapter 11, the law goes on to say that where there is no contract between the contributor and the magazine, the latter is "presumed to have acquired only the privilege of reproducing and distributing the contribution as part of that particular collective work, any revision of that collective work, and any later collective work in the same series." While this *could*, technically, give the magazine the right to print your article in every issue, it also says nothing about "first" or "exclusive" rights, so you could technically sell first or simultaneous rights elsewhere.

Generally, there is a kind of "gentlemen's agreement" about such things: magazines normally do not reproduce your work, even when they have the right to do so, without offering additional compensation, and writers don't resell the pieces elsewhere, at least *before* publication, without letting the editor know. Breaking this "gentlemen's agreement" can result in a bad reputation for the writer or publication that breaks it—but there is no *legal* redress.

As I indicated earlier, many magazines don't use contracts at all, though they *may* respond to a query with a letter of assignment, and may respond to a submission with an acceptance letter offering to purchase certain rights for a specific price. Because magazines normally pay so little, even if you do receive a contract it often doesn't pay to take it to a lawyer for review, unless you have serious questions about its implications over the long term.

To keep those questions to a minimum, and thus keep your costs down, you should develop a basic knowledge of publishing custom and practice. Know what rights you're selling (onetime rights or first serial rights or all rights—go back and look at chapter 11 if you've been skipping around), what you're getting paid, and when you're getting paid (on acceptance or on publication). You should also know the article topic, length, and due date, as well as the details of any kill-fee arrangements the publisher offers.

Now let's say you receive a telephone assignment, and neither a contract nor an assignment letter is forthcoming. Before you devote a lot of time, effort, and money to the article, *you* can draft a memorandum of agreement for yourself. It can be as basic as, "Per our telephone discussion of March 1st, I promise to write a 500-word article for you, on the subject of speaking at writers' conventions, for which you've promised to pay me $50."

This, when approved by both parties (or not refuted by the recipient), can be used to prove the existence of a valid contract—but it has holes in it that could cause potential problems.

Let's talk about those holes.

"I promise to write a 500-word article for you, on the subject of speaking at writer's conventions, for which you promise to pay me $50" covers *what* you will write, that *you* will write it, and *how much* you will be paid. But that's all it covers.

When is the article due? When will you be paid? If the publisher doesn't like the article, will you be paid anything? If the publisher never prints the article, can you sell it to someone else? Can the editors alter the article—and if so, how much? If it is so changed that it embarrasses you, can you withdraw permission to use your byline?

These problems are elemental and can be covered in a letter-memo by enlarging it to say something like this:

I promise to write a 500-word article for you, on the subject of speaking at writer's conventions, which I will submit no later than March 20th. You have agreed to pay me $50 for first serial rights in the article within thirty days of submission, unless you find it unacceptable, in which case you will pay me $10 as a kill fee and I will be free to sell the article elsewhere. If you accept the article but fail to publish it within two years of the date I submit it, the rights granted to you become onetime nonexclusive serial rights, and I may then authorize its publication elsewhere at any time with prior notice to you that I am doing so. In any case, I may authorize the publication of the article elsewhere thirty days after it appears in your publication without prior notice to you. You agree to submit galleys containing any editorial changes for my approval before publication.

This covers most of the problems that commonly arise in the course of submitting work to periodical publications. Book contracts generally anticipate, and attempt to settle in advance, many more potential problems. But for a short article that pays very little, you may just want to hit the high spots without scaring the editor out of the deal.

What elements are necessary to create a valid contract? Every contract requires an *offer,* an *acceptance,* and *consideration.*

- An *offer* is: "I will write a 500-word article for you."
- It can be *accepted:* "Great, when can we see it?"
- Or *countered:* "Sounds good, but we need 1000 words to fill a page,"
- And until it is accepted, there is no agreement, and neither side is bound.
- It should, to be truly enforceable, specify *consideration:* "We pay ten cents per word" or "Each contributor receives two copies of the book,"
- And should *not be illegal:* "We want you to include Top Secret documentation in the article" (You can't be held to writing it even if you've agreed),
- And the parties should be *legally able* to enter into a contract: You cannot hold someone who is a minor, or under a legal disability

(such as a judgment of incompetence), to an agreement, which is why you get a parent or guardian to sign for such persons.

If all those elements are present—offer, acceptance, consideration, legality, and capacity to contract—the contract will usually be enforced. Two cases in which it *won't* be enforced are:

- ▲ If you can prove that there was *no "meeting of the minds"*—if, for example, you offered to write an article on "publishing horror stories," and *you* meant horror stories about the publishing world, but *they* meant how to publish the kind of stories that Stephen King writes, *or*
- ▲ If there was *duress,* such as an editor holding your child hostage to make you sign, or, more likely, publishing the article and afterwards demanding an all-rights contract—which had never been your intention—as a condition of payment.

In such cases, the contract may not be enforceable, but you'll generally have to retain an attorney and go to court to get it invalidated.

Though magazines and newspapers often skip the formality of a contract, book contracts are almost always in writing.

Too often, the beginning writer doesn't worry about what is in a book contract because he or she is so happy to get it. If the writer does have a question, who does he usually ask? The editor who sent it, of course.

Talk about the fox guarding the chicken coop! Even if the editor has no malicious intent, he or she is seldom trained in the law and may merely be passing on misinformation received from another source— or premised on limited experience. A classic example is the editor who says, "We never enforce that," and then leaves that publishing house —or the house itself is bought out—and the next thing you know, they're enforcing that clause: "It says right here that you agree to give us your firstborn male child if you fail to deliver the completed manuscript on time. We're here to collect."

All right, it's not *quite* that bad, but if they never enforce a clause, why should it be there in the first place?

But you don't read the contract, right? That's what you have an agent for. Well, what if you don't have an agent? As I indicated in the previous chapter, once you have an offer, you can go out and get yourself an agent—which won't be that difficult, because you've done the greater part of the agent's work by selling the book. A competent agent should be able to negotiate the contract for you and may even employ an attorney if the contract contains a particularly strange or sticky clause.

What if your agent hasn't employed an attorney and doesn't seem to be giving you satisfactory answers to your questions about the meaning of the contract? If you have any doubt about what the contract means, don't sign it. Run, don't walk, to the nearest publishing lawyer. *Not* your family lawyer, who has probably never seen a book contract before, but someone who knows the publishing field.

However, to protect yourself, it doesn't hurt for *you* to know a few basic things about book contracts. And the three most important things you should know about a book contract are:

▲ There is no standard contract for the industry.
▲ Each publisher's standard contract is merely the starting point for negotiations.
▲ It isn't what's in the contract, but what's been left out of it, that can do you in.

Publishers' contracts are inevitably skewed in favor of the publisher. Most authors just don't have the clout to get *everything* they'd like until they hit the best-seller list repeatedly—like the best-selling author who once told me casually, "Oh, I just tell 'em what I want in my contracts, and that's what they give me."

Unless you have that kind of power, you'll have to do battle—and to do battle, you need to arm yourself. In this case, your armor is *information*.

The first thing you should ascertain is whether you have a legitimate contract. Remember Kozak's Rule #5—*they pay you*. I discussed vanity and subsidy presses in chapter 9, and unless your work falls into one of the three categories I listed on page 76, you should avoid these houses. As a rule, the publishing community *knows* which houses are subsidy presses and tends not to review books published by them. Generally, too, you are not eligible for most prizes or grants unless your work has been published by a "risk" house—one that was willing to take a *risk* on you.

Vanity presses often have distribution problems as well as credibility problems. I was once appointed trustee in the bankruptcy of a self-published poet who listed among his assets some 2000 copies of his book of poems. He had paid to have these published; now he couldn't pay anyone to take them off his hands. As trustee, my duty was to get as much as I could for his disposable assets and distribute the proceeds to his creditors, but I couldn't find a market for the books either. I "abandoned" them (with the permission of the court), which meant that he got to keep them—and I'll bet he still has 99 percent of them taking up most of his living space or costing him hefty storage fees.

Despite my rule that "they pay you," you should not assume that all risk houses pay you an *advance.* Even those that do pay an advance may not pay a very large one. But an advance is money paid to you in anticipation of the royalties your book will earn; it doesn't matter much if you get the money up front or after the book hits the stands, as long as *you* aren't paying *them.* The important difference between subsidy/vanity presses and risk houses is the commitment to publish the book at the publisher's expense. *You* have put forth the time and effort to write the book. If you are also paying for the editing, printing, and distribution, why should the "publisher" share at all in the proceeds?

Assuming that you have been offered a legitimate contract, what can you expect to find in it? Even though, as I indicated earlier, there is no such thing as a standard contract, there are certain things that most contracts contain.

The first is an identification of the parties—the name of the publishing house, and your name, and the tentative name of the book. If you are using a pseudonym, this is where you make it clear that your *real* name shouldn't go on the book itself.

In describing the book, the contract may specify a *length and due date,* and may include language that notes that the work has "never before been published"—which you may want to modify if the book is, for example, a collection of your previously published short stories. This is one of the places where you may need some professional assistance in choosing the proper wording to eliminate any possible misunderstandings.

One of the hairier conditions usually included at this point is the requirement that the manuscript must be *"satisfactory to the publisher."* This gives the publisher the final say in whether to accept or reject the manuscript—and the publisher's dissatisfaction need not be premised on any flaws in the manuscript. Books have been deemed unsatisfactory, for example, when a publisher is purchased by another company and wants to change the kind of books it publishes.

You cannot usually eliminate this clause, but you *can* make sure that the contract contains provision for you to rewrite anything that is "not satisfactory to the publisher" and sometimes even obtain language that allows you to keep the advance if the work cannot be made "satisfactory." Again, this may require professional help.

Basic to any book contract is a *grant of rights*. This section indicates what rights the publisher expects to receive. These may vary from something as restricted as "North American English language paperback rights" to something as broad as "all rights." I have a personal aversion to granting all rights to anything, but sometimes—in the case of elementary and high school textbooks, for example—this, or the even more all-embracing work-for-hire clause, may be customary. Modification of the proposed grant of rights may be possible with professional help—and clout. The clout is based on how badly the publisher really wants your book. You should never overestimate your clout, but don't underestimate it either—if the publisher is willing to make an offer, it has made at least a minimal commitment to the book and will usually be willing to make *some* concessions.

Closely related to the grant of rights will be a paragraph relating to the registration of *the copyright*. This often specifies that the copyright notice will bear the name (or pseudonym) of the author, and will be registered in the name of the author. The notice and registration provide extra protection in case of an infringement, but having the copyright is a rather empty honor if you've granted the publisher all, or almost all, the rights contained in the copyright.

No matter how many rights you've granted to the publisher, the book contract should contain an *out-of-print* or *reversion clause* that returns those rights to you under certain conditions. What conditions? The most common one arises when a book goes out of print. Publishers often require that you make a written demand that the book be reprinted, after which they normally have six months to comply. If they fail to reprint, you get the book rights back. Sometimes you can also negotiate for the reversion of subsidiary rights, such as movie rights or merchandising (T-shirt and lunchbox) rights, if they haven't been exercised within a designated period.

Additionally, the contract will often require that the publisher print the book within a specific amount of time—eighteen months to two years is probably the most common length of time. If the book hasn't been published by then, you may be able to take the rights back and sell them elsewhere. Again, a professional analysis of the words in this clause may be advisable to make sure they mean what you think they do.

One of the most important clauses in a book contract is the *warranty clause.* In it, you, as the author, guarantee the publisher that *you* are the person who has written (or compiled) the book, that you haven't libeled anyone on its pages or invaded anyone's privacy, and that you have (or will get) permission to use anything you have quoted within the text. If your guarantee proves false, and the publisher has to pay out money for legal defense or damages or both, you will usually be required to reimburse the publisher for all or part of its costs.

Even though you may have taken the greatest possible care in compiling the text, you may have accidentally created a problem that *appears to be actionable.* Perhaps you have made up a name for a baker who is poisoning his bread—and it turns out there *is* a baker by that same name, working in a town with a name similar to the setting of your novel. Or perhaps your story bears a striking similarity to a story by someone else, even though you may never have seen the other tale. You didn't intend any damage—indeed, you may not even be guilty of any fault—but anyone can sue anybody for anything, and the only question that results is whether the suing party will prevail in court. Whether or how much you will have to repay the publisher for its costs in defending such suits depends on the wording in the warranty clause.

One way to defend yourself against possible suits is to insist on a chance to review galleys. Most publishers will send you either page proofs or galleys (unpaged sheets of typeset columns) for review. This is done for your protection and theirs—one more person doing the proofreading can catch even more mistakes, and, as the author, you may be able to catch some errors in implication or meaning that someone else might miss. If you call the attention of the publisher to editorial changes that may create a legal liability, you've passed the buck back; if the publisher doesn't make your recommended changes and you are both sued, you can point out, in your defense, that *you* recommended that the questionable language or allusions be changed.

It is also possible to insist in the contract that *no changes* be made in a manuscript *without your authorization,* and that you be allowed to remove your name if changes are made without your consent. This should be included in the contract if you want to be able to hold the publisher to it. You might also want to include a guaranteed minimum period of time for you to review the galleys, since I've known publishers who wanted an entire book proofread and corrected within forty-eight hours, without any advance warning for the writer to clear his or her calendar.

Also related to the grant of rights are the *subsidiary rights* (or "sub rights") sections of the contract. These paragraphs itemize which rights in addition to the book rights the publisher wants, and how much of any money for licensing these rights the publisher wants to keep. For example, the publisher may want to control the sale of movie rights and may be offering you 50 percent of the proceeds. Perhaps you feel that you should receive 75 percent of any movie sale—or perhaps your brother-in-law owns a production company, and you don't feel you should be paying *any* commission to the publisher if the movie rights stay within your family.

And what if the publisher keeps control of the movie rights but never makes any attempt to sell them? Or what if it sells the movie rights to your children's novel to a porno house? Again, retaining creative control or regaining the rights when the publisher fails to act on them are both examples of things that can be negotiated into publishing contracts.

Now let's get to what most people think of as the important stuff: *how and when do you get paid?* A book contract usually spells out how much of an advance you will receive, and when you will receive it. There are generally three times that an advance may be payable:

- *On signing* (as soon as both parties reach an agreement, sign the contract, and the accounting department can get the check out).
- *On acceptance* (as soon as the publisher receives the manuscript and decides that it is, indeed, "satisfactory").
- *On publication* (on, or usually within thirty days after, the official publication date—which may or may not correspond to the date on which the first copy finds its way into your eager hands).

For magazine articles, payment is usually made either on acceptance or on publication—although anyone who pays on publication is rather like a customer who tells a tailor (because articles are often tailored to a magazine's specifications), "I'll take this suit now, but I won't pay you till I wear it." The tailor wouldn't let you get away with that, and you shouldn't let magazines do it, either.

Newspapers normally do pay on publication or shortly thereafter (in other words, whenever the voucher wends its way through the system to accounting and they manage to get the check out of the computer). However, newspapers usually buy pieces over the transom instead of making assignments, seldom require anything more than onetime rights and territorial exclusivity, and normally use your material shortly after they receive it, rarely holding on to it long enough for the "suit" to go out of style. At least *their* system is more like a thirty-day revolving charge account.

Books present a different situation. First of all, they take much longer to write than an article, if only because they are so much larger (I've heard about a three-day novel contest, but anyone who can write a novel in three days can probably write an article in three hours, so the proportions hold). Second, they generally pay more than articles. Third, they ultimately pay based on the number of copies sold, rather than on a flat-fee basis. And, fourth, the book advance presents the only time in the publishing world when you can get money before you write something, rather than afterwards.

A book advance may be paid at any of the three times I mentioned or split between them—half on signing and half on acceptance, for example, or one-third on signing, one-third on acceptance, and one-third on publication. Or, as I noted earlier, sometimes no advance is paid at all. When you receive one, however, remember that the *advance* is money *advanced to you against royalties to be earned.*

Royalties that are paid to you are based on a percentage of what the book brings in—but here the language can be tricky. You can earn a percentage of the retail price of each book, or a percentage of the wholesale price that the publisher actually receives, or any amount in between. And the percentages can vary from 2 percent for some paperbacks to 20 percent for some hardcover editions.

The percentage can even vary for a single book depending on how many copies have been sold—for example, 6 percent on the first 20,000 and 8 percent on all copies sold in excess of 20,000. In my experience, the amount of the advance is rarely negotiable unless the book is a hot property that more than one publisher wants; the royalty percentage is sometimes negotiable; and the figure at which the percentage changes is probably the most negotiable of the three.

Once or twice a year after the book is published, according to a schedule set forth in the contract, the publisher will add up the sales figures, determine how much you have earned, and issue a statement telling you both of these things. Once your book has earned back the amount of the advance, the publisher, after subtracting a "reasonable reserve against returns" of your book from stores, issues a check to you for royalties.

You can also earn money through the sale of the subsidiary rights I mentioned earlier. If your publisher sells the movie rights to your book for $10,000, and this amount is to be split between you and the publisher on a fifty-fifty basis, you have $5000 coming. But if your book hasn't yet earned back its advance, the publisher is usually allowed to use your share of such income to offset the advance before paying you.

The one thing that is almost always negotiable in a book contract is the number of *free copies* the author will receive. The only refusal to enlarge this number that I've ever seen was from the publisher of an expensive textbook.

In addition, the contract usually specifies that the author can buy *copies at a discount* price. Some contracts specify that these may be bought for personal use only and not for resale, but many contracts do not specifically restrict authors from selling copies themselves. Most authors learn to carry a box of their books in the trunk of their car for those occasions when someone asks, "Where can I get a copy of your book?" and they don't know of any local bookstores that are still carrying it.

When a book is deemed no longer salable, it is sometimes *remaindered*. Remaindered books are the ones you see for sale at cut-rate prices on special sale tables in your local bookstore. Sometimes you can negotiate for the right of first refusal on remainder sales—the right to buy your books at remainder prices before they are sold to anyone else. You may wind up with your garage or attic full of boxes of your books, but at least you will have copies around to give as bread-and-butter gifts when you are a guest in someone's house or to prop up a table with a short leg—there are a million and one uses for a remaindered book!

Just remember, if you don't stock them yourself, finding copies of the book can be a real problem—especially when a publisher files for *bankruptcy*. Although many book contracts contain a bankruptcy clause, current law often renders it useless. Again, a skilled negotiator can sometimes insert changes in the contract that will offer you more protection—or at least enable you to get your hands on undistributed copies of the book.

Some book contracts contain a section that restricts you from selling a *competing* book without permission of the publisher. The decision as to whether the book you want to write constitutes a competing work may be up to the publisher. Think twice about signing a contract with such a clause if you are an expert in your field and all your books are likely to deal with that field.

A closely related issue is the *option clause,* which may give the publisher the right of first refusal on your next book. If you cannot eliminate an option clause entirely, you should at least make sure it allows you to submit a book proposal, rather than a completed book, and that it doesn't bind you to accept the same terms for your next book that you did for this one. (With your first book, you are an unknown quantity, and you have a very weak bargaining position, but if your first book becomes a best-seller, you may be able to negotiate better terms in your next contract.)

I have seen people sign away all derivative rights, which means they can no longer use the characters they invented, or sign away their pseudonym, which means that other people may be authorized by the publisher to write books—usually other books in the same series—under that pseudonym. I don't think anyone should ever be so eager for a book contract that he or she signs something like this without at least attempting to negotiate some modifications—but people do it every day. As P.T. Barnum is alleged to have said, "There's one born every minute."

Given that there is no standard contract for the publishing industry, the contract *you* receive may be missing an important clause or may possess a fairly standard clause worded in some strange way that turns its meaning inside out. These guidelines are meant only to alert you to where *some* of the problems may lie. Model contracts are available to members from some writers' groups like the Authors Guild or the Science Fiction Writers of America, but such models are an ideal and, like most ideals, are often difficult to achieve.

Although most of the terms in any contract are negotiable, sometimes you'll run into a publisher who won't budge on something that you consider particularly important. At that point, you'll have to determine whether to go along with terms you find less than desirable or to reject the contract and look for another publisher. Only someone experienced in working with publishing contracts can tell you whether your contract is fair to both you and the publisher, or if one of you—usually the author—is giving away the store. Whatever choice you make should be based on as much information as you can garner and as much self-confidence as you can muster. It also helps to have a sharp negotiator in your corner, or to learn to be a sharp negotiator yourself.

14

Where Do You Get Your Ideas?

Back in chapter 1, I suggested that writers are people who are driven to write. We can't stop ourselves. So I never fail to be astonished when someone says to me, "I'd love to be a writer—but where do you get your ideas?"

Where *don't* you get them?

There probably isn't a writer anywhere who doesn't have boxes upon boxes, or files upon files, or notebooks upon notebooks, all filled with scrawled ideas for titles, character names, plot lines, or articles. Ideas come to you *everywhere*—most often when your hands are wet, or full of something live and slithery (like a half-washed dog or baby), or are braced on the steering wheel in heavy traffic. If you're lucky, they don't get away (the ideas, not the dogs, babies, or steering wheels) before you've forgotten them—which is *why* writers have all those little scraps of paper all over the place.

And what's *on* all those little scraps and *in* all those notebooks? Weird things that may or may not mean anything to you when you pick them up later. For example, at random from *my* notebooks are the following entries, in their entirety:

A Frog, He Would A-wooing Go

Name for a cowboy: "Redwood Boles"

Trichinosis from pork, bear meat, walrus meat. *Walrus* meat?

In search of the perfect suitcase.

I used that last entry to spin-off an article. As for the others, who knows? I might be stuck for a cowboy name someday, and the walrus meat might find its way into an adventure novel or a mystery story. Why I wrote down the title to the folk song about the frog, or what I might be able to do with it, beats me. But you don't have to hit with *every* idea—just enough ideas to keep you writing.

You don't always have to come up with ideas. Professional writing runs the gamut from drafting résumés and business letters to creating a Nobel Prize–winning body of literature. In between, there are technical writers who write computer manuals (you didn't *really* think the computers wrote them, did you?), copywriters who put together the advertising brochures that land in your mailbox, television and radio "continuity" writers, even the people who write the stuff on the side of the cereal box. The impetus for these kinds of writing comes from others: assignments to write a manual for a new software, to describe this sofa or that teapot so the public will want to buy them, or to tell the public they can have a "free" cereal bowl if they send in six boxtops and a check or money order for one dollar.

But what most of us mean, when we talk about writing, is *writing for print*—seeing our work published in magazines or newspapers or (please, Lord) books. Leaving aside books for the present, writing for the print media falls into three general categories: news, articles (or features), and fiction.

You don't have to come up with ideas when you write news—they happen! Most news stories are not only right there in front of you, they may even have come with a press release attached, telling you what to look for. Indeed, the bulk of the stories you see in a paper or on a local news broadcast may be *manufactured news,* made up of photo opportunities, press conferences (often held for no reason but to get someone's name in the paper), and "quasi news" like the annual avocado festival, which requires nothing more of a reporter than to dutifully write that the mayor ate his annual dish of guacamole (no fair harboring a secret wish for him to have an allergic reaction so you can write something different this year!).

Once in a while, a story *is* new, or is an "exclusive"—what used to be known as a scoop. For example, if you happen to be on the scene when a plane falls from the sky, or a bus falls off of a mountain, or three little old ladies hold up a bank at gunpoint, you may have a story—*if* you are a stringer for the paper. Generally, however, the paper will send a staff reporter to the scene, and instead of writing the story, you'll wind up being interviewed for the story the reporter is writing.

The one exception might be if you live in an isolated area and there is a major event (like a flood or a train wreck); you may be able to call in the details to a major paper before they can get a reporter to the scene. But they're unlikely to accept the story from you unless you've laid the groundwork first by establishing yourself as a stringer—that is, a non-staff writer from whom they've agreed to accept stories of local interest.

Unless you're on staff or are a stringer, you can generally forget about selling *straight* news stories. Obviously, then, the things that happen right in front of you are not the best source of writing ideas—or *are* they?

News reporting follows certain conventions, which I'll discuss in chapter 15, and, as I've noted, news can be difficult to sell. The alternative to reporting the news, in nonfiction writing, is to produce features or articles. This is what most people seem to want to write, anyway. Where do you get ideas for features or articles? Like the news, they can be right in front of your nose!

This is where you get to exercise your creativity. Among the kinds of features that sell every day are:

- ▲ *The nostalgia piece.* You know what this is: "I remember the Good Old Days" or "Remember when . . ."
- ▲ *The interview.* If the subject's name isn't a household word, tie the story either to a local appearance or to a timely event: "Astronaut thinks our city is out of this world" or "Three chefs describe their favorite holiday meals."
- ▲ *The background piece* that accompanies a news story: "This avocado grower has been coming to the festival for forty years."
- ▲ *The "how-to" article.* This can mean anything from "How to mothproof your woolens" or "How to make strudel in your microwave" to "How to teach your child to read before birth."
- ▲ *The travel piece.* This can be either descriptive—"Arctic port gives visitors a warm welcome"—or personal—"What it was like to spend a week in the rain forest."

You can also cross over, combining the how-to, for example, with a travel piece ("How to pack for a trip to the Arctic") or with a celebrity interview ("The cardinal's favorite recipe for Christmas cookies"). And where do you come up with ideas for articles like these? There are basically four sources:

- ▲ who and what you already know,
- ▲ who or what you'd like to know,
- ▲ what you think someone else would probably like to know, which *you* are able to find out,

and the fourth, wild-card source:

- ▲ things that flash into your mind for no reason whatsoever.

How you use these depends on whether you can *think like a writer* and turn them into a story.

Let's start with *who and what you already know.* Did you grow up on a farm in the days before farms were as mechanized as they are today? To a writer, that's the source of a nostalgia piece—or, if you are willing to do a little legwork, a feature on how farming has changed over the past fifty years.

Is your best friend coordinating the avocado festival? Would other people be interested in how she worries every year about whether the avocados will be ripe at the right time? Not only might she herself be a good subject for an interview, perhaps she can put you on to the little old lady who has been coming for so many years.

Want more ideas? Where have you been lately? Even a one-day trip to shop at a wholesale mall in the next county can be a travel feature ("A profitable day trip"). And if you've just returned from the Everglades where someone gave you a recipe for alligator pie, you might be able to do a feature on the Everglades in general, on the person who runs the alligator farm in particular, or a food feature about how to prepare alligator ("First you've got to catch one . . .").

Sometimes the kind of information that you use every day is *news* to others and might make a good feature. Do you get all six of your kids and your husband out of the house on time each morning? Have you come up with a maintenance-free ground cover for your back yard? Did you fix your leaking roof with bubble gum? Other people might like to know *how.*

You can also make your hobbies work for you. Joan Winston,

Jacqueline Lichtenberg, and Sondra Marshak were all *Star Trek* fans who managed, years after the original series was canceled, to turn their affection for the TV show into a book called *Star Trek Lives!* Joan then went on to write a book about how she and a group of friends had organized the first *Star Trek* convention. Sondra went on to coauthor a number of *Star Trek* novels. Inspired by their ability to make their hobby turn a profit, when I found myself getting hooked on *Hawaii Five-O* reruns, I managed to transform all those hours of watching McGarrett tell Danno to "book 'em" into an article and a trivia quiz.

In addition to exploiting *what* you know to come up with ideas for your writing, there's also nothing wrong with exploiting *who* you know. Is your cousin press secretary to a senator? Can you get an interview with her boss? If so, the next question is, where can you sell it? If you don't know anything about politics, don't try to ask him about his political philosophy. Maybe you can get a good feature about what it's like for him to be a "bachelor" five days a week, stocking his own refrigerator and doing his own laundry, and what kind of adjustment it is to come home to his wife and teenage children on weekends. That kind of piece might sell to a family-oriented magazine if he behaves himself, to a confession magazine if he doesn't.

Is a classmate from grade school now starring in a sitcom? If you can be objective about the way he used to beat you up for lunch money, maybe you can do an interview. If you can't be objective, maybe you can sell a "tell-all" piece ("Television nice guy wasn't always so nice")—just be sure you have your facts straight so you don't set yourself up for a libel suit.

You can also base articles on *who or what you'd like to know.* Curiosity may kill cats, but it produces writing ideas. Look at it this way: if something provokes *your* curiosity enough for you to follow it up or find out what makes it tick, don't you think it might also interest readers?

I mentioned earlier an article I once sold about jacaranda trees. I was in Los Angeles for a movie premiere when the infamous purple trees caught my eye. We don't have purple *trees* in Wisconsin. Purple bushes, sure—lilacs bloom for about a week each spring. And lots of purple flowers and weeds. But here were *trees* that looked as if someone had festooned them with purple feather dusters. And whenever I asked anyone what they were, the laid-back response I got was, "Uh, yeah, the purple trees. I don't know what they're called."

There turned out to be a story not only in jacaranda trees themselves—they grow only in three or four areas in the entire United States—but also in how I dug up the information on them. In that, I took Alex Haley as my example—he not only wrote his family's history, he also wrote about how he discovered it! Sometimes *how* you get the story can be as interesting as the story itself.

Writers need a high CQ—Curiosity Quotient. How high is *your* CQ?

Do *you* stop people walking their dogs on the street to ask, "What kind of dog is that?" Perhaps this is a new breed, or a newly popular breed. Do you want to know exactly what the dentist or the surgeon are about to do to you, and how they propose to do it? There are two possible features in that kind of information: factual, as in "The how, what, and why of gum surgery," and first person, as in "I survived hip replacement."

Sometimes you'll find out something about a person that makes you think you might want to know them. Minnie Pearl, of the hanging hat tags and loud "HowdEEE," was actually educated in a private women's college—and challenged convention to go on the stage. She sounded like an intriguing and independent woman, and I decided I'd like to get to know her. I managed to get an interview, and she was absolutely delightful. Other people were interested, too—I sold two articles based on that interview.

Curiosity prompts me to watch the mechanics working on my car until they chase me away, and to try to guess—by taste—the ingredients in exotic foods I am served. My curiosity, long before sushi became trendy, about the correct way to order and eat it resulted in my selling several articles on sushi bar etiquette once the trend caught on.

Whatever *you* want to know about, you can bet some editor, somewhere, will also want to know about—and so, probably, will a lot of readers!

Closely akin to this are things you think someone else might like to know that you might be able to find out. Perhaps *you* aren't particularly into lawns. Maybe you *hate* yours and prefer the idea of letting it return to the prairie it once was.

An idle fancy? Maybe. But if you hate taking care of your lawn, there are probably a lot of others out there who share your sentiments.

You may never want to see the word "lawn" again—but what do you think all those other lawn-haters might like to know about the grass in their yards? Obviously, the history of the lawn and the ecology of the prairie are pretty dull subjects—but that history becomes more interesting if you check out local ordinances to find out whether it's *legal* for you to let your lawn return to nature. What if you checked with an environmentalist group and discovered that was the best way to preserve the topsoil? As you can see, there are several possible articles growing under your feet, and a lot of environmentalists and people who hate to mow their lawns just might like to read them.

Sometimes you find yourself with the opportunity to interview a celebrity in whom you have no interest—the star of a TV program you never watch, for example. If you have any warning at all, make it a point to prepare. Read up about the person so you can ask intelligent questions. In the process of doing this, you may discover something about the subject that *you* want to know—something other reporters, dazzled by the more well-known aspects of the celebrity's career, may have missed. Some of the people I've only reluctantly consented to interview have turned out to be fascinating for *un*obvious reasons, and even the duds have responded positively when asked a question that's out of the ordinary. The trick in interviewing a celebrity is the same as in getting to know *anyone*—exercise your CQ to help you find common ground. You'll get a better interview, and you might even make a friend in the process.

Learn to think like a writer and you can make great use of that wild card I mentioned—the things that pop into your head for no reason whatsoever. Take the morning I was doing dishes, and, out of the blue, the title of T. S. Eliot's poem "The Naming of Cats" popped into my head. What if it were written, "The Naming of Katz"? What kind of feature would that be?

I thought about the fact that my grandmother left Russia as Rifke Tsofnis and arrived in this country as Rose Albert. The switch from "Rifke" to "Rose" I could understand, but how did she get the surname "Albert"?

I once asked her.

"I don't know," she confessed. "Maybe it was the first name of the guy who passed us through immigration, and he couldn't spell 'Tsofnis.'"

I was aware that you are allowed to change your name or its spelling when you become a citizen. But how many people had their names changed arbitrarily by immigration officers when they entered the country?

Suddenly, I had all the ingredients for an article—merely because the title of a poem popped into my mind as I washed the breakfast dishes.

What kind of quirky free associations do *you* come up with? They can be the source of articles and stories—the kind of ideas that, as novelist Jacqueline Lichtenberg suggests, you have to "beat off with a stick."

The difference between a writer and a "wannabe" is that a writer can almost always turn whatever is currently obsessing him or her into a piece of writing. *How* you do that depends on your individual style and inclination.

Here's how *thinking like a writer* works. The kids have come home from camp with enough laundry for an army. You feel as though you've grown rooted to the washer. Take your notebook with you, and while you wait for the spin cycle to finish, consider:

- Who *does* the laundry for the army? *How* do they do it? This is a possible article idea.
- Despite automatic washers, is it really easier to do laundry today than it was a hundred years ago? Do we do *more* laundry because we have the machines? Are our clothes as clean? This is another article idea.
- Many a romance has been sparked between people who struck up a conversation while waiting for their clothes to finish tumbling in the dryer. Perhaps this is the starting point for a romantic novel?
- If a spy "accidentally" leaves a sock containing a microdot in a coin-operated washer, his contact can pick it up without arousing suspicion. This can be the premise for a thriller or a comedy of errors.

What if your mechanic promised your car would be ready in an hour and you've already been waiting three? What are those guys in the garage *doing* to it?

- Well, what *do* they do, step by step, when you take your car in for a tune-up? This could make an interesting article, and here's your chance to be nosy and to make your mechanic clean up his act (would he really want his practices revealed in a national magazine?).

▲ What if the mechanic is hiding something in your engine, and setting you up so you'll have to bring the car back tomorrow? What he's hiding will be off the premises tonight, but will come back when you return, outraged, to demand the job be finished correctly. You've just set up a partial plot for a thriller.

▲ If you write humor pieces, you might want to speculate on all the things the garage *could* be doing with your car all this time.

You get the picture. There are writing possibilities in all of life's little annoyances. The trick is to see them from an angle that hasn't been used before, and to build a better mousetrap—present the information in a way that attracts an editor because it will probably intrigue or amuse his readers.

Where do ideas for *fiction* come from? They are often based on character or circumstance or setting. What you do is look at one or more of these factors, and ask yourself, "What if . . . ?"

Let's take character, for example. You have a friend who is obsessive about a particular actor. What do you think would happen if she met him? Is she easily manipulated—could he take advantage of her infatuation to turn her into a love slave (or, more likely, a gofer)? What if she's a take-charge person and his career seems to be on the wane because of bad management—do you think, if they met, she could turn it around? Would she put her own life on hold to do it? What if he took her devotion for granted and married some bimbo—would she stay on?

Suddenly, there is a story there. Understand, the characters in your novel *cannot actually be identifiable* as your friend and that actor, or you *could* be sued for libel. Nevertheless, you can build on the kind of personalities you think they have, and imagine them together, and see if the story doesn't construct itself.

Character-based stories are, in many ways, the easiest to write. Think of a kind of person, put him or her together with another kind of person, and immediately, certain actions are inevitable. Just keep asking, "What if . . . ?"

Circumstance-based stories are a little more difficult. Suppose one of your friends took his first vacation in years—to San Juan, days before Hurricane Hugo hit? Speculate—what if he had stayed just a day or two longer—what adventures might he have had trying to survive in an unfamiliar place where he couldn't speak the language? What difficulties might he have found trying to get a flight home? Would he, perhaps, have met someone—a dedicated doctor, an injured child, a beautiful looter—from whom he could have learned something about life or about himself? Circumstances—the hurricane, his trip—produce your story.

Sometimes you create a story based on a setting. A writer coming upon a crumbling mansion high on a cliff overlooking the sea, or set back on a wild moor, might be tempted to create a *Dragonwyck* or *Wuthering Heights* because of that setting alone. Looking at such a house, could you help but think, "What kind of people must live there? What would happen if a person like *me* came to live there? *Why* would a person like me come to live there?" And you're off and running.

All it takes is following through on the kinds of ideas that occur to all of us, every moment of every day—and learning to *think like a writer,* which means using those ideas in a productive, *disciplined* way.

15

Some Specific Problems in Nonfiction Writing

In the foregoing chapter, I noted that successful writing requires making use of ideas in a disciplined way.

Discipline? But isn't discipline the antithesis of creativity?

Not at all. Discipline is what sets the professional writer, who writes and sells, apart from the ranks of amateurs who *want* to write.

Discipline is learning what *doesn't* belong in your work and having the courage to excise it. I discussed editing your own work in chapter 5, but there's more to discipline than just editing.

First of all, there is *observing the conventions*. Certain kinds of writing require specific formalities—for example, footnotes and bibliographies are required in scholarly works. Some publications have their own customs—no first-person articles or *all* first-person articles, short paragraphs or long ones. If you want to write in those fields or for those publications, you must obey their rules, however arbitrary they may seem.

Second, there is *keeping your focus*. A charming vignette that doesn't further the plot does not belong in your novel, and nonessential details can distract the reader from the point of your article.

Third, there are certain *legal constraints* that apply to published materials. I've discussed some of these in chapter 12, but there are a few others I'll mention as we go along.

Any writer will tell you that the hardest thing to come up with is your opening sentence. It must attract the reader, tell him or her what the piece will be about, and set the tone for the rest of the work. You can get away with "It was a dark and stormy night" only on rare occasions; the rest of the time, more innovative wording is required.

I'll save the openings of fiction for the next chapter. In nonfiction writing, the opening is often called the "lead."

In straight newswriting, the lead has certain specific requirements. Strictly speaking, it should be a single sentence of thirty-five words or less in which you tell the reader the *who, what, where, when, why,* and *how* of the story you are breaking.

One more thing—you are never supposed to start your lead with "The" or "A."

There are few, if any, papers that impose strict adherence to these formal journalistic conventions anymore, but it is still a good idea to try to get as many of the six basic facts as possible into the first paragraph of a news story. This is because most newspapers still assume that stories are written in "inverted pyramid" form, with all the important information in the lead, and the least-important information at the end. Put a punch line in the last paragraph of a news story, and you are quite likely to have it lopped off. Because your story may wind up only a paragraph or two in length, those first two paragraphs had better be able to stand on their own.

A traditional lead about a breaking story will read something like this:

Information released today by the Office of the Surgeon General revealed that 70 percent of the American population is "on a diet" on any given day.

That's twenty-six words that tell you:

what—a study was released (and what it says),
who—the Office of the Surgeon General released the study,
when—today.

You can assume the *where* (the Surgeon General's office is in Washington, D.C., and the study refers to Americans) and the *why* (you'd have to have spent the last forty years in a cave not to know that almost everyone in the United States is concerned about his or her weight). The next sentence will probably tell you *how*: "In a study conducted by sixteen leading universities, in forty-eight cities and towns throughout the country, it was revealed . . ." But, actually, if only that first sentence appeared in the paper, the reader would still have a basic understanding of that piece of news.

What if this weren't breaking news, but a magazine feature on the amount of money Americans spend on diet plans and devices every year? You might want to start with a teaser:

> The Surgeon General recently revealed that 70 percent of the American population pays more for the privilege of going to bed hungry every night than the people of many developing countries pay for filling their stomachs.

Got your attention, didn't I? I've set the tone, and grabbed you, and you know the article has something to do with the cost of dieting. Hopefully, the headline will also have given you the same indication: "Putting Your Money Where Your Mouth Is—The High Cost of Dieting." Now I can go on to say how much the average diet plan costs, how much more expensive a low-calorie dinner is than a normal one, quote a few people on why they feel this is cost-effective for them, and quote a few doctors on whether these plans really work in the long run.

I assume that when you are reading the article, which is being written for a magazine rather than the front page of a newspaper, you will probably be sitting down, not standing on a swaying subway. So I also assume that you will be willing to take more time with my in-depth story than you would with a news flash. You won't be angry if you have to read to the second or third paragraph to find out what I'm really talking about.

But you *will* be angry if I digress and start to talk about my memories of favorite childhood foods. In that case I've given you a false indication, from the headline and the lead, that I was going to talk about what a diet costs monetarily, not emotionally. This brings us to:

Kozak's Rule #7: *Always play fair with your readers.*

Basically you play fair with your readers by sticking to your subject and writing about what you say you're going to write about.

▲ ▲ ▲

Are you having trouble coming up with any lead at all? That's a not-uncommon problem among writers. One solution that works for me is to go ahead and write the conclusion of the article: "Thus it's obvious that in the land of plenty, plenty of people want *less* for their money, rather than more. And they're willing to spend more to get less."

Guess what—if you drop the first four words, you could use those two sentences for your lead. Support the thesis with facts, throw in a few quotes, and write a new conclusion when you get to the end. In feature or article writing, your first and last paragraphs can often be exchanged without doing a lot of harm to the piece. Keep that in mind when a lead won't come to you, and it may help to move things along.

Once you've got your lead, a story often writes itself. Assuming you're not writing in an inverted pyramid—in which case each succeeding paragraph should be more detailed and less important than the last—you have a lot of freedom to expound on your subject according to any pattern that strikes your fancy. If your lead has done all it should, the rest of the story will often follow automatically. In no time at all, you'll be able to come to the end, tie up any loose ends you may find, and exit gracefully.

But what if the story *doesn't* seem to want to flow? Help *is* available, in the form of certain tried-and-true methods.

First, sum up what you are trying to say in one sentence: "Americans waste a lot of money trying to get less food value out of what they eat." Type this on a card and tape it above your typewriter or word processor. Check every sentence or paragraph you write to see if it supports that thesis. If it doesn't, you are digressing; throw the rascal out.

A corollary to this is to go back and look at your lead. Perhaps you were so busy being clever that you never got around to having it do what a lead is supposed to do—set the tone for the piece and tell the reader where it is going. Somewhere, in paragraph five or eleven, you will find the main thrust of your article.

Congratulations. You have just "buried your lead."

Disinter it. Move it back to the beginning, even if you have to discard your clever opening for something much more mundane.

Now try going forward. You probably won't have any trouble at all.

What if you're *still* having trouble carrying the story forward? You may have skipped ahead too far. Go back to the lead and lay out, in logical sequence, what steps you need to get from the lead to the conclusion. You will probably find that you have skipped over one or two, and your conclusions didn't follow because they weren't premised on anything.

If you're still having trouble, fall back on two formats, one or the other of which will usually see you through to the end of the article. The first is the "army method."

Anyone who has ever gone through training to be a military officer has learned this method of structuring an article or speech. The format: "Tell 'em what you're gonna tell 'em, tell it to 'em, and tell 'em what you told 'em."

Sound familiar? In many cases, it may be the most workable solution to the problem of setting complex facts before the reading public. Summarize the article, expand on that summary with facts and examples, and then summarize again.

The second tried-and-true format is the "trends method," familiar to all who have ever written a history or sociology paper in college. This is a formulaic means of identifying and expounding on any social development.

Here's how it works. First, identify a social tendency that you think you can prove in your article: diet foods are costly, yet Americans seem to buy more and more of them.

Now support this thesis with facts and quotations. Organize them by smaller trends contained in the larger ones.

When at all possible, stick with the "rule of three." Three trends— "Americans eat too much, exercise too little, and eat the wrong foods" —are better than one. If this causes your topic to be too broad, you can stick with *one* trend—"Americans spend too much on diet foods, and then defeat the purpose by eating other things in addition." But again, use the "rule of three" to back up your single trend.

You do this by finding *three people* who are an example of the trend, and *three things* each of them does that makes them typical of the trend. For example, if "Many Americans spend too much on diet foods," I give you as examples Tom, Dick, and Mary. The percentage of their income that each of them spends on food is twice the national average.

Tom (the first example) is a bachelor who lives alone. (1) He finds that cooking from scratch takes up too much time and doesn't taste as good. (2) He buys diet dinners because he is watching his weight—but he hasn't lost any weight, because (3) he also drinks a lot of beer and eats a lot of snacks while watching a lot of television.

Dick (the second example) likes to cook and (1) buys a lot of "light" foods with which to do so. But (2) he travels a lot on his job, and most of them rot in his refrigerator while he is out of town, so (3) when he gets back he winds up ordering in a pizza.

Mary (the third example) is a single mother with custody of her two children, so she tries to cook nutritious meals for them. She (1) buys low-calorie foods for herself, but either (2) she doesn't cook them because there is enough left over from the children's meals, or (3) she *does* cook them and eats the leftovers as well.

Conclusion: buying diet foods is a waste of money for these people. This conclusion is supported by the actions of three people who serve as examples, and I have shown three facts about each that prove they are *good* examples.

Fair warning: I made up these people *and* the Surgeon General's statistic for this chapter. I'm writing a book about *writing,* not a book about dieting (my *sister* wrote the diet book).

I put in that disclaimer so that no one would think that my made-up facts were true. Disclaimers can get you out of a lot of hot water. Janet Cooke, who won and then gave up a Pulitzer Prize in 1981, *might* have been able to keep both the prize and her job if she had noted in print that the child she was writing about was "a composite, drawn from the experiences of several children."

Positing a hypothetical situation in a news story is perfectly acceptable, so long as you clearly identify it as hypothetical. Generally, when you write *news* stories or even *news* features, there is no room for fabrication. There is also no room for your opinions; save them for the editorial page. What a news story is supposed to give the reader is what *Dragnet*'s Sergeant Joe Friday always asked for—"Just the facts, ma'am."

Just what *is* news?

Journalism students and cub reporters (who seem to have been replaced by "newspaper interns") are often told, in words attributed to various nineteenth-century newspaper editors, that when a dog bites a man, it isn't news, but when a man bites a dog, you have a story.

Maybe that was true in the nineteenth century, but I've seen newspapers and television stations get a lot of mileage out of dog-bite stories. "Help find the grey dog that bit this woman so she'll know if she needs rabies shots," and "Pit bull kills child" are typical—and no one would dispute that they are *news.* "Man bites dog" is probably a publicity stunt and doesn't warrant any attention unless it's a really slow news day.

People who stage publicity stunts or send out press releases generally *want* to see their names in print. This is not necessarily true of people who grant you an interview, so you may be tempted to disguise their circumstances, or alter the facts somewhat, in order to protect their identities. What you wind up doing is treading a fine line between journalistic ethics and their right to privacy. Altering the facts to suit your story, rather than to protect the identity of your subjects, is definitely a breach of journalistic ethics. But where does the one leave off and the other begin?

What may be the dividing line between disguised fact and permissible fiction is the amount of space devoted to a subject. If I want to write an article about the problem of truancy, I can make up typical or composite examples and give each a single sentence in a much longer article:

- ▲ Hughie has difficulty reading and feels lost in the classroom;
- ▲ Dewey is hyperactive and can't sit still for a full forty-minute class;
- ▲ Louise has a boyfriend who tells her that if she loves him, she'll skip school and spend the day with him.

But it still may be a good idea to note that they are composites, though the reasons they give are typical of those given by truants for cutting class.

If you use *real* people as your examples, and if they are private citizens, unless their circumstances have turned them into public figures (as victims or perpetrators of a crime, for example), they possess a right to privacy. Because they may not be happy with having their circumstances revealed—even if they consent to an interview—they may want you to change their names for your article. When you do so, journalistic convention decrees that you *say* so: "Sara (not her real name) lives in a cardboard box beneath the 12th Street Bridge . . ."

But if people request such anonymity—*especially* if they request anonymity—you might do well to have them sign a document saying that you may use the facts of their case in your story so long as you change their names. This is because it is possible that merely revealing their circumstances may give away their identities.

A simple release might read as follows:

I, _____, grant permission for _____ to use any and all facts that I have revealed to him/her in the course of an interview conducted on _____, and any subsequent interviews, in any work he/she may write for print, so long as my name is changed and my actual address is not revealed.

This will probably suffice, as long as the person signing it is not a minor or under any legal disability (such as a judgment of mental incompetence—watch out for *this* when interviewing subjects like the residents of halfway houses).

Most people don't bother to get this sort of release when they do an interview, because they assume that the act of giving the interview implies consent. You should be aware, however, that—even in the absence of a request from the subject to change his or her name—there are certain circumstances in which it may be *illegal* for you to use a person's name in print. In some states, court records in "sensitive matters" may be sealed, which means that you may not print the names of victims of certain crimes (usually sexual assaults) if you obtain them from those records. In other jurisdictions, it is illegal to print the names of minors accused, or even found guilty, of a crime. Depending on circumstances, even a release may not protect you if you use the real name. Check with a lawyer—or, if you can't find a knowledgeable lawyer, check with the district attorney—in your area before you publish the name of any crime victim or accused criminal.

It is also a good idea to keep in mind that in our judicial system a person is innocent until proven guilty in a court of law. Thus, until there is a verdict of guilty, even someone who stabbed another person in front of ten witnesses and was arrested with the bloody knife still in his hands is always the "*alleged* killer."

The rules for naming names are very complex. Entire courses are taught in journalism schools about this subject—and a single judicial decision can change all the rules with the stroke of a pen. This is an area in which all journalists should tread with care, double-checking with their editors if they have any doubts about how and whether to use a name or an identifying descriptive phrase.

Freelancers are at a particular disadvantage, when compared to newspaper and magazine staffers, because only staffers have credentials. It is nearly impossible to obtain credentials for part-time feature writing, but it remains a possibility when covering news. *News,* in the vernacular of the sixties, is "what's happening," and very often it is rather routine: "The city council voted on the budget and authorized three tavern licenses today." This kind of information may not be earthshaking, but it did just happen, and it is important to those who live next door to one of those taverns, or whose pet project may have been left out of the budget.

Generally, such stories are written by newspaper staff members, who are assigned a "beat." If a reporter's beat is City Hall, he or she writes about aldermanic debates, ethics scandals, and the mayor's fundraisers. If the assignment is the courthouse, the stories will be about arrests, trials, and, once in a while, charges of impropriety leveled against a judge. The reporter who draws the zoo beat gets to write about the new lion cub. But occasionally, when a paper has a "beat" it covers infrequently—suburban town board meetings or high school athletic competitions come to mind—it may hire "stringers" to cover these events.

Stringers are truly the lowest people on the newspaper totem pole, and their status is epitomized by the way they are paid. Although a stringer sometimes reaps a small salary for covering, say, a weekly suburban school board meeting—whether a story results or not—it is more likely that the stringer won't be paid unless the paper actually runs the story. This puts stringers in a double bind: they don't dare miss a meeting, because if they miss a big story, their value to the paper drops to less than zero; on the other hand, they could be putting in an awful lot of time and effort for nothing unless the paper prints their work.

Nevertheless, being a stringer can garner you two kinds of credibility: first, with the paper, which will be more likely to take an article from a stringer than from a freelancer they don't know; and second, with the public, because the paper for which you are stringing will probably provide you with some sort of identification, like a press card or general letter of introduction.

Never underestimate the power of credentials. If you don't have them, it can be virtually impossible to get a story; with them, you can get interviews, admission to private functions, a backstage look at a business or an attraction—and if the paper you are stringing for turns out not to want the story, maybe, just maybe, you can sell it somewhere else.

▲   ▲   ▲

Credentials can also sometimes get you on a "junket." Motion picture studios, television networks, resorts, cities—sometimes even *countries*—sponsor trips to enable journalists to familiarize themselves with an area or film, in the hope that a number of stories will find their way into print as a result.

This presents an interesting ethical problem for the journalist. If studios or networks are willing to pay your air fare to Los Angeles, put you up in a first-class hotel, and allow you to charge meals, drinks, room service, and telephone calls, all so you can see their new movie and sit in on a group interview with its stars, do you *dare* to pan it? Enough newspapers have found there is at least a suggestion of conflict of interest in such trips that many forbid reporters to accept freebies, instead requiring them to pay their own way.

Freelancers, unless they are members of professional societies that have adopted such codes of ethics, are generally under no such constraints. Only their personal moral codes apply. But because many writers treat such tours as paid vacations, and may not bother to attend the interviews or write the stories, sponsors often make it difficult for nonaffiliated writers to get on a junket. Without credentials, you normally must prove you have an assignment before they will include you. This can make things very difficult for freelancers who need the basic information that the junket will provide before they can formulate a query and obtain an assignment.

When and if you do get on a junket, you may find you have to deal with what I call " reporter guilt." I get a good case of this when someone gives me an interview, and I write it, and then, for some reason, the publication for which it was written doesn't publish it (one magazine, for example, went out of business—I ask you, was *that* a valid excuse for failing to publish my article?). *How* can I ever face the person who was nice enough to grant me an hour of his or her time?

Of course, my reporter guilt gets even worse when I am on a junket. My way of coping with this kind of guilt is to run around like a chicken without a head, desperately trying to get to every scheduled interview, taste every typical buffet, look at every part of the ship or hotel, and visit every site that even remotely qualifies as a tourist attraction. Sometimes I even attempt to obtain a couple of extra interviews that may not be on the general schedule, but which I think I may be able to sell. Everyone else is having a high old time, and I am wearing myself out trying to obtain the facts for stories that I may never be able to use.

It's true that, as a freelancer, I am not constrained to write only what *one* editor wants. Since I sell to many publications, any strange angle or odd fact that I discover *could* result in another sale. But because I might strike out and sell no articles as a result of the trip, I tend to feel better if I am *working* the entire time and thus not accepting the junket under false pretenses. This also helps me to convince myself, if I decide to pan the resort or the movie, that I am within my rights as a member of a free press.

This moral position may not be necessary for everyone, but it is for me. I know other writers who figure they are on the junket to have a good time, and if having a good time makes them write more favorably about the place they've visited or the movie they've seen, they can't help that, any more than I can help the fact that exhaustion may sour *my* viewpoint. All I can say is that, unless the publication for which you are writing has a position on the acceptance of any freebies, *you* will have to decide for yourself.

Whatever kinds of articles *you* decide to write—whether you're reporting what happens in the world around you or coming up with the tidbits one reads while standing in the checkout line at the supermarket—if you are a good news reporter, you will have, it is said, a "nose for news." This generally means you have the kind of nose that you are willing to stick into other people's business. Being a professional journalist gives you a license to do just that.

This can be a lot of fun if you play by the rules, or an invitation to real trouble if you don't. How you play the game, and what it ultimately costs you, is up to you, but it helps to learn the rules before you play, so that you know when you are breaking them. If you have any doubt about these rules, and if you are serious about journalistic writing, whether for newspapers or for magazines, think about checking into the courses offered at your local journalism school in areas such as journalistic ethics, legal issues, and technical requirements.

16

Some Specific Problems of Fiction Writing

Rules—can there be rules for writing fiction? Isn't fiction supposed to spring, unfettered, out of your imagination?

Of course it is—and that's one of the rules. You can't write up your neighbor's life, change the names, and call it fiction, because *that* isn't fiction. Anyway, if your neighbor's life is that interesting, you should be interviewing him and writing an article in which you stick to the facts. Writing up someone's real-life adventures as "fiction" can, if he is not a public figure, invade his privacy. And describing a real person to the extent that he is recognizable but making up events can be construed as libel.

Fiction should come from your imagination, which is why it can be fun to write. In the world of your novel, you are a god. If you want it to rain, you make it rain. On reflection, if you think the scene in question would be better played in sunlight, you can change the weather with a few strokes of your pen.

Authors have the power of life and death over their characters. Have you tired of your hero's arrogance? Kill him off, and let your heroine marry his best friend. Or bring him back to life. Sir Arthur Conan Doyle grew tired of Sherlock Holmes and threw him down a waterfall; the public clamored for more tales of the great deducer, and Sir Arthur resurrected him.

This power can be hard to accept if you are used to sticking to documented facts for articles and newswriting, but it is required of the fiction writer. *You* should control the story, and not the other way around.

Once you realize that *you* control the story, it is possible to eliminate digressions. For example, the details of a minor character's shopping spree have no place in your narrative unless they disclose something about one of the *main* characters or impart information that carries the plot forward. A scene that does neither of these things annoys your readers, who wait impatiently for its connection to the plot to be revealed, and feel cheated when it isn't. Scenes like that can—and should—be cut from your narrative. Doing so is an inherent part of Kozak's Rule #7: "Always play fair with your readers."

You play fair by tying up all of the loose ends of your story. Leaving a piece of the plot unresolved is like going out in public with your shirttail or slip hanging out. The reader keeps thinking, "But whatever happened to Laura? She went out to get that package from the car, and we never heard from her again. Did she win that scholarship? Did the pizza she had in the oven burn?" And in worrying about that loose end, the reader forgets everything he or she liked about the rest of the book.

This doesn't mean that you can't throw in a few red herrings, distractions *intentionally* put in to keep the reader from guessing the outcome of the plot. But a *valid* red herring is put there for a reason: Laura went out to fetch a package from the car. Therefore, she wasn't in the house—where your detective could keep an eye on her—when the garage burned down. This puts her among the possible arson suspects, which is her purpose for being in the story—to keep people from knowing, too soon, who really did the dastardly deed.

But she is more than a red herring if she never returns from the driveway; she is an annoying distraction. Bring her back in the house, let her take her pizza out of the oven, and several chapters later, let her announce to everyone that she did, indeed, get her scholarship. The reader will pay just enough attention to her to be uncertain of the identity of the arsonist, but won't become obsessed with her.

Playing fair with your reader also means you lay a foundation for your denouement. If the cavalry is going to come over the hill to save your hero, you had better mention, early in the story, that the cavalry is somewhere in the area, though no one knows just where. If your heroine is trapped in a tower for twelve chapters, she can't suddenly remember that she has a rope ladder under her skirt in chapter 13. You don't take your characters to the verge of nuclear Armageddon and then resolve their problems with the cop-out "But it was all a dream." If you must do that, at least lay a foundation: mention, somewhere in the early part of the text, that your hero had been having trouble sleeping because of the rumors of war and had tried a new kind of sleeping pill that was known to produce vivid dreams.

While you must play fair with your reader, it is perfectly all right—in fact, necessary—to manipulate his hopes and his emotions through your fiction. A surprise twist of plot will often delight a reader, *so long as you have laid the groundwork* for what happens.

By this, I do not mean to imply that endings must be *happy.* Indeed, frustrating endings and tragic endings may stay longer in your readers' memories. But endings *must* be premised in logic, *must* follow on what came before. In real life, a promising hero is sometimes killed by the random descent of a flowerpot from a windowsill, but such an ending does not a satisfying story make.

Thus, you must lay your groundwork before you play god—but then the clay is yours to do with what you will. Remember that writing is a *craft,* and as is the case with any craft, though you may come to this one with basic talents, your skills will be honed with practice and by learning from both the triumphs and the mistakes of those who have gone before.

If you are supposed to be in control of your fiction, what do you do when your characters insist on taking over their own lives? Actually, this is a good sign. It means that you have created characters that are strong and real, but, even so, you should never let them get the upper hand.

Do listen to them when it's relevant, though. For example, if, as you set down a bit of dialogue, a character seems to be protesting, "I would never say *that,*" listen to her; she may be right. The speech patterns you have given her have probably become ingrained in your subconscious, and what you're hearing is your own instinct. Trust it.

Sometimes your characters start drifting off into scenes you haven't planned. This may mean it's time to wrest control from them. I say *may* because sometimes what they do is logical and will carry your story forward. Again, those characters are creations of *your* subconscious, and their insistence may really be your own dramatic instinct coming through. An extra line or an extra scene can make all the difference in clarifying a character's motivation or showing another side of him that will make your denouement more poignant.

But there are times when such a scene is really an unnecessary detour, when, even if you, not the characters, initiated the scene, judicious cutting is in order. A lot of aspiring writers make the mistake that I call "writing the history of the planet"—the equivalent of a nonfiction writer burying the lead. You can flip through the opening chapter and see immediately that their story really starts on page two, or page twelve, or even page fifty.

Frequently, a writer can throw out those first pages of the book with no deleterious effect—indeed, he or she may *have* to do just that to arrive at an appropriate starting point. Charles Dickens could start *David Copperfield* with "Chapter 1. I am born," but that was in an earlier, slower-paced era. James Michener can get away with starting his novels with the history of a continent, but he has established that as his personal style. Readers have come to expect it, and either look forward to it or skip over it, flipping pages until they find the action. But because readers are impatient and *you* have not graced the best-seller lists for four decades, like most other writers *you* will need to start in the middle of your adventure to hook the reader.

Think about it. You pick up a mystery, and it opens with an elderly woman chastising her little dog for digging a hole. She looks a little closer, and, lo and behold, the dog has dug up a body. You're hooked, right?

But would you be hooked if you'd just spent fifty pages learning about how the woman had acquired the dog, housebroken it, and taught it to fetch before you ever arrived at the dog digging in the neighbor's yard? Unless you were a dog trainer, would you bother to read past the first paragraph?

Those fifty pages are what I mean by "writing the history of the planet."

So if you're writing a contemporary novel that takes place in New York, don't burden the reader with the details of the purchase of Manhattan from the Indians, unless those details comprise a short, wry introduction to the fact that people have been "doing deals" in the Big Apple ever since. If a bit of history is important to your story, you can usually work it in, by reference, at an appropriate place. It doesn't belong at the *beginning* of your novel.

Many books and courses on fiction writing suggest that you should create a biography for your characters, describing their homes, personal histories, and favorite foods—but this is so *you* can get to know them well enough to write about them. There is no need to spring all this on the reader when you are introducing a character.

Think about it—do you really need to detail where your hero went to grade school, whether he played soccer there, what he does for a living, and how long he has held his current job, in order to explain that he is tired of his current life and harbors a secret dream of making it big in show business? Save the background for later in the story, and jump right in with a line like, "He got stuck in his office late that Wednesday, which is why he was on the corner when the red limousine passed by."

The background of your character doesn't belong in your book except by reference. Work in a sentence from it here and there, where it may be relevant, but don't introduce all the details to your reader on the first page. After all, how many people, upon being introduced, show you their last five years' tax returns and their high school diploma? If real people don't do this, why should a fictional character?

Brilliantly though you may have worded your summary of your hero's life, excise it from the opening of your story. Save it the way you save your canceled checks and tax returns, for reference only. Leave it off his "Hello, my name is . . ." badge.

One way to introduce background facts is through confession. Sam is sitting in a restaurant, explaining to Janis why he can't marry her—because his parents had a bad marriage, and his first marriage was just like theirs.

But what if, for dramatic purposes, you don't want Janis to know his reasoning? What if you just want Sam to remember it? "Recalling how bad his first marriage was, he decided to cut things off with Janis now" is not very dramatic. Instead, you can use a *flashback* to carry you to a different time and place:

> Somewhere on the other side of the room, a busboy dropped a loaded tray. The clatter of breaking crockery reverberated in Sam's memory.
>
> His parents' home—house was a better term, for there was no love there—was filled with the sound of breaking crockery every Saturday night. His father would cash his paycheck and stop off about a block from the house, at Pete's Bar and Grill. Supper would grow cold, and night would fall, and eventually, without the presence of the head of the household, everyone would go to bed. Inevi-

tably, Sam would awaken to the sound of breaking dishes. It was a scene that happened so often, it was etched indelibly in his mind.

"How are we going to pay the rent? You've spent the rent money again," his mother would scream.

"I earned it. I'll spend it any way I want to." Sam's father's voice was, as always, slurred with the effects of alcohol.

"If you don't care where your children live, what about yourself—if we get evicted, you'll be out in the street too, you know."

"I know plenty of women that'll take me in—better women than you, Velma."

Velma's response was the crash of breaking crockery.

This kind of scene gives you the opportunity to *show, rather than tell,* the reader what has happened. And although we speak of "telling" a story, in the best fiction, you want to *show* your readers, as dramatically as you can, what happened, rather than *telling* them. Flashbacks are a way of doing just that.

In the preceding vignette, you were introduced to Sam, Janis, and Velma. You probably took no real notice of their names, concentrating instead on the action taking place. This is as it should be—but might not have been if I hadn't taken great care in naming them.

There is a real art to naming a character. You tend to get to know *real* people over a period of time, and once you do, you forget how incongruous their names may seem. A football hero named Percy? You probably call him by his last name or by a nickname like "Killer." Was the cutest girl in your eighth-grade class christened "Bertha"? You probably called her "Buffy." Or, because of her, for you the name "Bertha" came to be forever associated with petite blondes.

Unfortunately, your experience was not shared by anyone except the members of Homeroom 202. To the rest of the world, a Bertha is large and definitely *not* cute. Name a gorgeous heroine Bertha, and the reader will cringe every time he or she sees the name in print. Worse, the reader will disregard your descriptions as irrelevant, and when a reader starts treating even *part* of what you write as irrelevant, your story starts losing its credibility.

So how do you choose a name? Start by asking yourself what you want to convey by it. Some names are neutral—Carol, Joan, Barbara, Tom, Larry—except to that small portion of the population for whom the moniker will always mean their older brother or ex-wife. Some names are strong—Alexander, Alexandra, Nicholas, Elizabeth, and Catherine come to mind (the names we associate with royalty tend to have a regal ring). Some names are considered sexy, like Vanessa or Grant, and others have a connotation of innocence, like Beth or Tim.

The power of a name can change—Bruce once evoked a brawny Scottish warrior; now it tends to suggest a San Francisco waiter. It doesn't matter what *you* think of the name, but how the public at large has come to regard it. Give a strong character a weak name, and, unless part of your plot is the fact that he has to overcome it, your reader will read into the character what the name suggests to him.

Names are also generational. Jennifers are common now, but they are seldom called Jenny, a name that tends to connote a generation the same age as the twentieth century; the name has lost the sweet youthfulness it had for Leigh Hunt when Jenny kissed him in 1838, or for Robert Nathan, when he wrote "Portrait of Jenny" a century later. A contemporary character named Jennifer would not necessarily be innocent.

She would also probably have been born after 1970; a Kimberly would be slightly older. Like these, other names can put your characters into a certain age group. American Debbies were probably born between 1947 and 1956—classic baby boomers. Linda and Judy were probably born between 1943 and 1947, Beverly slightly before that, Shirley and Dorothy between 1925 and 1935, and Anita between the close of World War I and the mid-twenties.

Robert and David transcend generations, as do Anne and Elizabeth. But a Jason would have been born after the Vietnam war. Kevin would be older, and Scott older still (he and Greg were probably born in the fifties).

While there are exceptions, these names generally connote certain age groups to the rest of the population. Name the heroine of your World War II romance "Tammy," and no one will believe your story. Call her "Dorothy," and your reader will have no trouble picturing her in a polka-dotted jacket, with her hair in a snood, as she waves good-bye to her sailor (who is named Frank, Bill, or Jimmy, but *never* Brian or Kyle!).

In addition to pinpointing his generation, your character's name can indicate his regional or ethnic background. Sometimes this is obvious:

José and Carmen are usually Hispanic, Klaus and Elfrieda are German, and Boris and Olga are Russian. But sometimes the distinctions are more subtle: while Jesus is probably Hispanic, Christ is often Greek.

And just as there are names that some ethnic groups seem to have a lock on, there are others that they almost never use. I've yet to meet a Jewish Dawn, for example, or a non-Hispanic Jesus. Mohammed and its variations seem the special province of the followers of Islam—and, while Americans may think a Japanese name like Emi or Tai or Midori sounds nice for a girl child, I've yet to run into anyone without Japanese blood who named a son Kenji or Otaro.

Cross these invisible lines with a character's name and, unless the crossing is intentional (to point up the uniqueness of your hero, for example), your story just won't ring true.

You can play generational "begats" with ethnic as well as nonethnic names. Within a black community, it would be easy to find Willie and Althea, who begat Odell, who married Vanessa and begat LaTrisha and Travis. In any Jewish community, you could locate Jake and Belle, who begat Esther who married Irv and begat Rochelle and Mark. *Their* kids are probably named Kimberly and Jason.

A name can convey instant clues to a character's background. For example, what does it imply about his family when a German under the age of forty-five is named Adolf? What does it tell you about an American black when he changes his name from Rufus to Hassan—or to Kwame?

The predilection for dual names in the American South has become a kind of in-joke in recent years: you just know Joe-Bob is going to arrive in a pickup truck with Betty Sue sitting beside him. But while Billy Jack may be Joe-Bob's best friend, Bill is working on a ranch Out West, Jack is sailing off the New England coast, Joe is a produce wholesaler in New York, and Bob is plowing a field somewhere in the Midwest. Betty, for that matter, is hanging out the laundry in Iowa, while Sue is selling real estate in Los Angeles.

Ethnic and regional names can cause additional problems when they appear in *print,* conveying a first impression you didn't intend. In real life, when a man tells you his name is "Yan," it may take a moment or two for it to register that his background is Middle European, and his name spelled Jan. But if you meet him on paper as Jan, you may picture a petite woman for several paragraphs until the mistake is cleared up. By then it may be too late to erase the image—I *never* succeeded in thinking of the rabbit called "Hazel" in *Watership Down* as a male!

▲   ▲   ▲

Because few people will spend more than a day or two with your character, the first impression a name conveys may be the *only* impression they ever get. Naming characters is just as difficult as naming children. Having a baby name book or two around can help; I've been known to name characters out of a dictionary of musical terms or off the list of post offices in Wisconsin.

One of the complications of naming characters is that you are naming not just one person but the entire town. Unless it's the point of your story, having more than one person in town named Peter or George is going to confuse your reader—*and the one thing you want to avoid at all costs is confusing your reader.*

To minimize confusion, watch out for "Russian Novel Syndrome" —too many alternate references to the same character. Mary Jones can be referred to as "Miss Jones" or "Mary"; but if you also call her "Mimi" and "Mims" and "the duchess," you're going to have a lot of readers who think she is several different people and can't follow your plot.

Watch out, too, for rhythms, first letters, and *last* letters. If every name has two syllables stressed in the same way, it can become hard on the ear; you want an Ann and a Mel•ind′a and even a Lou•ise′ among the Ca′rols, Ma′rys, and Sha′rons. It goes without saying that Martha, Matilda, Melanie, Marnie, and Maxine in the same story will drive your readers crazy, but so will Am*y*, Bett*y*, Cand*i*, and Tamm*y*—especially if they're involved with Ton*y* and Harv*ey* and Larr*y*. (This kind of thing can slip by you all too easily.)

One last problem with names. It is all too easy to libel someone by accident if you give your character the name of a real person. *Never* name a character after someone you hated in grade school or the guy who got the promotion you think should have been yours. *Never* take the name of a real person out of the phone book. Indeed, if you set your story in a particular town—for example, Smallville, Ohio—check to see whether there really *is* a Smallville, Ohio. If the town exists, get hold of a telephone book, and make sure that the owner of the gas station isn't named "Jack Thomson" or whatever you have named the gas station owner in your novel. Disclaimers to the contrary notwithstanding, giving a character the name of a real person in a real place with a similar profession, however inadvertent your action may have been, can leave you open to a libel suit.

You can be just as vulnerable to suit if your character is named "Jack Thompson," and he owns a garage rather than a filling station. Checking for coincidences can save you a lot of trouble.

Of course, you can't avoid the possibility that the name of *some* real person might show up among the names you have chosen. In a city the size of New York, for example, there is probably someone with a name similar to any name you might choose.

One way to at least partially protect yourself when writing fiction is through the use of a disclaimer: "All events portrayed in this book are purely fictional and any resemblance to any person or persons living or dead is purely coincidental." Another is to choose a name that belongs to a *lot* of people, so that no one of them can make a case that you obviously meant *him*. Just to be on the safe side, however, it never hurts to check the phone book of the city where your story is set to make sure that there is no Dr. Tom Jones, and if there *is*, he is a paleontologist, not an oncologist like your character, and his home and office are nowhere near those you gave to the character in your book.

What about thinly disguised renditions of famous events, where the names are changed and the writer makes up the details? An example would be a novel about a young president who is shot in the prime of his life in what just happens to be the hometown of the vice president who succeeds him. Spin off from there: the vice president was behind it; the vice president was the real target; the vice president has a heart attack and the Speaker of the House becomes president; the president had *himself* shot because he was dying of cancer; the president's twin brother was the real victim—you name it, someone has probably written it. The variations on the theme of the assassination that shook America in 1963 are still coming.

Such a story is known as a *roman à clef*, and the category is sometimes referred to as "faction"—a cross between fact and fiction. In both cases, barely disguised real people—often public figures—have conversations, make love, and do various other things that they may or may not have done in real life.

Closely related are stories that include appearances by real people —usually famous people—on their pages. For example, your character wins a spelling bee and gets to meet the president, who shakes her hand and tells her how the future depends on good students like her. Or your characters could run into a movie star in a restaurant, and the movie star might punch your hero in the jaw.

How much of this sort of thing you can get away with depends on a large number of factors, including whether the persons portrayed are dead, whether your reference to them is innocuous, and whether the story is clearly intended to be fiction and designed to entertain or is more likely to be taken seriously and thus has placed the person you have portrayed in a "false light."

Each case will turn on its own merits, and the person you have represented on your pages may or may not prevail. Such lawsuits are really the modern equivalents of duels. A couple of centuries ago, besmirching a man's honor in the pages of your novel might have meant having to meet him in an open field at sunrise; today the satisfaction demanded is usually your money rather than your life. Anyone who feels his or her honor has been besmirched can bring a suit; and even if no damages are awarded, defending such suits can cost you a pretty penny. A word to the wise, then: use real events or real people with extreme caution.

Back in chapter 11, I mentioned that characters can be protected under the section of the copyright law that grants a copyright holder the sole right "to prepare derivative works based on the copyrighted work." The more delineated a character is, the more it is likely to be protected. *How* delineated is hard to say—but if the characters are recognizable, like Scarlett O'Hara or Sherlock Holmes, you can usually assume that using them will, while copyright protection continues, be a violation of their creators' copyrights.

As in every area of the law, there are exceptions; parody, for example, is permitted to a degree. And, of course, you can use someone else's characters if you have obtained permission, or if they are in the public domain, like Romeo and Juliet. (Where some stories concerning a character are in the public domain and others remain covered by copyright, it has been held that you may use those attributes of the character that are expressed in the public domain works, but not those in the works still protected by copyright. However, *some* characters—particularly cartoon characters—may be protected by *trademark law,* and this protection can outlast copyright protection, so be careful.)

When you create a work using someone else's characters, your work will be protected *to the extent that it is original.*

How does this work? Let's say you write a story about Juliet's childhood. You can't claim ownership of Shakespeare's characters—Juliet or the Nurse or Tybalt—but you *can* copyright your story about their early adventures. And although your story about Darth Vader's school days may infringe on George Lucas's character right, no one—not even Lucas—may print *your* story without your permission; that would be an infringement of *your* rights.

I've said you can't use someone else's characters without permission. Why would you want to?

Sometimes you just can't help it. You've been watching your favorite television program every week, and suddenly the plot for an entire episode pops into your brain, full-blown. Perhaps you've plotted out a puzzling case for Sherlock Holmes. Or you just *know* how Scarlett got Rhett back, or what Scrooge did the day *after* Christmas. What do you do with those stories?

Write them. You might as well, because they're going to drive you crazy until you do. After you've set them down, take a good look at them, and determine whether you can remove them from the world you've borrowed. If your story is about Scarlett and Rhett at Melanie's funeral, you probably can't; but if it is about Prissy facing the choices that freedom brings her, perhaps you can make it *any* freed slave in 1865. Change the name, change the setting, and the story just might become an original work with no connection at all to the story that inspired it—in other words, your own.

Those stories that *can't* be removed from a derivative world can, if they are written for a functioning series (whether book, movie, or television), sometimes be sold *to* that series. James Bond movies appear every year or two, *Star Trek* novels appear every month, and some series authors permit or even encourage other writers to contribute a book or an episode.

Science fiction author Marion Zimmer Bradley, for example, encourages her fans to write in her *Darkover* "universe" to the point of authorizing some of their collected stories to see print commercially. She feels this is a good way for new writers to get started, because it can be much easier to hone your fiction-writing techniques when you don't have to *create* the characters or their world. Keeping the characters in character and sustaining your plot with enough finesse to hold reader interest can be excellent training.

If you've developed a derivative story that can't be removed from the world you've borrowed, and commercial publication isn't feasible, you have two alternatives. The first is to treat the work as an exercise in learning *how* to get a story down on paper, bury the manuscript in a drawer, and move on. The second is to see if there is a fanzine that will take it.

Fanzines are fan-published magazines whose poetry and fiction are based on established characters and situations existing in popular books, movies, or television shows. They originated in the science fiction field, where they have long been considered the sincerest form of flattery. Now *zines,* as they are affectionately known to their devotees, have begun to extend to other genres as well. Many a vintage television series has developed enough of a following to have zines of its own.

While using someone else's characters could be construed as infringement of the original author's copyright, many authors are not bothered by such fan activities. *Star Trek* creator Gene Roddenberry, recognizing that it was the enthusiasm of fans—held together by, among other things, the exchange of fanzines—that brought about the resurrection of the old *Star Trek* series as a movie ten years after its cancellation, has called fanzines "the lifeblood of the [*Star Trek*] movement."

Although some authors, like Jacqueline Lichtenberg and Marion Zimmer Bradley, encourage their fans to create fanzines based on their works, other writers have been known to take legal steps to stop such publications. However, most writers leave the zines alone. After all, the average fanzine has a run of no more than 500 copies. Usually produced in offset, fanzines pay contributors only in free copies. They are a labor of love, and publication standards vary widely. Nevertheless, the publication of your training exercise in a fanzine can produce enough adulation from fellow fans to keep you at the typewriter in hopes of earning more strokes—not to mention the added solace of discovering that you aren't the only person obsessed with what childhood traumas caused Darth Vader to grow up to be the villain of *Star Wars.*

There is another kind of derivative work that can be an excellent exercise in learning to write fiction. This requires a piece of modern electronic equipment—a VCR.

Find a movie or a television show that you think is particularly dramatic or well-paced. Tape it. Then—and this is strictly an exercise, *not* something that you're writing in the hope of selling it—turn it into a piece of narrative fiction.

Play back a scene and describe it the way you would if it were a novel. Not just, "The two cowboys walked into the center of the street.

'Draw,' said the tall one. Shots rang out . . .'' Really *watch* the scene, and you'll discover that there's a lot more going on:

> A hush settled on Main Street as Smith strode out to take his place under the blazing sun. He tossed his head back defiantly and squinted into the distance. A lone horseman approached.
>
> The two old men who had been playing checkers in front of the General Store hastily gathered up the pieces and the board and retreated inside. Mrs. Kelley dashed out of the hotel and grabbed young Willie, who had been hiding behind the horse trough, and half-pulled, half carried him to safety.
>
> The rider slowed to a trot. His horse's hooves kicked up miniature cyclones in the dusty street. He drew to a halt in front of the livery stable, dismounted, and threw the reins over a hitching bar, then turned to face Smith, who nodded at him.
>
> "Wesson," Smith said. It was an acknowledgment of the other man's presence, nothing more.
>
> Wesson squinted up at the bronze sky, then fastened his eyes on Smith. His steady gaze never wavered as he, too, took a position in the middle of the street, about forty feet from his rival.
>
> A tumbleweed rolled along the street, barely disturbing the yellow dust. Neither man moved. The moments stretched on endlessly, as the whole town held its breath.
>
> At last Wesson broke the silence. "Draw," he commanded . . .

When you write fiction, you see scenes like that inside your head and just describe them, one after another. As you describe all the details, you create the world, the characters, the events. And if you describe them well, your readers can see them too.

Sometimes, though, it helps to practice on a scene you can actually see, over and over again, by replaying it on your VCR. As I said, this is meant to be a practice exercise, but there are *some* popular series that have commissioned novelizations. So there *might* even be a market out there—although I wouldn't hold my breath until I found it, if I were you.

One scene after another, you build a story. You build the story by building tension, so that the reader is carried forward, asking, all the time, "What will happen next?"

You want the reader to wonder that from the very first moment, which is why you create a dramatic hook. Look at that first sentence in that little western scene: "A hush settled on Main Street as Smith strode out to take his place under the blazing sun." You don't know who Smith is, but you know that whatever he is taking his place for is enough to reduce the rest of the town to silence. *What will happen next?*

You also want to pace the story so that while the action is enhanced by description, the descriptions do not become burdensome. The tension should continue to build, smoothly, without the reader becoming aware of when you switch from description to action to dialogue.

Dialogue, too, should be varied—not just "he said" and "she said," but with action interspersed:

> "Where *is* it?" Tom demanded. He strode across the room and grabbed Peter by the lapels, pulling him to a standing position. "Where *is* it?" he repeated menacingly.
>
> "Please, the suit. It's a four-hundred-dollar suit." Peter smiled his most congenial smile. "The suit—"
>
> "Sure you spent four hundred dollars," Tom sneered. "Four hundred dollars of *my* money. Where *is* it? What did you do with it?"
>
> "*Your* money is long gone. I spent it months ago."
>
> The wind seemed to go out of Tom's sails. He let go of the other man's lapels and slowly dropped his hands to his sides. "You spent it months ago," he echoed dully.
>
> "Months ago," Peter confirmed. "*Your* money, I spent months ago. Now, Louie's money, *that* I'm spending *today.*" He removed a fat wad of bills from his back pocket. "On you. On what I owe you." He began to count out hundred-dollar bills while Tom stared, just stared at him in absolute astonishment.

Note that it is not always necessary to attach "he said" or even "he demanded" to a quotation. Peter smiles his most congenial smile, and you know who is saying the words next to that statement. Two quotations later, Peter isn't even identified at all, but since there are only two people in the scene, and the two surrounding quotes belong to Tom, this statement is obviously Peter's.

And through it all, these men are *doing* things: striding across the room, grabbing lapels, smiling, pulling out a wad of money. There is action interspersed with the dialogue, so the dialogue never interrupts the action, and the action never breaks up the dialogue.

Dialogue should be the simplest thing to write, but many people have difficulty with it, perhaps because they aren't listening—*really* listening—to the way real people speak.

No one speaks in full sentences all the time. Sentence fragments are more likely. Look at the previous example: "Please, the suit." "The suit—" "Four hundred dollars of *my* money." "Months ago." "On you." "On what I owe you." Not one of these examples is a complete sentence, with a subject and a verb (and perhaps an object). But they all sound more like *real* conversations than any full sentences could.

The descriptive phrases interspersed in the dialogue break the pace and suggest when the character may be inserting pauses in his lines. You can also do this with punctuation:

"Take us," he said, "out of orbit, Helmsman."

or

"Take us—out of orbit, Helmsman."

You can show a lot about a character by the *way* he phrases something, the rhythm of his speech: "*Your* money, I spent months ago." The use of colorful phrases—" 'I'll be hornswallered,' he said"—can also mark your character. Despite the rules of grammar, real people say "ain't." They also swear—which means you can put profanity inside quotations when you would never dream of doing so in your text.

Real people also speak with accents, but it is seldom a good idea to attempt the portrayal of an accent in print. You usually don't succeed in conveying the pronunciation, but you do succeed in confusing your reader—which, as I noted earlier, is the last thing you want to do.

A character who says things like "Keer fer a chaw ev my t'backy?" forces the reader to stop and translate, breaking the rhythm of your text, so you are generally better off writing dialogue without dialect. Instead, you can use action, description, and a careful choice of words and expressions to convey the kind of dialect you are hearing in your mind's ear. For example: "'Care for a chaw?' he drawled, holding out a hunk of chewing tobacco.''

Pacing, phrasing, punctuation, and selective breaks are often the best indicators of an accent. One exception might be a specific word that can serve as a signature note for a character—something mentioned early on and then used throughout the work:

> He insisted in calling each of the young men "Master," but he pronounced it oddly, with a broad "A," though more Massachusetts coastal than British: "Maawster." The first time he addressed little Timmy that way, the child burst into tears. "I am *not* a monster," the child protested, "I'm not. I'm not."
>
> "Of course not, Maawster," Riggins replied, trying to soothe him, but Timmy only wept the louder at the second use of the term.

Giving a character a signature note, can, like the bassoon in *Peter and the Wolf,* announce his presence. It can also help define him, help make him *real* to your reader—and the more real he is, the more the reader will respond to him, care about him, and care about your story.

Sometimes it is actually the character who tells your tale. I'm not speaking only of a first-person narrative:

> I got back to the office and my secretary was nowhere in sight. But in the waiting room was this gorgeous blonde with legs that didn't stop. I pretended to ignore her, but she saw through me. As I walked by, she purred in a husky voice, "If you're Mr. Shamus, I have a thousand dollars for you."
>
> "And if I'm not?" I replied, my hand on the doorknob of my private office.
>
> "I'm sure something can be arranged."

It is also possible to get inside your character's head in a *third-*person narrative, by reading his thoughts and looking through his eyes:

> He opened his eyes slowly. The shade was partway up, and the streetlight cast a pale glow through the window—just enough to see that he was not alone. There was a woman huddled in the corner,

behind the radiator. She was sitting against the wall, clutching her knees, her eyes as big as saucers.

He fingered the lump on the back of his head. "Did *you* do this to me?" he asked her.

The saucers turned into dinner plates. "Oh, no," she told him in a breathy voice. "I found you there."

Finnegan attempted to sit up, but stopped when the slight movement of his head sent shooting pains through his skull. Pain momentarily blurred his vision. When it cleared, he touched the lump again. It was swollen to the size of an egg.

She couldn't have done this, he told himself. *She's a skinny kid, and a blow this hard took a lot of power.* Aloud, he asked her, "How long you been sitting there?"

This is known as telling the story from a character's point of view. We are actually inside Finnegan's head, reading his thoughts. We also see through his eyes and are privy to his opinions of what he sees. Obviously, then, *we* cannot see what *he* cannot see. If someone comes up behind him, we won't know it, unless—

Suddenly, he saw her stiffen. Her eyes went even wider, and focused on a spot just behind him. Someone, or something, must be there. Steeling himself against the pain he knew must come, he rolled over and came to his knees facing the door. What he saw was a grotesque shape advancing toward him.

The light snapped on, and the grotesque shape became his secretary, carrying an armload of packages.

He glanced over at the clock, which read half past eight, then back at her. "Long lunch hour again?" he asked her.

Modern literary convention suggests that when you are in one character's point of view you cannot suddenly shift to another character's point of view. Some people do it, but it is seldom done well. As a rule, it is confusing to the reader to use more than one point of view in a single scene. You need a scene break—skipping an extra line will suffice— before you can shift to another person's point of view.

Again, the same restrictions apply; you can now read *her* thoughts, but you can only see what *she* sees:

He wasn't such a bad-looking guy, except for that bump on his head. The woman who had turned on the light, though, looked cheap—

from her overlacquered hair to her garish red nail polish to her open-toed shoes with their run-down heels.

From Finnegan's comment, Claudia gathered that the woman with the packages worked for him. . . .

We have now been inside Claudia's head as well as Finnegan's. Therefore, they must be fairly important to the story. Unless you are telling the story from the viewpoint of an omniscient narrator, there is an unwritten rule that anyone important enough to have his or her viewpoint revealed is going to be important in the story.

What this means is if you write the opening scene from the bus driver's point of view so that you can describe the two main characters without having them look in a mirror, that bus driver had better show up again. If he does not, you are breaking Rule #7, and not playing fair with your readers; they expect to see him again since he was important enough to have his thoughts revealed.

For some reason, point of view seems to be one of the most difficult writing skills to master. It is one of those things that is unnoticeable when done right, and jarring to the reader when done wrong. Mastering point of view can mean the difference between a sale and a rejection, so it is worth taking the time to learn.

One more thought about plots. All stories are variations on a relatively small number of basic plots, or combinations of two or more of them. Plots are not copyrightable, since there is no copyright in an idea, but *the way* in which you express a plot can, indeed, be protectable by copyright.

The test for infringement is "access plus *substantial similarity.*" Obviously this is a subjective test, with room for human prejudice, compassion, and error. But the test for *substantial* similarity is premised on the number of corresponding details that exist in two works —with one exception.

That exception is *scenes à faire.* These are scenes that have become generic to a type of book, and which no writer can claim. Thus the fact that in two different westerns, the cowboys wear spurs, ride horses, rope cattle, live on ranches, and go into town to drink at the saloon on payday, does not prove that one is violating the copyright of the other, because these details are part of *all* westerns. Similarly, all soldiers wear boots and helmets and slog through the mud and dig foxholes.

These are the conventions of a genre of writing, and no one writer can lay claim to them.

The problem lies in distinguishing between generic scenes and scenes that showed up for the first time in the book you have been accused of copying. Again, if there has been no *access*, there is no copyright violation. But if you *had* access, and didn't realize that the scenes were unique rather than generic, you're probably guilty not only of infringement but also of having violated the first axiom of writing. As I said very early in this book, writers *read*. One of the benefits of reading is knowing what has gone before.

The line between a generic scene and an infringement may be a fine one. Reading widely can be the best way to learn to differentiate between the two.

Reading not only widely but *like a writer* can be a good way to familiarize yourself with the way in which other writers handle pacing and transitions, combine description and dialogue, or subtly introduce background facts. Don't just read, but carefully *analyze* the works of a writer you like. Look for flashbacks, pacing, and the way dialogue is handled. Learn from what has gone before.

One last point on the subject of reading other writers: most professional writers do *not* read the works of other writers *while* they are writing. It is too easy to find yourself borrowing someone else's style or voice. Cornelia Otis Skinner, in her essay "The Ape in Me," discusses how easily and embarrassingly she found herself picking up other people's accents when talking with them. Reading other writers' works while working on a project of your own can do the same thing to your writing style.

Read to learn techniques, read to learn what has gone before—but if you really want to be a writer, find your own voice. There's a lot of competition out there, and only by telling a unique tale, or telling your tales in a unique way, will you stand out from the crowd. Just don't stand so *far* out of the crowd that no one can figure out what it is you're doing.

17

Out Beyond Fact and Fiction

Most people, when they say they want to write, mean they want to write *prose*, and so far, that's the kind of writing I have discussed. But there are, of course, many other kinds of writing.

There is, for example, advertising copywriting, which includes not only creating the text found in a magazine or newspaper ad, but also coming up with an entire ad campaign, or a jingle and script for a commercial. Copywriting also includes the descriptions that appear under the pictures in all those catalogs in your mailbox—and even extends to those letters that tell you "You may already have won . . ."

Some people who write for a living create brochures for local businesses or ghostwrite speeches and articles for people who may have expertise in their field but can't put sentences together to convey it. Some writers write résumés. If you want to make your *living* with your pen, these are some of the ways to keep the wolf from the door.

There are also many other kinds of writing that do not fit into the prose category. You can write television or radio scripts, theatrical plays, greeting card verses, jokes, fillers, and poetry, to name just a few. Each of these categories has its own rules for format and submission, and selling your works in these categories is subject to the age-old salesman's directive that *you need to know the territory.*

Let's start with poetry. You were raised on it in the form of Mother Goose verses and other nursery rhymes. They taught you the cadence and the use of the language. But the poetry that makes it into print is—usually—not at all like the nursery rhymes you grew up chanting.

What makes a poem? There have been entire treatises written on the subject. And I must confess that I am not the best person to ask, for like Sir Max Beerbohm's Zuleika Dobson, I only know what I like. I like a lot of Robert Frost's work—"Fire and Ice," "Stopping by Woods on a Snowy Evening," "The Road Not Taken," and, particularly, "A Considerable Speck"—but I have a tendency to skip over most of "The Death of the Hired Man" and "Birches." I think there are two or three good lines in each of Walt Whitman's poems, and harbor the secret opinion that the world might well have been better off had Wordsworth died as young as Keats. Sometimes I prefer a humorous "verse" to an enigmatic "poem." But those are *my* opinions—and, as I have told any number of clients who have asked my opinion of their poems, poetry is in the eye of the beholder.

Nevertheless, there are certain constants in this field as there are in all areas of authorship. If the words *sing,* if they *haunt* you, if they stick in your memory as aphorisms of truth or beauty, they are probably poetry. But if you want them to be *published,* you need to know what the community of poets and publishers currently considers to be poetry.

Once again, this means that you have to *read what has gone before,* although in the world of short poetry, wide reading can have a down side. Poems—particularly short poems—sometimes pop into your head nearly full-blown. This spontaneous generation can spark the nagging fear that your latest creation just might be rooted in a work by someone else that you once saw but have—at least consciously—forgotten.

Despite this hazard, you *have* to read the poems that make their way into print, not only so you will know what the current arbiters of taste are arbiting, but also so you will know *where* to send the kinds of poetry that *you* are writing. Poet Esther Leiper, whose column on writing poetry appears in *Writer's Journal,* suggests that there is probably a market for whatever kind of poetry you may want to write; the trick is finding it—which means studying the market listings and, where possible, the publications themselves.

Reading market lists and magazines is really the only way to know who is publishing what kind of poetry. Reading current poetry and critiques of current poetry are the only ways to learn what rhymes are acceptable (or whether rhymes are acceptable at all) to the poetic Powers That Be, whether meter is in vogue this year, or cadence, or totally free verse, and which subjects are taboo and which are daring. I'm not suggesting that you shouldn't, in the words of old Polonius, "to thine own self be true"—just that, if you want to see your work *in print,* you may have to pander to the preferences of publishers.

If you find yourself writing a lot of poetry, you should invest in a copy of *Poet's Market,* another annual volume from the folks at F & W Publications; this book provides current information on publications that buy poetry and those that sponsor poetry contests, along with their particular requirements. Since time may have passed since even the newest issue of *Poet's Market* went to press, it is always a good idea to send for writers' guidelines for any listed publication, and to familiarize yourself with one or two of the most recent issues of any poetry magazine before making a submission.

You might also want to keep up with the current state of poetry by reading Judson Jerome's column in *Writer's Digest* or Esther Leiper's column in *Writer's Journal,* or by subscribing to *Poets and Writers Magazine* from Poets and Writers, Inc. (see the Selected List of Writers' Organizations for the address).

This is how you learn about the markets—but how do you submit to them? As with prose, you *type* your works, using standard (not italic or germanic) type, in black ink on 8½-by-11-inch white paper, on one side of the page. Very short poems can be double-spaced, very lengthy ones single-spaced; sometimes the best compromise, according to poet Angela Peckenpaugh, is a space and a half between lines. Double-space between stanzas. Start each poem on its own page and give each one a title.

Put your name and address on each individual poem (and your name on each page, after the first, of a lengthy poem)—unless you are submitting to a contest that specifies some other format to insure anonymity. Unless you *have* only one poem, submit at least three poems at a time. Unless your poems are book-length epics, it's all right to fold them in thirds, but *never* smaller (use a business size—number 10—envelope). Enclose a cover letter that tells something about you and lists the poems submitted. And, of course, *always* enclose a SASE.

One of the things that you will notice when you scan the poetry markets is the telling phrase "pays in contributors' copies." Very often, poetry doesn't pay at all; when it does, it may pay something like a dollar a line. Obviously, you aren't going to get rich from the publication of your poetry.

How do poets make money, then? For most of them, writing poetry is a labor of love, and they do it *in addition* to their other occupations. A few poets break through, and their work becomes nationally known. How do they do it? There are a number of routes.

One way is to enter contests. Poetry contests abound, and most of them are financed the same way lotteries are: each entrant pays a fee, and the fees finance the prizes. If you *win,* you may make back ten or twenty times the entrance fee. Esther Leiper's helpful booklet on this subject, *How to Enter Poetry Contests to Win* (Inkling Publications, St. Paul, Minn., 1984), is now out of print, but a copy may be available in your local library.

Winning contests or having your poetry published in prestigious literary or "little" magazines helps you to develop a reputation as a poet. The prestige you garner from frequent publication and multiple prizes may enable you to win fellowships and grants, or a teaching position at your local college or university. It may also enable you to get on what Angela Peckenpaugh has termed the "poetry circuit." Poets "on the circuit" can make money by giving readings of their poetry. You can do this even if you are *not* on the "circuit" by setting up your own readings at libraries and bookstores, but such sponsors may not be as receptive and attendance may not be as great as they might be if you bore the proper imprimatur. As a result, you may not earn as much as a recognized poet.

If you can get a small press to publish a "chapbook," or booklet, of your poems, you can sell it at your readings and increase your earnings. If you can't find a publisher, consider that giving regular poetry readings probably places you within the second exception to my rule against self-publishing (I'm talking about *self*-publishing here, not paying some vanity press ten times the printing cost to bring out your book). Indeed, if you can afford the initial printing costs, it may make financial sense to self-publish books that can be sold in conjunction with your readings so that you can reap *all* of the profits from those sales.

Self-publishing normally does not afford you the kind of credibility that publication by someone else does, especially when it comes to applying for grants and fellowships. However, if your poetry has already been published widely, a self-published collection will not necessarily be seen as unprofessional.

▲   ▲   ▲

What if you write light verse, and none of the traditional poetry markets will take you seriously? Take heart—some newspapers and general-interest magazines buy humorous verses as fillers. And sometimes you can sell such verses to the greeting card market.

Greeting card companies buy humorous verses, and they also buy more serious verses for occasions like Mother's Day, religious holidays and events, and sympathy cards. They also buy the one-liners, quips, and concepts that make up the text of most of the cards you see on the stands today.

Again, in writing for greeting cards, as in other kinds of writing, you've got to know the territory. A partial list of greeting card markets can be found in *Writer's Market;* you can also order a directory of greeting card publishers from the Greeting Card Association, 1350 New York Avenue N.W., Suite 615, Washington, D.C. 20005 (send a SASE to find out the price of the current edition). Another way to locate greeting card markets is to look through the card racks in your local shops until you find a line that appeals to you and then ask the retailer for the address of that publisher.

To find out what kind of submissions a company wants, you can obtain its writers' guidelines and a market list upon request (if you enclose a SASE). This is a good idea, because you may learn that the company requires a submission agreement before even looking at your materials. By signing this agreement, you usually waive any right to sue, should your idea prove similar to one they already have in development, and you may be asked to warrant that your idea is original and that you own the rights to it. A helpful addition to the guidelines is the market list, which tells you *exactly* what a publisher is looking for at any given time, both in style and in subject matter.

The key to successful sales to greeting card companies is to understand what each company wants. As verse writer Gail Hagen notes, "Even humor is *not* the same—each company has a distinct personality." For this reason, it is not always possible to sell an idea created for one company to any other company if the first rejects it.

Negative responses are often swift, but positive responses may take many months. Sometimes a company will test market an idea, either by showing it to consumer groups picked at random from passersby or by offering it in a limited geographical area, before making a commitment to purchase the verse. If the company does buy your work, it will probably purchase all rights, generally *won't* publish your byline, and will usually pay you a flat fee (probably in the $75 to $150 range).

Greeting card submissions have their own etiquette. They require the usual SASE, and a simple cover letter specifying how many ideas you're enclosing. But greeting card verses are submitted on 3-by-5-inch or 4-by-6-inch cards (white, of course, and unlined). Some format guides suggest that you type your name, address, and telephone number in the upper left-hand corner as you would on the first sheet of a manuscript; then type the card verse, indicating the inside and the outside message. Other format guides recommend putting your name and address on the back of the card, and the verse on the front (again, the verse should indicate the division between inside and outside messages).

If you have a title for the card, you can type that above the verse, but to avoid confusion, a code number may be better. This goes either on the upper right-hand corner or on the back, depending on which format you choose.

Keep the code simple—"B" for "birthday," "BJ" for "juvenile birthday." "BJM" for "juvenile birthday (male)," for example, would code the card "For a Big Boy on His Birthday." Assign the card a number so that you can distinguish it from your other "juvenile birthday (male)" cards. This enables you to keep track of which cards have been sent to which company and lets a company offer to purchase "Card BJM-3" without any confusion as to what is being bought.

One last caution. Unless you are also an artist (and by this I mean a *real* artist, whose work is salable), do *not* illustrate the card. Don't even suggest any art unless the suggestion is absolutely necessary to the card concept.

While we're on the subject of illustrations, another cautionary statement: *do not* offer to illustrate your manuscript unless you are a professional artist. *Do not* submit a sketch of the cover you want along with any manuscript. *Do not* draw happy faces (or any kind of faces) on the manuscript or the submission letter.

Where photographs are important to your text ("An Illustrated Guide to the Inns of Vermont"), you can and should submit sample photos with your proposal—but make sure they are copies, and keep the originals. Identify photos and slides with your name and address *and* a typed caption (for magazines, this can be taped to the back of black-and-white stills or typed on a sheet to which you've taped a pocket for your slide; for books, common practice is to submit the captions on a double-spaced manuscript page, coded to correspond to the labeled art or photos). Make sure that you have the necessary releases, and tell the editor that the releases have been obtained, but don't send copies until you are asked.

For picture books, unless you are, indeed, an artist, leave the choice of art up to the publisher. And if you *are* an artist, *never* send the originals of your art to the publisher with your initial proposal. Arrangements can be made to submit them later, with proper precautions taken against their loss, if the publisher wants to see them.

What about scripts? These fall into three basic categories: theatrical plays, radio scripts, and scripts for motion pictures and television. The latter can be subdivided even further depending on subject matter (fact or fiction) and running time (half-hour sitcoms as opposed to two-hour feature movies).

Tight writing can be even more important in television scripts, where you are trying to make your point in a limited period of time, than it is in prose writing. What is also important, in any kind of script, is *believable* dialogue. As in fiction writing, your characters should speak the way real people do. Watch out for lengthy monologues, hook the audience, build to a climax, and you'll carry the day.

What are the rules for writing a script? Let's start with theatrical plays. These can be fact-based (historical dramas for high school students or even for a Broadway audience, as was the case with *Evita*) or totally fictitious, serious or humorous, and can require a large cast or only one actor (*Mark Twain Tonight* and *Vincent* come to mind). Who will produce the play may determine the form it will take: high school plays like to cast as many willing students as possible, and usually have more females available than males, while the cost of putting together a play for a professional run may be considerably reduced if the cast is smaller and doesn't require a walk-on by a live elephant.

Perhaps you are expecting me to say, at this point, that a play requires action—but *Waiting for Godot* did not. Perhaps you are expecting me to say that a play requires repartee between the characters—but a one-man show does not. For every piece of conventional wisdom about playwriting, there is an exception.

Your play may be that exception, but—as with prose writing—you have to know the rules before you can break them, so don't expect to make it to Broadway with your first play. Start, instead, by putting together a little sketch for your daughter's Brownie troop to perform the day they "fly up" to become Girl Scouts. When you see their actual performance, you'll get a better feeling for what works and what doesn't, and you can move on to bigger and better things from there.

The unpaid market for plays is endless. Your church would probably be delighted if you would write a Passion Play for them. Your town council would probably be just as pleased if you created a play about the town's first settlers for its centennial. You can cut your teeth on plays like these, but you'll probably learn even more about what goes into playwriting if you try out for a bit part at your local community theater group, or offer to hang around doing props and scenery for their latest production.

Not that the format for theatrical plays is difficult to learn. It hasn't changed much since Shakespeare wrote *Hamlet*. The name of the character goes flush against the left margin, in capital letters. His or her lines are typed in upper- and lowercase letters, indented about five spaces on the left but running across the width of the page. Stage directions are in parentheses. (Shakespeare's stage directions were in Latin; instead of "Exeunt," *you* can say, "They leave.")

Probably the most important trick in writing a play is to show as much of the action as possible through the dialogue you write. Keep stage directions to a minimum—after all, how the characters move on the stage is ultimately the director's prerogative. *Do* include the entrances and exits of characters, and instructions that are necessary to the action, such as "the telephone rings" or "a shot is heard offstage" or even "Ralph hides the book behind his back" or "Lillian feigns surprise." But don't bother to tell the actor to furrow his brow or scratch his head, because he won't do it anyway unless you're also serving as director—and maybe not even then.

Keeping the action moving right along without boring or confusing the audience is an art that takes practice, but, luckily, there are almost always a lot of amateur thespians around who are willing to give you the opportunity for that practice. Once you think you've got the hang of writing for them, you can try submitting to local, regional, and university theaters, and even to theatrical producers (although this last might best be done through an agent who knows the business). Local and regional institutions don't pay *much,* but they do pay—and some of them even sponsor contests with fairly substantial prizes.

It is also possible to have your play *published* in book form or as part of a collection ("Christmas Plays for Sunday Schools"). Lists of play publishers can be found in *Writer's Market* and in the latest edition of *The Writer's Handbook* (published by The Writer, Inc.). The authors of published plays generally receive royalties from the sales of such books and may receive additional royalties when the plays are performed. But because your rate of pay may vary for different uses of the work, and because you may someday want to rewrite the play and try for Broadway, be careful of what rights you sign over to anyone who offers to publish your play.

Radio, television, and motion picture scripts each have their own special formats which can be difficult to learn. These scripts have places not only for dialogue and action, but also for sound effects and camera directions like "fade in" or "dissolve."

Nothing is going to get you marked as unprofessional faster than submitting a script for one of these markets in improper format. As in other kinds of writing, failure to follow the normal submissions procedure can also get your script returned to you unread.

There are lengthy discussions of the way to construct proper script formats in *The Writer's Digest Guide to Manuscript Formats* by Dian Dincin Buchman and Seli Groves, *Writing the Script* by Wells Root, and *The Complete Book of Scriptwriting* by J. Michael Straczynski (who also writes a column on scriptwriting for *Writer's Digest*). The problem is that unless you are familiar with radio, television, or movie production, you may have difficulty understanding the terminology.

How can you learn what the terms mean, short of taking a master's degree in film production at U.C.L.A.? This is another job for your VCR!

One of the simplest things you can do is obtain a film or television script (many of these have been published or are available from the studios) along with a tape of the finished product (the film or the television show). Sit down in front of the television with your remote control in hand. Open the script on your lap and follow it as the tape plays.

If you have any doubt about what a "two shot" might be, freeze the frame when you get to it, and study that scene until you figure it out. The same goes for a "fade in" or "int. day" notation. You can do this at your own pace until the jargon becomes clear to you.

The exercise with the VCR will enable you to put necessary directions into your screenplay. It will also give you a clear understanding of why *I* don't have a great desire to write scripts.

It has to do with what I want to say when I write. I like to put in details and descriptions as well as dialogue—I like to create pictures out of words for my readers to see in their own minds. Scriptwriters don't really get to do that, because the details of the action are up to the actors and the director, and the point of view can be changed by the cameraman or the film editor.

In short, a film or television production is a group effort. I prefer to work alone.

I want to be able to tell you that a character "winced when the full sunlight hit his face. He reached up, covered his eyes with his hand until the pain of the sudden light receded, then slid his hand down his face, slowly, feeling the stubble that had grown there. *How long have I been asleep?* he wondered. *What day is this?*"

In a script, the scene would be rendered like this:

```
3    EXT. DESERT - DAYLIGHT

     The full sunlight falls on Joe's face.   He winces,
     covers his eyes with his hand.

                    JOE

          Ouch.

     Joe slides his hand slowly down his unshaven face.

                    How--how long have I been
                    asleep?  What day is this?
```

Despite the way I see the scene in my mind's eye, the actor has the prerogative to wrinkle his nose rather than wince. The director can decide to shoot from ten feet away or with the camera right in Joe's face. The emotion is inserted by the performer and the director.

And the interior monologue must be voiced—either by Joe, directly, as I've indicated above, or by a voice-over indicating his thoughts. If Joe merely stares into the distance, you have no idea what he is thinking—and no action to engage the viewer.

This need to engage the attention of the viewer is why television shows and movies are so filled with action. Introspection doesn't play well on the screen.

A totally different technique is required for radio, where you can *hear,* but cannot *see,* the action that is taking place. To get the scene across to the listener, you need actions that make noise—or a narrator who can describe what is happening. Thus, in a radio play, you can have a horse gallop up or the contents of Fibber McGee's closet descend on him, but there is no way to illustrate the sunlight on Joe's face unless someone mentions it. Since a narrator can prove an intrusion, if I were dramatizing that scene with Joe for radio, I might choose to have *him* narrate.

MUSIC: Transition/Fade in

JOE: The sun hit me full in the face, blinding me. I
          reached up to cover my eyes and suddenly became
          aware of the stubble on my face. How long had I
          been asleep? What day was it?

Unfortunately, this puts the events in Joe's past, with Joe doing the reflecting. You lose the immediacy of action taking place in the present, and you also reveal the answer to the question of whether Joe is going to survive. Obviously, he has survived to tell the tale, in retrospect, to the audience. It's a subtle point, but one the radio writer should be aware of.

There are fewer constraints with prose, which is why I prefer it as a mode of expression. On the other hand, in a piece of prose, I can tell you that "the song running through his head was Mozart's Minuet in G," but you may not remember what that minuet sounds like. In radio, television, and film, I can play it for you, so you know exactly what music I mean.

Dramatizations are often derivative works, based on a book or story that came before or premised on the adventures of a set of characters in an ongoing series. And they are usually collaborative works, with the end product encompassing the contributions of actors, directors, editors, and sound and video technicians, as well as the writer or writers. Because of this, the film industry makes broad use of work-made-for-hire contracts.

The compensation a writer gets for a film or television script is normally subject to industry-wide minimums established in negotiations with the Writers Guild of America. Most Hollywood film companies and television production companies have signed this contract, and you can expect to be paid at least the minimum established by the Guild contract if you write for them—even if you are not a member. You can sell your first script without joining the WGA; after that, you must apply for membership in the Guild in order to obtain further employment as a scriptwriter with any production company that has signed the Guild contract.

However, your local television stations, whether commercial, cable, or public, may not be WGA signatories; this means that they will probably pay you less—a lot less—than the WGA contract mandates, but they also won't require you to join the union.

Even if you are not a member of the WGA, you can still register your scripts with them before sending them off to an agent or a producer. This is *not* the same as copyright protection which, if you think back to what you read in chapter 11, protects only the way an idea is expressed, but not the idea itself.

In television, you seldom submit a finished script—and, even when you do, it is likely to be altered considerably in the production process. Your ownership may therefore be merged with the contributions of some other writer or writers, or even the director, the producer, and the star. When a finished product has such confusing paternity, a suit for copyright infringement may not be possible.

Instead, if someone lifts your idea, your recourse may be to the law of unfair competition or to the arbitration proceedings of the WGA itself. To avail yourself of either remedy, you will need proof, both of the basic elements contained in your script and of the fact that the idea was conveyed to the person or production company that used it. To prove access, you will need a record of letters, phone calls, and other contact. To establish the form and content of your scripts or treatments, you should *register* them with the WGA before pitching or submitting them.

Currently, Guild registration costs $10 for nonmembers. Technically, writers west of the Mississippi should register with the Writers Guild of America West, 8955 Beverly Boulevard, Los Angeles, Calif. 90048, and those east of the Mississippi with the WGA East, 555 West

57th Street, New York, N.Y. 10019, but registrations are not rejected if you send your materials to the wrong office.

After it receives your materials, the WGA will send you a registration number, which should be placed on the title page of your script or treatment before you submit it. This puts others on notice that you've registered the work and that pilfering it (or the basic ideas contained in it) may get them into trouble, since you can establish that you possessed the material, in the form deposited, on the registration date.

In addition to this registration service, the WGA has an approved agency contract, and, for a small fee (contact the Guild for the latest price), will also send you a list of agents who have agreed to abide by the terms of this contract in dealings with writers. Agreeing to abide by the terms of the Guild contract is no guarantee of an agent's competence or ability to sell your work, but at least you know that you'll be dealt with fairly. Just to be sure, you can obtain a copy of the current contract from the WGA and compare it to the one you have been offered. As always, don't sign anything you have questions about until those questions have been resolved.

Finding an agent to sell your scripts can be as difficult as finding a literary agent, but a good agent is probably more necessary in the television and movie industry than in the publishing world. This is true for several reasons:

- ▲ Many producers will not read unsolicited scripts or treatments, even if you've signed a submission agreement, unless those scripts have come from an agent.
- ▲ The volatility of the television market almost requires that you be represented by someone with inside knowledge of which series are buying and which are complete for the season, which shows accept scripts from outside writers and which are written by a staff team, or which have been canceled and which have been renewed.
- ▲ If you don't live in Los Angeles, you are away from the centers of power, and it can be almost impossible to pitch or sell a script. Having an agent who is on the spot there or in constant communication by phone, fax, and plane can bridge this gap.
- ▲ Some of the better-connected agents are able to put together package deals, allowing you to glide in on the coattails of another

of the agent's clients or pushing your script as the ideal vehicle for an actor the agent also represents and whom the studio may want.

Note that your *literary* agent may not have the knowledge or the desire to sell television or film scripts. He or she may employ a script agent to do that, or you may have to place your book-length works with one agent and find another to handle your film scripts.

In the movie and television industries, scripts are "pitched" to producers. To pitch a script, you (if they will let you or your letter in the door) or your agent must be able to boil it down to summaries of different lengths, depending on how interested the producer is when he or she hears the initial description. The longest of these summaries is not unlike the narrative outline you may have created for your novel (see chapter 9), but you must also be able to boil a script down to its smallest essence for a successful pitch.

How does this work? Basically, though your script may run from twenty-five to more than a hundred pages, you will need to condense it to eight or ten double-spaced pages for a "treatment"—a detailed narrative outline of the plot, scenes, and characters.

The treatment, in turn, should be boiled down into a one- or two-page synopsis for presentation to a producer. But before you get even this far, you or your agent—usually your agent—will need to summarize the entire plot in one or two sentences, much like the descriptions you find in *TV Guide* listings.

What does this kind of boiled-down description sound like? The Five Books of Moses might be pitched: "God creates the world, populates it, and cuts a deal with one group of people that he saves from slavery and gives a bunch of laws to." Anything longer than that and the producer will probably have taken a phone call or started to practice his putting in the corner of the office.

If you don't have an agent, but have managed to find a producer who is willing to read your unrepresented script, be prepared to sign a release form or a submission agreement. This is to protect the producer in case your script turns out to resemble something the producer already has optioned or in development.

If you are writing an *original screenplay,* you may submit it any-where, and all that matters is that you tell a good story in a professional manner, and don't propose special effects and cameos by stars that would make the production too costly to take on. Any producer who is willing to look at your original script *may* be willing to option it.

If you want to write *an episode for a television series,* you must sub-mit your script to the producer of that series. You start with a query let-ter that, just as in magazine querying, establishes you as *professional,* and with the special credentials necessary to write for *this* series. These credentials could include the fact that you are an avid fan and have never missed an episode—at least you'll have established your fa-miliarity with the series and its characters. If you want to submit a script to a show about doctors, it might help to note in your query that you are a surgical nurse or paramedic.

If you want to write for a series, it is important that you know what the characters are like and that you keep them in character in your epi-sode. Although the best way to get to know the characters is by watch-ing the series, by the time you have a handle on it, the show may be on hiatus or canceled. Another alternative is to obtain a copy of the series "bible"—a booklet that contains basic character descriptions and de-velopment, along with a statement of the philosophy behind the show. There are two problems with this approach: the series bible is often not available to unrepresented writers, or even to agents that the producer doesn't know; and a series often outgrows its bible as it develops. Nev-ertheless, the bible can help you to keep your characters in character and your plot on an acceptable course.

In your query, ask what kind of release form this particular producer requires. Assuming the producer's response to your query is positive, submit your script (or treatment, if that is what the producer has asked to see), accompanied by the signed release form, and note on the enve-lope that there is a "release form enclosed." Include the usual SASE for the return of your manuscript.

Make sure your submission is in the proper format for the series in question. The Straczynski and Root books mentioned earlier in this chapter provide excellent and expert advice on writing and formatting scripts for movies or television.

One last, related note regarding selling story ideas to Hollywood. Pro-ducers buy different rights from different writers: rights to just the story (often based on the treatment), rights to the first draft of the script, rights to rewrites, and rights to the final draft of a script. The same writer may or may not be employed to handle all of these steps.

Not all ideas for screenplays come from treatments. Another source of ideas is books, both nonfiction (like *Wired*) and fiction (like *Heartburn*). When your book is "sold to the movies," what the producer usually buys is an *option* on the right to produce it. This means that despite the numbers that may be bandied about, you have not sold the movie rights for half a million dollars or whatever figure they are citing in *Variety* or *Publishers Weekly*. What you have sold is the right to decide to make a movie—and that right goes for considerably less.

You may receive as little as $500 for an option, which will probably be good for six months to a year, and which can probably be extended for additional six-month periods for an additional fee, as specified in the option agreement. Only when the producer *exercises the option* and goes into production will you receive your half a million dollars (less your agent's cut).

However, even though the money won't come until the option is exercised, *the option agreement contains the contract* that specifies what rights, royalties, interests, and control you will have if the movie is made. The best advice anyone can give you, then, is that if you are offered an option on the film rights to your book, *have the option agreement, deal memo, or contract negotiated by an attorney familiar with the industry*—even if it costs you as much as you're being paid for the option. This may help you get the rights back if the option is never exercised, and may save you a lot of aggravation if the movie is, in fact, made.

Don't be dazzled by the numbers. As in any sale of your writing, it's the rights that count. And don't let anyone convince you that the deal you're being offered is the only one you'll ever get. If one producer has evinced an interest, another will probably do so sooner or later. The thing to remember is that there are sharks out there in film- and televisionland; if you're bound and determined to swim with those sharks, hire your own shark to defend you from them.

18

Galley Slaves

Writing for anything but a daily paper is not a career for the impatient. The publishing world grinds slowly, despite deadlines for individual pieces. It can—and usually does—take a year for your finished manuscript to become a published book. And while articles *may* see print sooner, I have had them disappear in limbo for as long as four years at one national magazine.

I once produced a piece of doggerel about the length of time it took for my already-sold writing to come out in print. I called it,

Waiting for the Galleys

The two great fears with which I'm smitten
Are dying before my work gets written
And managing to do my stint
But dying before my work sees print.

Galleys, or proofs, are printouts of typeset articles or books which are sent to the author so that he or she can double-check them for accuracy before they are published. This does not mean that the author is necessarily the final arbiter of wording or punctuation. Galleys pass through the hands of a proofreader (who is supposed to catch mistakes in spelling and punctuation) and at least one editor (who may change a piece for style or length). Nevertheless, galleys represent both the author's last chance to correct a mistake and, generally, a signal that publication is near.

You do not always get to see galleys on articles—although, when your reputation as an expert is on the line, you should insist on it. I generally make and keep a photocopy of my corrections so that, if necessary, I can prove that I *tried* to have the text changed, even if the publication didn't abide by my wishes. This can be important, for example, if it comes down to allocating fault in a lawsuit.

Galleys for articles may come fairly quickly, but, as my poem suggests, the galleys for a book may not come for many months after the manuscript has been turned in. After such a long hiatus, you may be horrified at what you wrote and feel tempted to change almost all of it. Your contract may preclude that; most contracts specify that if you change more than 10 percent of the copy on the galleys (except for the correction of printers' errors), *you* have to pay the cost of resetting the type. It may not be as expensive in these days of computer typesetting as it was when type was set by placing individual lead letters into metal trays. But it is still a good idea to make as many corrections as possible *before* the work gets to the galley stage.

Sometimes your horror at what the galleys look like is justified—and it isn't your fault. Although it is possible to have a phrase inserted into your contract to the effect that "no one but the author may make changes in the Work," often this is modified with the words "except for ordinary copyediting." And many contracts specifically grant the publisher the right to edit your work.

Some editing has always been customary in the United States, and major editing is legal where the author has given the publisher that right by contract, but in many European countries authors have the "moral right" to object to changes in their work. Indeed, the moral right of authors in the integrity of their work under the Berne Convention (which the United States ratified in 1988 *without the moral rights provisions*) is "inalienable," surviving even the assignment of the entire copyright.

Who generally makes changes in a work? There are normally three people charged with this duty. The first is the editor who bought the work from you. Known as the *acquisitions editor* or *content editor*, he or she is in charge of making sure you cover everything that needs to be covered, that your angle or slant is on target, and that the tone of your work is what the publisher wanted. A content editor may suggest large or small changes, or even complete revisions, before deciding the work is acceptable.

The *copy editor,* on the other hand, is concerned with details: spelling and punctuation, grammar and clarity, redundancies and dangling modifiers. The copy editor is also supposed to see to it that your manuscript is consistent—that the spelling of each character's name is constant, that details like a character's eye color don't change between chapter 1 and chapter 3 without explanation, and that no one rides off on a horse that is still in the barn. It is the copy editor's job to see that your writing is correct in style and reads smoothly.

The *proofreader* is there merely to correct the printed copy for errors in spelling and punctuation, and, occasionally, an improper homonym—for example, "two" where you meant to use "too." The proofreader may work from the copyedited manuscript as well as from his or her own knowledge of correct spelling and usage. It is the proofreader's job to make sure that all quotes and parentheses are closed, that names are capitalized, and that words are spelled correctly.

If you submit copy to newspapers, it will often be edited without any contact with you whatsoever. Sometimes you won't even know your piece has seen print until you receive your check in the mail.

When you write for magazines, the galleys that reach you will usually be in final, typeset form, ready to go to press—and some of the changes that have found their way into your copy may astonish you. This doesn't mean that these changes are necessarily bad. See chapter 5 on how you can learn from an editor who has tightened up your copy.

However, in book publishing, the content editor and the copy editor have separate and distinct responsibilities. The copy editor—often a freelancer and therefore free of supervision—is generally not charged with the responsibility for making major changes in the manuscript. Indeed, he or she is supposed to query the author about changes in the text. Typically, these queries are written on little paper flags attached to the margins of the manuscript. However, some copy editors seem to be frustrated writers who forget that the publisher bought the book from *you,* not from them, and who insist on rewriting your manuscript, whether they have the authority to do so or not.

An example? When the galleys for my first novel came, I discovered that all of my italics had disappeared. Most of these were italics that I had used to indicate the direct quotation of a character's thoughts. (*Grr,* she thought bitterly. *A pox on all copy editors.*)

That copy editor had also altered the punctuation—and therefore my meaning—in almost all of my dialogue. Thus,

"It's disappeared," he gasped.

became

"It's disappeared." He gasped.

This was not the same thing, nor was it what I had intended.

Perhaps it was naive of me to assume that my carefully crafted manuscript could be transferred, intact, to print, despite my very clean copy (so clean of errors that my content editor had remarked on the fact). Certainly, grammatical errors had, on occasion, been edited *into* my articles, and I had come to accept that as part and parcel of being a professional writer. But to wreak such havoc on a *book* manuscript my content editor had praised as being "thoroughly professional" boggled my mind.

Theoretically, the cleaner your manuscript, the more likely it is to survive the copyediting process. "Clean" means that words are spelled properly, the facts are correct, the writing is grammatical, and there are a minimal number of typos or written corrections on any given page. It also means that the manuscript is in the editorial style that the publisher prefers (for instance, whether the numeral "12" or the word "twelve" is used is a matter of editorial style). Many publishers have style books that explain to authors their preferred style in various matters. Others refer you to *The Chicago Manual of Style,* one of the basic texts of the industry (if you don't have a copy, and you are serious about writing, for heaven's sake, go out and *buy* one!).

But the theory broke down where my novel was concerned. Despite my clean copy, my manuscript was mauled—a process which one editor suggested, rather facetiously, might have resulted from its very cleanliness. He claimed that if a writer made a couple of obvious errors on each page, the copy editor would keep occupied and not mess with the parts of the manuscript that were none of his or her business.

When I complained to the content editor about everything I'd had to change back before the novel could go to press, she suggested that for the second novel, I submit a style sheet of my own to guide the copy editor. This would give me the opportunity to explain some of the unusual usages in the novel, a space opera full of telepathic communications that required the extensive use of italics.

I dutifully submitted just such a sheet with the second novel. It specifically requested that the italics remain untouched and listed the words I had invented along with the odd plural forms some of those invented words took.

Unfortunately, I soon learned that some copy editors need a specific note advising them to query you on any changes in wording. Since most responsible copy editors query the author on anything more substantial than routine spelling, grammar, or house style changes, a note requesting that you be consulted theoretically shouldn't be necessary. But I neglected to make the request, and the copy editor neglected to query.

The lesson to be learned might well be "Bribe your copy editor with chocolate to keep him or her from mauling your manuscript"—but I think it is really, "Request queries even though you think that procedure should be obvious, just in case the copy editor isn't inclined to consult you."

Among the things that disappeared from that second novel were several carefully crafted puns that the copy editor apparently didn't get, but the most outrageous alterations were two quotations from *Hamlet* that had been changed to comply with what the copy editor seemed to think was more appropriate style.

As I noted when I sent those proofs back, it was one thing to copyedit *my* prose, and quite another to tamper with the Bard's. But I have to admit that if my efforts were going to be sabotaged, at least I could take comfort that I was in good company.

When your carefully crafted article sees print, under your byline, in a form that bears no resemblance to the manuscript you submitted, is there anything you can do?

As I mentioned earlier, in some European countries, you may have the "moral right" to object to these changes. But when the United States ratified the Berne Convention for the Protection of Literary and Artistic Rights, which contains moral rights provisions in its text, Congress sidestepped the issue of moral rights by stating categorically that ratification does not "expand or reduce any right of an author . . . to claim authorship in a work; or to object to any distortion, mutilation, or other derogatory action in relation to the work that would prejudice the author's honor or reputation."

Sneaky—the new law neither expands nor reduces those rights that currently exist.

And as the wording suggests, moral rights fall into two categories:

those that affect a work's integrity and those that affect its paternity. The question of whether the United States *can* adopt the Berne without the moral rights provisions will ultimately fall to the courts to decide. Until that happens, the moral rights Congress neither expanded nor reduced must be protected by other areas of law.

This does not mean that there is no recourse through the copyright law. The section of the copyright law that gives the author the exclusive right to prepare derivative works based on his or her work may apply. You, as the creator of a work, own this right unless you sign it away.

Usually, we think of derivative works in terms of, say, a film version of your novel or a second book using characters from the first. However, if your work is so distorted that what finally sees print could be construed as a separate and distinct work based on your original, you might be able to claim that the editor produced an unauthorized derivative work. The key word here is *unauthorized;* look to your contract to see if you signed away ''all rights'' or specifically gave permission to edit.

This derivative-works route might give rise to an action for copyright infringement if you haven't surrendered the right on which it is based. But even if you have signed away the right to make editorial changes, if those changes are so drastic that their publication could damage your reputation, you might be able to sue for libel. This goes to the *paternity* aspect of moral rights law—the right to have your name on a work that you created, or the right to have your name removed from a work that isn't yours.

Any court awards under this theory will depend on a number of factors including whether you have developed a provable reputation (either as a writer or as an expert in the field about which you are writing), how many people who know of you are likely to have seen the publication, and whether the changes are actually damaging—or even apparent. If they are so slight that no one would notice them, you won't have a case. And even if the changes are striking, they *may* have improved your text. As agent and former editor Sharon Jarvis notes, ''Any author, no matter how famous, should realize that not everything he or she writes is wonderful—and that an objective eye is always needed.''

Obviously, if the editor massacres a manuscript that is garbled or obscure, you should be grateful for the bloodletting. Before you run for the process server, review all changes objectively; you may be happier with them on your second reading. Then again, you may not. But cool down before you make a final decision.

▲   ▲   ▲

What else can affect the paternity of your writing? Sometimes a piece is still basically your work, but your name has been left off of it—or worse, someone else's name has been substituted. It is always a good idea to do a little checking and find out whether the omission was intentional or inadvertent. If it was the latter—perhaps an intern or a secretary attached the wrong name—a formal correction in the next issue might be sufficient consolation.

Again, your remedy depends on what rights you've signed away. But if no correction is forthcoming, you *might* have a case under trademark law, which forbids one person's "passing off" another's work as his own.

The best protection against this kind of misunderstanding is to be careful of the terms of any contract you sign and to insist on the right to review the galleys of your work. In these days of easily available overnight mail services and fax machines, time pressure and distance are no excuse for failing to send galleys. You can read and return them just as quickly as someone a block away from the editorial offices.

While it is true that you can proofread the galleys for a short article rather quickly and fax them back the same day, reading the galleys for a book will take much longer. For this reason, it is a good idea to put into your book contract not only a provision that galleys will be sent to you, but also a clause giving you a minimum amount of time—two weeks is reasonable—in which to read them and get them back to the publisher.

I learned this lesson from personal experience when the galleys from my first book—the one with the missing italics—arrived on a Thursday with a note saying they had to have them back by Monday. I was booked solid with legal work, and I wound up sitting up all night for two nights so I could get the galleys to the "overnight" service by Saturday noon, when the last pickup that could ensure Monday delivery was scheduled.

And I've learned to include another clause in my book contracts as a result of my experience with my second novel. I now require that the publisher call to tell me that galleys are being sent. This is because one set of galleys arrived at my office the day after Thanksgiving, again on a short deadline. But the publisher never warned me that they were being sent, so I had no reason to go in to work—and I never knew they were there until the following Monday.

▲ ▲ ▲

What do you do when the galleys arrive? You proofread them, making whatever changes are necessary using traditional proofreaders' marks. These changes are written in by hand, so if your handwriting is totally illegible, you may have to practice printing or cursive script in order to avoid compounding errors by putting in unreadable corrections.

These corrections go in two places—in the text itself (at the site of the error) and in the margin (to call attention to, explain, or give you more room for your correction). Generally, your corrections of errors should be done in red, and any changes or additions should be done in dark blue or black ink. The production editor—who supervises the copy editors and proofreaders—will usually let you know what color he or she wants in a cover letter accompanying the galleys. (This is the same letter that tells you you have to get them back by the day before you received them.)

Additions or corrections to the text are written right on the galleys. Notes to the typesetter—like "tr" for "transpose" and "ital." for "change to italics"—should have a circle around them, because anything that is not circled will generally be added to the text.

Most proofreaders' marks are consistent throughout the industry, but some publishing houses have their own idiosyncratic systems, so it always helps to ask your editor for a chart of the marks your publisher prefers. The list provided here, with the example of how to use it, includes the most basic marks that *are* standard for the industry.

Proofreaders' Marks

WHAT THE MARK MEANS:	HOW TO USE IT IN THE TEXT:	WHAT GOES IN THE MARGIN:
Insert	insrt	/e
Delete	deleteє	e
Delete and close up	deleєte	℈
Close up	clo se up	◡
Insert space	insert|space	#
Change to uppercase	change to uppercase	cap
Change to lowercase	change to Lowercase	lc
Italicize	italicize	ital
Set in bold type	boldface	bf
Change from italics	change from italics	rom.
Insert period	insert period	⊙
Insert comma	insert comma	⋏
Insert colon	insert colon	⋏
Insert semicolon	insert semicolon	⋏
Insert quotation marks	insert quotation marks	ꞌ / ꞌ
Insert double quotation marks	insert marks	ꞌꞌ / ꞌꞌ
Insert apostrophe	womans work	ꞌ
Insert hyphen	half eaten	=
Insert dash	insert a dash	⊥M
Insert ellipsis	is never done	⊙/⊙/⊙/⊙
Insert parentheses	it is parenthetically	(/)
Start new paragraph	proofing. This is not	¶
Run on (no paragraph)	proofing. This is not difficult	no ¶
Transpose letters	tranpsose	tr
Transpose words	This is difficult not to	tr

Using Proofreaders' Marks

] Address at Gettysburg[

bf /center
tr
⌃ /tr
tr
lc ///
that /

lc   FØURSCORE and seven ago years our fathers brought
ℰ forth on this continent a new nation, concieved in
cap liberty, and to dedicated the proposition that all men are
⊙/⌗ created equal. Now we are engaged in a Great Civil War,
testing whether nation, or any nation so conceived and so
dedicated, can long endure. We are met on a great battlefield
of that war.⌐

no ⌗
rom

⌐We have come to dedicate a portion of that field as
a final resting-place for those who here gave their lives
lℓ that that that nation might live. It is altogether fitting
and proper that we should do this.

But, in a larger sense, we cannot dedicate—we cannt
consecrate—we cannot hallow—this ground. The brave men,
/d living ans dead, who struggled here have consecrated it far
above our poor power to add or detract. It is rather for
us to be here dedicated to the great task remaining
before us . . . that we here highly resolve that these
dead shall not have died in vain, that this nation, under God,
shall have a new birth of freedom; and that government of the
people, by the people, for the people, shall not perish from the
earth.

o̲ /
⌃
ᶴ /
|⊙|⊙|⊙|

⌗/ ;̂

—A. Lincoln   *ital*
November 19, 1863   *ital*

19

A Working System to Keep You Working

Early on in this book, I suggested that only *you* can decide what kind of writer *you* want to be—whether you want writing to be a career or a second job or a hobby, whether you want to write for money or just for the satisfaction of seeing your work in print. But no matter which path you take, sooner or later you're going to have to come to terms with the detritus of writing, which consists mostly of paper.

All writers live with paper. It piles up in the corners of rooms, then spreads insidiously, and soon you are inundated with the pulp of a million trees—*unless,* that is, you can manage to get organized. And the secret to getting organized is to think of your writing as a *profession.* Indeed, I've always been convinced that my professional approach—which has its roots in the organization of my law office—was largely responsible for my having made the transition from amateur hobbyist to professional writer in a relatively short time.

You don't need to start *big,* but you need to handle even one lone story as though it were part of a large group of works—because it could be, and you don't want to have to go back and organize your first twenty sales two years from now, when you're trying to beat six deadlines at once.

What you need is a system.

I have one that works for me. I've modified it bit by bit, over the years, and you can modify it too, to make it work for you.

▲   ▲   ▲

"A place for everything and everything in its place," my grandmother used to tell me. The first part of that philosophy is the hard part—how do you find a place for everything in your tiny studio apartment, or in a house shared with an active family?

If space is truly at a premium, I suggest you *think vertical*. If you can find the space for a file cabinet, buy a *five-drawer* file cabinet, because it takes up the same amount of floor space as a two-drawer cabinet, but holds nearly three times as much. Need space for your reference books? Consider installing a shelf across the end of a hallway, above the door frame.

Or buy some of those drawers or bins designed to slide under a bed. Do *not* slide your writing materials under the bed in an *open* carton; they'll get dusty and will look decidedly uninviting the next time you pull them out to work on them! Always, in fact, store your materials in closed boxes or file drawers, because papers left out become not only dusty but brittle and flyspecked—and someone is always grabbing the top sheet to scribble a phone number on. Look at it this way: taking care of your notes and drafts is a way of taking yourself seriously as a writer, and if you don't take yourself seriously as a writer, why should anyone else?

By taking yourself seriously, I *don't* mean you should quit your job or rent an office or invest in a $10,000 computer system. *That* constitutes an awful risk for someone who has never been, and might never be, published.

But a cardboard file storage box (you can buy one in a stationery store for as little as a dollar and a half), a box of file folders, and a ream of paper do not constitute a major investment. And while a word processor or a memory typewriter can save you the task of retyping each draft, and a personal copier can save you the trouble of making carbons, owning a typewriter with clean keys and having access to a local copy shop are all the basics you need. The extra equipment merely makes you more efficient.

In addition to *some* kind of typewriter or word processor, these are the things no working writer should be without:

▲ a file cabinet or stacking file boxes
▲ file folders (one-third cut have large enough tabs and enough variety to make files easy to locate in the drawer or bin)

▲ file folder labels in different colors (I'll get to the reason for these later)

▲ paper clips, both standard and extra-large

▲ a ream of good quality, 8½-by-11-inch white paper for submissions

▲ any 8 ½-by-11-inch light-colored paper (I use the back of old letterhead stock that the office next door was going to throw out) for drafts or for manuscripts that you intend to photocopy (you can submit the photocopies if they *look* like originals)

▲ a card file with three sets of dividers—two alphabetical and one designating the months of the year

▲ file cards and ledger cards that fit in the card file

▲ a cash journal (any small, two-column ledger will do)

▲ a looseleaf notebook

▲ book and magazine storage space

▲ a recent edition of a good dictionary

▲ a recent edition of Bartlett's *Familiar Quotations*

▲ a thesaurus or synonym finder

▲ reference books on English usage and grammar

▲ stationery (in white, cream, or gray, please—dark colors are hard on an editor's eyes, don't photocopy well, and tend to mark you as a dilettante) with your name, address, and phone number printed on it (you can design this with press-on type or have anyone with a computer desktop publishing system make you a master. A copy shop can then reduce or enlarge the master as necessary to run stationery, envelopes, or even business cards)

▲ envelopes imprinted with your return address, in both standard business size (number 10) and 9-by-12-inch size

▲ blank envelopes in both sizes to use for SASEs

▲ a wall calendar on which you can note deadlines

▲ a postage scale and a supply of postage stamps in different denominations (unless you live next door to your local post office branch station)

▲ the current issue of *Writer's Market* (and any other market book that might apply to the kind of writing you are doing)

▲ a subscription to *Writer's Digest* and to any magazines that you've targeted as markets for what *you* are writing

An answering machine is also useful, and I can't live without Post-it™ notes and a bulletin board myself. I also find a two-hole punch and a box of three-inch prongs (they're called "fastener bases") very handy for keeping correspondence in order within file folders.

A word to the wise: if you're going to buy all this stuff, introduce yourself at your local stationery store; tell them you're a writer and you'd like to open a business account. Often, they will grant discounts and even allow you to charge your supplies and pay for them on a monthly basis. It never hurts to ask.

The one good thing I got out of the college writing course I took was the habit of a daily stint. We were required to write 500 words a day—even, the professor told us, if all we did was write the word "no" 500 times. Now, 500 words a day is not a lot. It probably comes to less than two typewritten, double-spaced pages. But there are times when the muse is on vacation, and the only thing you *can* write is the word "no."

Nevertheless, if you let a day go by without writing, it can turn into a week, and then a year, which is how those piles of paper get covered with dust. The important thing is to keep your hand in even if you're not churning out manuscript pages. Writing a query letter is still *writing*— and so is editing something that you wrote the day before.

If you're not on a deadline, and can't think of a thing to write about, this may be the perfect day to thumb through *Writer's Market* to see who might be interested in something you have already written. (Remember, if you haven't assigned the reprint rights, you can sell and re-sell an article as many times as the market will bear.) And sometimes, as you read the market listings, you realize that one of your older or un-sold pieces could be reworked for a publication you've just come across. You can query them now or, if you're not up to writing letters today, make a note to query them later and continue with your market research.

Market research—how do you match up your story ideas to the publications that might buy them? One of the best ways is to check the listings in *Writer's Market* to see what a publication *says* it buys. All the information in this volume is gleaned from forms sent in by the listed publications.

I have a system for using *Writer's Market*. I purchase the annual volume as soon as it arrives in my bookstore. I skim it immediately, just to see if any changes have been made in the way the listings are presented. Then I decide what sections of the book I am most likely to want to consult.

I index these by typing a one-word tab ("Women's" or "Travel," for example) and taping it to the edge of the first page of that section of the book—staggering these tabs on the edge of the book makes them easier to read. Then, having marked the categories I am likely to want to sell to, I begin my *serious* perusal of the listings.

I first look to see how much a publication pays, and *when* it pays for articles. It is all well and good to sell or resell an already existing piece to any market that will take it, but if I am going to *create* an article for a specific market, I want the exercise to be worth my time and effort. I sold my first article for a penny a word paid on publication, just to get a print credit, but I'm not about to do that now that I know I can command better prices and payment on acceptance.

Next, I check out the kind of rights the publication purchases. I don't mind selling first serial rights, but, on the principle that such practices should be discouraged, I *never* sell all rights or accept work-for-hire assignments. However, I've found that not all publications that *claim* they buy all rights or make work-made-for-hire assignments actually do so—and even when they do, this stance may be negotiable. As a result, I tend to treat the listing as a warning flag cautioning me to make sure that both the publication and I know what rights are being bought and sold; however, I don't automatically rule out a publication that claims to buy more rights than I am willing to sell.

If a publication pays enough, and preferably does so on acceptance, I look for an offer of guidelines, sample copies, or both. I send for the guidelines (and, if I am unfamiliar with the publication, for a sample copy) to discern whether I can match the style and provide the kind of article the publication seems to want.

Only then do I send a query letter, and, as a result of this careful market research, my queries *often* garner assignments. And when I get an assignment, I make sure that its terms are clearly understood by both of us, sending a letter-memo to them if they don't send an assignment letter to me.

All this may seem more pragmatic than romantic, but starving isn't really romantic. Neither is spinning your wheels with no result. The approach I've outlined ensures that I will seldom expend postage or typewriter ribbons without getting a monetary return, for while it may be very gratifying to see your work in print, it's even more gratifying when you've been paid for the piece. I think I'm worth it—and if you can write well, so are you.

▲   ▲   ▲

If, as I do, you write articles on assignment for many different publications, and sometimes resell them, keeping track of queries, assignments, resales, and copies of your work can start to take up more time than writing. So I have derived a system to cope with this and free up as much time as possible for writing. That's where those supplies I listed come in.

The basic system is organized around that old standby, the card file. I use large cards—5-by-8-inch cards seem to work best for me—and color code them—white cards for queries, yellow cards for articles I'm circulating (either for resale or because I wrote them without a specific assignment), blue cards for fiction or poetry.

I write the title of the piece on the top line of a white, yellow, or blue card, whichever is appropriate, and then divide the card into columns: a wide one for the name of the publication to which I've submitted it, and three narrow ones for the date sent, the date a response is received, and any commentary, such as "assigned" or "oversold, try in six months" or even just plain "no." If, when I first send out the query or submission, I have ideas for alternative markets, I list them on the card. Thus, if something is rejected, I can send it right off to the next name on the card.

These cards are filed alphabetically by title, using one set of dividers.

Behind the monthly dividers, I use pink cards to mark assignment due dates and green ones as "ticklers" to remind me about a contest deadline, an upcoming conference, or an idea I can sell at some future time. When I create an assignment card or tickler card, I mark it at the top with the due date (or the date of the conference). Sometimes these cards merely carry a short note—"Work-for-hire piece due at *Writer's Digest.*" Other times the information may be more detailed: the date of a conference, the price, the place, the address for registration, and the contact person may all be listed (you can cut this off the flyer and glue it to the card to save time).

I normally file these cards a month or two earlier than the date on them. If a conference is in June, but registration closes in April, I file the card in the March or April section. If a newsworthy event is taking place in November, and I want to sell it to a national magazine with a four-month lead time, I will file the reminder at least six months ahead, perhaps even seven or eight. I find it also helps to glance through *all* the cards from time to time, just in case there's something I should be getting out sooner than I had originally planned.

Every publication that has ever bought a story from me or given me an assignment gets a ledger card, filed alphabetically behind the third set of dividers.

The ledger cards come already divided into columns. I can enter the amount a publication owes me for an article on the day I send it off (or on the day it is accepted, if it wasn't written on assignment). When I get paid, that goes on the next line, zeroing out the balance.

I cross-enter the payment information to these cards from my cash book, where each payment I receive is entered as soon as I receive it. Billing information is a little more haphazard, since I don't always send a statement (which would be the logical source of the amount due). My operation is still small enough so that I can enter the amount a publication owes me directly from an acceptance letter or from the cover letter I send with an assigned piece; when acceptance is first acknowledged by a publication's mailing me a check and contributor's copy, I merely enter the amount due and the payment at the same time.

The next step in my system makes use of the file folders and those color-coded labels I mentioned. (You can actually buy colored files now, but they are much more expensive than the old standby manila ones.)

I use a purple file label on the files that hold my notes. Thus, I have a "purple file" on Florida attractions, another on Milwaukee history, and another on *Hawaii Five-O* background information. I've written articles on all of these subjects and might want to do others some day, so I always keep my notes. Sometimes I have had to go to expansion files—the kind that are closed on the sides and expand to one or three inches—to hold bulky notes and lengthy drafts; when I do, I sometimes divide these into subfiles by inserting ordinary files into them. This is a way of keeping all my notes on a given subject in one place, accessible if and when I need them, and *not* all over the house or office.

When I query a publication for which I have never written, my copy of the letter goes into a "miscellaneous writing" file. If the response is negative, the rejection letter goes into a general "rejection slips" file, alphabetized according to the name of the publication, so that if I ever want to write to them again, I'll know what *kind* of rejection slips they send. The slip may even yield the name of an editor or associate editor I can write to. If all I receive is a form rejection slip, I note the date I received it and the piece it concerned on the rejection slip before filing it with the others.

If the response is positive, I open a file with a red label for that publication. All correspondence with them will henceforth go into the "red file," along with photocopies of the galleys for the article when I get them.

Rough drafts of my articles usually wind up in the "purple files," but the final draft, as submitted, gets a file of its own, with a blue label. The name *I* have given the article is the name that goes on that label.

My original printouts of book-length works go into the kind of box that paper comes in because what I submit is a clean photocopy. I try to keep these originals as pristine as possible in case additional copies are needed, so I usually make an extra photocopy, on colored copy paper, which I keep in an expansion file so I'll have something for family and friends to read if they want to see "how the book is coming."

There is a temptation, when you finally receive copies of publications containing your articles, to run around showing them to people—at least the first few times it happens. This is a good way to misplace or damage the magazines and to mess up your record keeping.

The first thing I do when one of my published articles arrives is to *log it in.* I use the looseleaf notebook for that, entering the articles about three to a page in the order in which they are published. I use standard footnote style for the entry, like this:

"Work for Hire: A Red Flag for Writers," *Writer's Digest,* August 1989.

If I later sell reprint rights, I note that directly underneath the original entry, citing the name the piece was given when it was reprinted, the publication in which it appeared, and the date.

The title is one of the complicating factors in any writer's record-keeping system. It is generally an editor's prerogative to change the title of an article, so the name it bears in print may not be the name it bore when it was sent out. By trial and error, I have found it more efficient to file tear sheets alphabetically by the headline they had when they were published than under my original title, although this sometimes makes it hard to place my hands immediately on the tear sheet. However, if I can remember approximately when the piece appeared, I can look it up in my notebook with the chronological listings, find out what name the editor gave it, and easily locate the clip.

A word about those tear sheets. Never *tear* them out of the publication, as was done in the old days. First of all, if you want to register your copyright in your published work, you will need an intact copy of the publication—and I think, wherever possible, you should keep an archival copy as well.

What I do is *photocopy* the article after I've logged it in. If the article just fits on a photocopied page, I add my copyright notice (if it does not already appear on the article), my name, address, and phone number. That becomes my master copy. If the text as published doesn't fit neatly on a standard page or two, I or my secretary will cut and paste the master to a more convenient size before adding the identifying information.

The master is kept in the file and used to make the photocopies we send out as samples of my work. We usually keep about half a dozen copies in the file with the master. These files have green labels, which, as I mentioned earlier, bear the title under which the article saw print.

I file my archival copies of all publications in which my works have appeared in chronological order in the cardboard magazine bins you can buy at any stationery store. These bins are also available in plastic, but the less expensive cardboard ones serve just as well. Oversize publications, such as newspaper supplements, are kept in a couple of stacking drawers I purchased at a local department store. This storage system enables me to lay my hands on the original publication in which my work appeared almost as easily as I can find the tear sheet.

As with any system, there are a number of things I have always meant to do with this one but have never gotten around to—or have avoided doing because it would take too much time. One of those is cross-coding my published articles by subject matter. The problem is that too many of the pieces fit into multiple categories: one article called "Mr. Sulu's Sukiyaki," for example, could be listed under "food," "celebrities," "entertainment industry," "Japan/Japanese," "Star Trek," "science fiction," "recipes," and "George Takei." That would mean eight entries, and entering them would take up entirely too much time.

And for a long time I have meant to create a list of everything I've sold, broken down by the publication in which it appeared, but, again, this would take more time than I'm willing to devote to it.

I know that I could set up this kind of record keeping on a computer, but entering all that data at this stage of my career would take time— and I must confess that I harbor the fear that the computer will "eat" my information. I prefer hard copy that I can lay my hands on, and, of course, for the tear sheets, I *need* hard copy anyway.

But even without this additional cross-referencing, the system seems to be working. Perhaps it will also work for you.

20

Death and Taxes

It's an old saw that death and taxes are always with us. If you're a writer, the rules for both that apply to you may be different from those for your steadily employed friends.

Let's start with the problem of taxes. You can make the Internal Revenue Service and every other taxing authority extremely happy by keeping good records. Keeping them happy will keep *you* happy—it's as simple as that.

Back in chapter 19, I mentioned entering all payments that you receive for your writing in a cash book or journal as soon as you get them. There are two reasons for this. The first is that the I.R.S. holds *you* responsible for reporting all your income from your writing endeavors. Obviously, if you work for yourself, no one is going to send you a W-2 form. If all receipts are entered in your cash book, it is a simple matter to total them up at the end of the year.

The second reason for keeping a running record of all income is that if the I.R.S. ever audits you, the first thing they will want to see is the kind of system you have for keeping track of receipts. If you can show them that your entries are, indeed, systematic, they aren't likely to hang you out to dry—at least for *that* part of your return.

They do have at least one way of finding out if your entries are honest. I mentioned that no one is going to send you a W-2 form—but publishers who pay you more than $600 in any given year *are* required to report what they paid you to the I.R.S. using form 1099-MISC. Sometimes companies that pay you less than that also file a 1099-MISC, but it isn't required. The I.R.S. totals up all of the 1099s with your name on them to make sure that your gross receipts equal *at least* that amount. If they don't, you're inviting an inquiry at minimum, and probably an audit.

Along with the record of what comes in, you have to keep a record of what goes out. This is because your taxable income from your small business (writing) is determined by deducting the permissible expenses of your writing career from your gross writing income.

This used to be easy: you simply wrote checks for everything. Your checkbook was your record of expenses, and the canceled checks were proof of payment. Nowadays, the cost of checks makes their use for small purchases an extravagance; besides, charge cards are quicker and often more acceptable. So how do you keep your records of expenditures?

I know of two ways. One is to write down everything as you spend it (or at the end of each day) in a ledger, noting the date, the amount spent, and the purpose. Then file the receipts away by category of expense (such as supplies, rent, or travel), cross-referenced to the appropriate ledger page.

Most of us don't have the time to do that.

What's the alternative? At the very least, take all of the receipts (including charge slips) that pertain to your writing and drop them into a file marked with the year you spent them; you can sort them out when you do your taxes. You should also retain your telephone and charge card bills so that you can document what portion of them was incurred for business purposes. Cash outlays can be entered in your pocket calendar, but because parking meters and pay phones don't usually issue receipts, be sure to add a note as to the payee and purpose of the expense, especially when there isn't a receipt. If you intend to deduct automobile mileage, you should keep a log of the dates, times, and distances you drive for business purposes. The important thing is to be able to document anything you deduct.

To deduct the expenses of your writing activities from your income, your writing must be a business rather than a hobby. There are a number of tests that the I.R.S. uses to determine whether you are operating a business in which you at least *intend* to make a profit. These include how much time you devote to the business, whether your losses are due to circumstances beyond your control (like a publisher going bankrupt and not paying what it owes you), and how businesslike your operation is (the real reason for adhering to systems like the ones I've outlined in chapter 19 and in this chapter).

If you show a profit on your writing, whether it is a business will not normally be questioned; it is only when you take in less than you spend that you need to prove your motives.

Assuming that you qualify as a business, how do you file your taxes? Self-employed writers should use Schedule C to show profit and loss from a business. This schedule replaces the W-2 you would receive from an employer and should be attached to your Form 1040.

If you net more than $400 per year as a freelancer, you must also file a Form SE, on which the amount of social security tax you must pay will be figured. This, too, should be sent in with your regular Form 1040 when you file your taxes.

Freelancers usually receive payment in full for their work, with no deductions taken out. If the payment, or cumulative payments, from one publisher are high enough, however, that publisher may be required to withhold as much as 20 percent—unless you provide your social security number. To avoid any problems that might later arise, many publishers ask you for your social security number before they'll send your check. To expedite getting paid, it sometimes helps to put your social security number on the cover letter that accompanies your submission.

If nothing is being deducted, you will probably owe taxes at the end of the year. The I.R.S. wants to make sure you'll have the money when the time comes, so—depending on how much you are likely to owe—you may also be required to make quarterly payments by filing Form 1040-ES on the fifteenth of January, April, June, and September each year.

The Internal Revenue Service will provide you with two helpful books, *Tax Guide for Small Business* and *Your Federal Income Tax,* upon request. These are reissued every year to include any changes in the rules. They're free from your local I.R.S. office, so if you're a working writer, you should probably make it a practice to stop down and pick up the newest version every January.

The share you send to the Internal Revenue Service is not the only tax you may owe. A freelancer who earns enough may be required to pay state and local income tax as well. You can get information about your tax obligations by calling the information office of the appropriate taxing authority. Look under the city or state listings for a heading marked "tax" or "revenue."

In some places, you may be required to pay an annual property tax on the equipment used in your business. And if you sell copies of your work—for example, if you have self-published a book—you may be required to collect a sales tax on every volume you sell. This sales tax must be paid over to the state or municipality at monthly, quarterly, or annual intervals, depending on how much is involved. Again, you will have to check with the appropriate taxing authority—state or local or both, depending on who assesses the tax.

One of the fundamental ways to avoid problems with tax collectors is to take the time to set up a proper bookkeeping system. Investing in the services of a good C.P.A. to help you do this can save you both time and money in the long run. Your accountant can also help you to obtain whatever taxpayer account numbers you may need, since each taxing authority generally assigns its own number.

You may need additional identification numbers if you employ others who are not engaged in business for themselves. Even if your assistants work only part-time, hiring them makes you an employer. Employers are required to deduct social security tax and withholding taxes and pay them over to the I.R.S. and any other applicable taxing authority. Employers are also required to pay unemployment taxes, based on the gross salaries of their employees, into a fund that will cover their unemployment insurance if you ever lay them off. Employers are also expected to provide a safe workplace, and in most jurisdictions, must carry worker's compensation insurance to pay the employee for on-the-job or job-related injuries.

If you retain the services of others who are in business for themselves—termed "private contractors" by the I.R.S.—*you* may be required to file a Form 1099-MISC for *them*. This form is also used for documenting payment of office rents that total more than $600 to the same person. (If you use a portion of your home for your business, check the *Tax Guide for Small Business* for current rules on deductibility.) A Form 1099-MISC is also required for anyone to whom you paid more than $10 for royalties or permissions. One copy of each Form 1099-MISC must be sent to the person you paid; you keep a second for your records, while a third is submitted to the I.R.S. with covering Form 1096.

As you can see, what people engaged in their own businesses do for the most part is fill out forms.

If you want to avoid close encounters with unnecessary forms, and want assistance in filling out the necessary ones *correctly,* turn again to your accountant—not only to get your system set up correctly in the first place but also, if you can afford it, to keep it running efficiently. The monetary cost of handing over this chore to an expert will almost always be offset by the time and frustration you'll save.

The tax man may be forever waiting in the wings, with his hand out for a piece of your pie, but what if you never get your hands on that pie in the first place? If death and taxes are always with us, so are deadbeats. When you operate your own business, you soon discover that some people will go to extraordinary lengths to avoid paying a legitimate bill.

Publishers are no different from the population at large (except for being generally more literate). Some pay their just debts as soon as they incur them; others live by what most freelancers would have to agree is the worst and most common of lies: "The check is in the mail."

Of course, it isn't. It's sitting on someone's desk in Accounting or on the floor under an artist's table in Graphics. Or it has to be signed by the associate treasurer, who's on maternity leave. Meanwhile, the wolf is at *your* door.

There *is* an etiquette to extracting money that is not forthcoming for your work. You start out with the person you've been dealing with all along—the editor—and you start out being pleasant. Drop a note that says something like,

> Dear Charlie:
>
> Your assignment letter says you'll pay me $500 *on acceptance,* and I have to assume that my article was accepted, since what I am enclosing with this letter is my corrected galley proofs. Can you get those guys in Accounting to shake a leg? My bookie wants his bread.

You'll usually receive one of three basic responses to this kind of letter: the check, an apologetic note from the editor saying, "I'm *trying* to pry it loose for you—tell your bookie to hold his horses," or something decidedly unbusinesslike, such as, "The story isn't officially accepted until the editor-in-chief countersigns the contract, and he's been in Nepal for six weeks. We think he'll be back next month, but then it takes about a month for Accounting to process it."

If you receive a letter like this, it means that you are dealing with a publication that has no respect for writers, doesn't understand the meaning of its own contracts and commitments, and is using your money, interest-free, for as long as possible. I suggest that you make it *im*possible, *imm*ediately.

Unless the publication has always made timely payments to you in the past, which would mark this as an aberration, they probably stiff their writers all the time. You don't *need* a market like that, and you should probably write them off as far as any future sales are concerned. But if you've already written something for them, what you *need* is to be paid.

If the editor still seems to be on your side, enlist his or her help in getting the check through channels as expeditiously as possible. Sometimes, however, the editor can't be bothered with mundane things like making sure writers get paid. The remedy for that is an end run.

There is a definite art to the collection process. First, double-check your contract. Does it say, specifically, "We will pay on acceptance"? Do you have a note from the editor that says, "The piece looks great— we'll run it in the March issue"? You've met the conditions of the contract; *they* have breached it.

But what if there is no correspondence? This makes things harder, and it is why I suggest that you always send a letter-memo to confirm a telephone assignment. However, the lack of a written contract needn't stop you from calling Accounts Payable and politely asking the clerk you reach, "Could you check on the status of a payment, please? I'm a freelance writer, and I was supposed to get my check two weeks ago for a piece in the March issue."

Sometimes the clerk can find the check request and expedite payment, in which case it was worth the cost of the call. But sometimes Accounts Payable will not be able to find any record of you at all. What this tells you is that the system broke down before the check request got to Accounting. Call the editorial department back, ask to speak to the editor-in-chief, and politely ask what can be done to get your money to you.

On occasion, the accounting clerk finds the check request but informs you, "It's in the computer. It'll be issued next Tuesday." If you are really desperate, and the payment is really late (and large enough to merit the extra effort), it is possible that you can persuade *someone* to cut a check by hand and send it by overnight mail.

But what if you are willing to wait until Tuesday, and it becomes a week from Tuesday, and then a month from Tuesday, and there is still no check? Consider a trip to court. This is where you will need your documentation—the better the paper trail you can lay before the court, the more likely you are to recover.

There may be certain jurisdictional problems if you choose small claims court and the publisher is located in another state, so you should probably check with an attorney to find out the rules for small claims court in your state. (If the amount in question doesn't warrant retaining a lawyer, sometimes you can obtain rudimentary assistance from the clerk of courts or a local lawyers' hotline.) However, if a publication is sold throughout the country, you *might* be able to bring the action in your own state, under what is called a "long-arm statute." This would enable you to bring the suit in your own hometown, forcing the publisher either to come there or to hire a local attorney to defend the suit. It may be cheaper to pay you what you have coming.

Of course, there are times a suit is just not possible: you don't have the documentation to support your claim or you can't get jurisdiction or the sum is too small for all that effort. If you are a "cash method" taxpayer—that is, if you do not declare any income until you receive it—you can't even deduct the bad debt from your taxes. What do you do then?

Sorry to say, you let it go. Some writers get back a little of their own in creative ways—Harlan Ellison once mailed a dead gopher to a publisher who, he felt, had done him dirty.

I'd encourage you, instead, to just walk away. Go down to the gym and batter a punching bag, or go out for a run or a swim. Then put it behind you and get back to your *other* writing. I think it's sometimes less costly, in time, money, and emotions, to chalk the whole thing up to a learning experience than to exact revenge—but then, I *like* gophers.

Sometimes there isn't even anyone to whom you can send a gopher. This can be the result of a worst-case scenario—a publisher who has gone out of business. Often a publisher just fades away, but sometimes it will file or be forced into bankruptcy proceedings. In either case, you're unlikely to see any money; and where a *book* was involved, it can actually cost you money to get the rights back or get your hands on copies.

Where a publisher just fades away—where mail comes back marked "Moved—unable to forward"—there isn't much you can do. But what do you do when a publisher goes bankrupt?

A bankruptcy is a kind of financial death, and, as in the case of a death, the estate must be distributed to those who have a share coming. In the case of a bankruptcy, the law draws priorities: the first in line are the I.R.S. and other taxing authorities, landlords, and employees. Anyone with a *secured* claim (for example, someone who has a lien on a piece of office equipment) gets to take the security (that piece of equipment). Banks often secure the inventory of a publishing business, which means they can seize that inventory—all the books in the warehouse, for example—to satisfy that lien. Only after priority claims and secured creditors have been taken care of do all the other creditors get to split up the pie in proportionate shares. Usually, this means you get paid pennies on the dollar—if you get paid anything at all!

There are two kinds of business bankruptcies. In one, referred to as a reorganization or a Chapter 11 proceeding (this is the chapter of the Bankruptcy Code that governs it), the publisher stays in business, trying to keep creditors at bay, until times get better or the crisis that forced the bankruptcy passes. It pays its secured creditors and may sell off some of its assets—including contracts with some of its authors— so it can keep other assets like its business equipment. Current expenses usually get paid, but past debts are usually settled according to a plan approved by the court, under which, again, the unsecured creditors may receive only a few cents for each dollar of indebtedness.

Many Chapter 11 proceedings fail and are converted to the other kind of bankruptcy, a straight, or Chapter 7, proceeding. Sometimes the publisher files under Chapter 7 in the first place. A Chapter 7 proceeding is a financial death with no hope of resurrection—the company goes out of business, and the creditors split up whatever corpse there may be.

In either case, the court in which the bankruptcy petition has been filed will generally send you (or your agent) a claim form. Unfortunately, a publisher's financial affairs are sometimes so muddled that the court is not supplied with a full list of those to whom money is owed. If you know that a publisher who owes you money has filed a bankruptcy petition, it never hurts to write to the court to obtain the deadline for filing claims and the appropriate claim form.

Fill out the claim form, listing what you are owed, and file it with the court before the deadline (it doesn't hurt to use certified mail to prove it got there). Then wait.

And wait.

And wait.

Eventually, if your claim is not challenged, you may receive a percentage of what is owed you—usually a very small percentage. That's all you get; the debtor (the current term for what used to be called "the bankrupt") is excused from paying any more on your claim than the percentage the court has approved.

Of course, individuals can also file for bankruptcy. When they do so, the law allows them to keep certain property as "exempt." The secured creditors claim their secured property, and the court assesses the costs of administering the bankruptcy. Then the unsecured creditors divide the rest.

It is important for writers who are considering filing for bankruptcy to be aware that their copyrights are property, and hence are a part of the estate that the creditors get to split. Royalties that have been earned but not yet paid will also be subject to claims by creditors. A writer contemplating a bankruptcy has very special problems that probably warrant hiring an attorney who is a bankruptcy specialist, rather than going to a low-priced bankruptcy clinic.

When I started this chapter, I also mentioned death. For writers, estates can get a little more complicated than the classic will (held valid) that read, in its entirety, "Give the works to Mabel."

Copyrights—and all the rights contained in them, such as book rights, first serial rights, and sequel rights—are property. But because a copyright is infinitely divisible, it is often impossible for a writer's heirs to know which rights can be bequeathed and which may have been sold, stolen, or given away before the author's death.

For this reason, one of the best things you can do for your heirs—and yourself—is to maintain an up-to-date list of whatever rights assignments you have made, including the date and the person or company to whom you made the assignment. It also helps to make an extra copy of any long-term contracts you may have signed and clip those to the list of assignments. Then make sure your heirs or your personal representative knows where to find this information.

You can leave your copyrights to the heir of your choice by will, or you can trust in your state's laws of intestate succession to pass the rights to your next of kin. But whichever course you take, you should be aware that the U.S. Copyright Law creates extra rights for authors and their heirs. With those rights come extra responsibilities for their protection.

Knowing which copyright law applies to your works is one of those responsibilities. For pre-1978 works, for example, whether you are still alive on the renewal date can have a profound effect on who owns the rights for at least the next twenty-eight years, and perhaps even the full forty-seven remaining in the term of copyright.

It works this way. If any of your works were published before January 1, 1978, the copyright is good for only twenty-eight years. It must be renewed in the twenty-eighth year in order to take advantage of the full term—seventy-five years—that the new law provides. If you have signed away your rights for the full term and all renewals, and if you are still alive on the renewal date, the person to whom you assigned the rights gets to renew them. But if you are dead, and your spouse or children didn't sign that contract, *they* are the ones who get to renew the copyright in their own name—*if they know enough to do so.*

There's a different provision in the law for works that were already in their renewal term on January 1, 1978, when the new law went into effect, and for those old law works that are renewed after that date. If the renewal right was assigned before 1978, because the total duration of old law copyrights (including renewals) was fifty-six years, you—or your heirs—can now take back the rights to such works in the fifty-sixth year. But to do this, you or your heirs have to know when the work was first published, when it was registered, and when it was renewed—and by whom. *You* have to keep those records for your heirs since *they* probably won't even know what to look for!

Another interesting provision of the new law allows you—or your surviving spouse and children or grandchildren—to terminate *any* assignment of rights made after January 1, 1978, in the thirty-fifth year after it is made. This termination right cannot be signed away. However, it is not automatic, and if you take no action in that thirty-fifth year, the right of termination dies. Again, a list of when you assigned those book rights or the exclusive movie rights to your novel will make it possible for you—or your heirs—to take the proper steps to get them back.

Making a list of renewal and termination dates, and the proper persons to notify, can help you as well as your heirs. And putting a cover letter with that list, telling those who come after you what to do to preserve their rights in your works, can keep your lasting legacy from lapsing into the public domain.

21

Stepping Out

In some ways, writing is the most gratifying of careers. You can reap satisfaction from a single project over and over again: when you finish it and it really looks the way you hoped it would, when it is accepted for publication, when the check arrives, when you first see it in print, and when other people comment favorably after having read it.

It can also be a frustrating business when your work doesn't sell, when pieces that *have* sold sit in limbo for years without ever seeing print, when an editor butchers them, and when a promised check fails to arrive.

More to the point, writing is a lonely business. Often, the only interaction you have is with your typewriter. Communication with editors is generally accomplished by mail, sometimes by phone, almost never in person. Even if you are collaborating on a project, you will find you are spending large blocks of time alone. And while you are trying to whip a major project, like a novel, into a shape you wouldn't be embarrassed to show to anyone, the lack of any feedback can wreak havoc with your confidence.

Worse, what seems to you to be a tragedy—like a period when the words won't come—may be regarded as a return to sanity by your friends and family. ("You can't write today? Good. The lawn needs mowing.") So, sooner or later, there will come a time when you find yourself crying out for the company of someone who understands you, someone who can empathize with your problems or give you a word or two of practical advice.

You can find that companionship in a number of places: a local writers' group or press club, a national or statewide writers' organization, a writers' conference or a special interest gathering (like those held for science fiction, romance, or mystery fans), a book fair, or a seminar. You can apply to stay at a writers' colony, or you can organize your own version of the Algonquin roundtable with a few phone calls to other local writers you may have met from time to time. Which you choose depends on what kind of input you feel you need.

Local writers' clubs are the most basic of writers' groups, and usually the most informal. Very often these are gatherings of "wannabes"— amateur or beginning writers who meet in a church or library basement to critique each other's work. Once you start selling a lot of your work, you may find that you have outgrown this kind of association because the only criticism that counts for the professional writer comes from editors, your conscience, and the reading public.

Members of some local groups avoid passing judgment on each other's work and meet merely for companionship (and if a little market information gets passed along, that's a lagniappe). I go to lunch about once a month with a small group of women who, like me, are published fiction writers. We gather for good fellowship and mutual encouragement, but have resisted formalizing the structure of our very informal group because it might stop being *fun*. Still, in our meetings we reinforce each other as writers—and it's nice to know that if there's a signing party for one of our books, we can count on *some* people to show up.

Locally sponsored workshops and seminars, or the local visit of a national writing seminar, are other places to meet fellow writers and even to pick up a few tips. Some of the larger writers' conferences are attended by agents, editors of national magazines, and publishers' representatives. In addition to the social and educational benefits they provide, these conferences are great places to make contact with people who might be interested in representing you or buying your work.

At some conferences, you may pick up not only information but free book bags or free copies of books to put in them. I once attended a romance writing seminar at which they gave out purple pencils. But the best thing to come away with is the knowledge that *you are not alone*. Many a collaboration effort has been spawned by people who first met at a writers' conference; probably a number of marriages have resulted as well.

Conferences can be large, like the annual American Booksellers Association convention and World Science Fiction convention, each of which may draw ten to twenty thousand attendees. Or they can be small, like a one-day seminar at your local community college. They may draw the biggest names in the field or merely consist of a gathering of local talent.

Sometimes the talent at the conference is *you*. If you've been published often enough or in prestigious places, or if you've won a few awards for your work, you may be invited to participate in a panel or speak about your experiences. Conferences afford you an opportunity to promote your works, to give readings from them, or to sign autographs (always a heady experience).

Is there a down side to attending writers' conferences? They *can* become addictive. I know of one writer who attends every conference in the Midwest, and—perhaps as a result—hasn't written anything in years. Conferences, like everything else, can take you away from your writing, therefore ultimately defeating their purpose.

How do you find out about these conferences? One of the best sources is the May issue of *Writer's Digest,* in which conferences for the next year are listed, by state, with the dates, places, and the names of the people to contact if you want to register. Shaw & Associates of Coral Gables, Florida, publishes an annual *Guide to Writers' Conferences.* You can also call the outreach department of your local college or university and ask if they are sponsoring any writing seminars or conferences. Chances are they have one scheduled.

Once you attend one conference—any writers' conference, I'm afraid—or subscribe to a writing publication or join a writers' association, you'll get on a mailing list. And, as is true in the rest of our society, if you're on one mailing list, you're on them all. Soon your mailbox will be filled with all sorts of announcements about conferences, seminars, courses, and books to order by mail. The problem won't be *finding* the conferences, but finding your checks and rejection slips among all of their circulars.

What if your problem isn't loneliness, but finding a little peace and quiet? Consider hiding out in a writers' colony.

These retreats may house from as few as four or five to as many as two or three dozen writers. At some you'll get a room, at others a cabin or a suite. Some provide communal meals, some box lunches, and others cooking facilities.

Residence at a colony is by application only. Approval may be conditioned on the amount of work you have published, the number of awards you have won, even the *kind* of project you are attempting— and, sometimes, your financial need. Getting into a writers' colony can be very much like applying to college all over again.

Like colleges that provide financial aid, there are colonies where, if you can't pay the rent, your residence is free. But don't figure on moving in permanently; most colonies allow only limited stays (from one to six months is the general range).

At some colonies, you can bring your family; others admit you and you alone—even your canary can't come along. The advantage of going, of course, is that you'll be writing in an area ostensibly as conducive to encouraging the muse as can be found (if, that is, *your* muse thrives in a rustic setting; most writers' retreats are out in the country). If you live alone and are between apartments, there might also be a financial advantage to hiding out at a colony for a while. But, of course, if you have responsibilities that tie you to the outside world, staying at a colony may merely mean that you have to conduct pressing business by phone, and the phone will not necessarily be in your quarters.

As is the case in any small community, you may find that you are distinctly at odds with the other residents. Still, if distractions at home are keeping you from finishing a project, and you don't need access to the New York Public Library on a daily basis for your research, a writers' colony may provide a much needed respite and just might result in a completed project or two.

Then again, if you need the pressure of other obligations to keep you creating, you could be better off staying home. Only you can be the judge of whether a writers' colony will work for you. Just don't burn your bridges by selling your home or subletting your apartment, and remember to bring along your ruby slippers for emergency exits.

Should you join a statewide or national writers' organization? That depends on whether the benefits outweigh the costs.

The benefits of joining a local press club, for example, can include reciprocal admission to the facilities of other press clubs—useful if you travel a lot to cities that have such facilities, useless if you do not. On the other hand, if you are a working journalist or are hoping to become one, you might want to join the press club just to be privy to the grapevine of job opportunities that may be opening.

Both the National Writers Club and the organizations that are part of the Cassell Network of Writers (Florida Freelance Writers Association, Georgia Freelance Writers Association, and Texas Freelance Writers Association) regularly provide up-to-date market information to their members. Groups like the Science Fiction Writers of America supply their members with specialized market lists.

Some groups, like the American Society of Journalists and Authors (ASJA) and the Authors Guild, have developed model contracts and may have enough clout to foster the adoption of at least part of those contracts as industry standard. Concerted lobbying efforts by these groups or the collective efforts of their members have resulted in changes in the laws affecting writers.

ASJA and the Society of American Travel Writers have established codes of ethics by which their members agree to abide. Membership in such a group can improve your credibility with an editor who doesn't know you, and may make the difference between getting or not getting a sensitive assignment.

Membership in some writers' associations makes you eligible for group insurance, an important consideration for self-employed freelancers who may not be able to obtain reasonably priced insurance any other way.

How "professional" a group is, and how much clout it has within the industry, depends to a degree on its membership standards. For some groups, "professional" membership may be predicated on having three announcements published in a church bulletin; for others, merely selling your novel to a risk publisher won't be enough—until it actually sees print, you will have to be satisfied with affiliate status. And while some groups are truly professional societies whose members elect officers and set policy, others are no more "clubs" than the Book-of-the-Month Club is.

Whichever is the case for an organization *you* are interested in, what may really discourage you from joining are the annual dues and initiation fees. Make certain that the association offers enough advantages to compensate you for these charges.

Formally organized associations often sponsor contests for published or unpublished writing. Often, these contests and the prizes for winning them are funded by the entry fees. And sometimes the standards by which the entrants are judged are downright embarrassing. If you enter such a contest without prior knowledge of the type of work it supports, you may spend the rest of your career hoping no one finds out that you won. (Even though a prize is a prize and a credential is a credential, do you really want to tell anyone you won second prize for an unpublished article in the Chowderville County Writer's Club contest?)

Generally, the smaller and more obscure the group, the higher the fee for entering their competition. Applications for grants from the National Endowment for the Arts are free, while some poetry contests can cost as much as $10 per entry. Incidentally, some poetry "contests" serve as blinds for subsidy presses; everyone willing to pay the entry fee wins, but what you win is the publication of your poem, and the right to purchase the overpriced book in which it will appear. (I once came across one of these that added insult to injury by insisting on an all-rights assignment as a condition of the publication the author had "won.")

So what about legitimate grants and fellowships? How do you get your hands on that money?

Some of the really big ones, like the MacArthur "genius" grants, find you, you don't find them. Others can only be won if submitted by your publisher; still others require the author to apply.

Some awards, like the Pulitzer and Sidney Hillman prizes, are given for published work. Others, like the Writers of the Future Contest and the Nelson Algren Awards, are for unpublished works. Grants are usually awarded for works in progress.

Some prizes are given only to never-before-published authors; others require you to establish your professional status by submitting an entire string of published works, and may even require that the submitted works be published within the last five or ten years (no sitting on your laurels if you want one of these).

Awards are also awarded by category: children's book, medical reporting, or investigative reporting, for example. And switching fields is not encouraged—if you want a National Endowment for the Arts grant for a fiction work in progress, for example, you have to establish your eligibility with proof that you have already published a substantial amount of fiction; journalists need not apply.

Sometimes the terminology on the application is murky. Is it enough to *come* from the state or region sponsoring a regional award, or do you have to reside there? Can you live outside and have written about that region? Or do you have to be a resident *and* have written about the area?

The contest committee of one state arts board whose briefing I once attended suggested that you should talk with the administrator of any grant before applying to obtain helpful hints on what kinds of references and résumés are taken most seriously. Sometimes it also helps to take a look at the work of recent winners; however, if the jury changes annually, there may be a vast difference in criteria used in judging. This is a good reason to reapply the next time the award is offered, although it may be embarrassing to go back to the people who wrote your recommendations and ask them to write another letter *this* year. (Some grants, like those from the Alicia Patterson Foundation, require as many as *four* letters of recommendation!)

The more prestigious grants *always* require that qualifying publication be by risk publishers; local groups making awards may be willing to consider self-published works.

For the most complete and up-to-date information about contests, fellowships, and grants, check the annual listings in *Literary Marketplace* or a biannual book called *Grants and Awards Available to American Writers* published by PEN American Center. Then write to the sponsoring organization itself for application blanks and informational materials.

Because book royalties are based on the number of books sold, authors have a vested interest in promoting those sales. This is why you see them on TV talk shows, hear them on call-in radio programs, and meet them at signing parties. When your income is based on as little as twenty-one cents a book (6 percent of a $3.50 paperback), you need to sell volumes of volumes to put bread on the table.

Promotion becomes the name of the game. And because you can't count on your publisher's overworked publicity department to push every book by every author every day, the best way to make sure *your* book doesn't fall through the cracks is to take on the task of promoting it yourself.

So important is promotion that some writers even hire publicists at their own expense to help them with the task. A good publicist can set up press interviews (more likely to be read than book reviews) and speaking engagements, and may even get you on talk shows. But if you're really a shrinking violet and don't feel you could possibly remain coherent in the presence of Oprah or Sally or Phil (not to mention Johnny, Pat, or Arsenio), there are still a number of ways you can promote your book without leaving the safe haven of your home.

One of the best ways to help sales is to get your book into the hands of receptive reviewers. You can and should supply your publisher with a list of people (beyond the usual book review editors who will already be covered) who should receive copies—the book review editors of your local papers, the editor of your college alumni magazine, and anyone else you think might be likely to mention the book in print.

Another example: if your publisher supplies you with book jackets or covers (paperback publishers frequently send you dozens of them), you can trim them to postcard size and mail them to all the people on your Christmas card list. (But save one to frame and hang in your office or living room.)

If your book is a paperback, you can phone the distributor who supplies paperbacks to newsstands and grocery stores in your area and let it be known that you are a local author. Thus alerted, the distributor may order extra copies of your book, make sure that they have a prominent position on sales racks, and leave them there for longer than the usual three weeks of a paperback's shelf-life.

Sometimes a distributor goes even further in promoting a local book. To each copy of *Birthrights,* a novel about a brewing dynasty by Milwaukee authors Vicky Hinshaw and Reva Shovers (writing as Summit Wahl), the local distributor affixed a blue-and-white sticker that read, "*Birthrights* was brewed in Milwaukee."

You should also contact local bookstores to alert them to the fact that you live in the area and your book is about to be published. But be forewarned—they are likely to offer you the chance for a signing party.

Even the shyest author would do well not to balk at the suggestion of an autograph party, because all you really need to do is scribble your name in each volume as it's presented to you. This can be very heady, especially when a lot of people show up. It's even better when someone stops by who has actually read your book, loves it, and remembers details! Even authors who suffer from terminal shyness can become addicted to that kind of experience.

Of course, it can also be very embarrassing when the only person who comes up to you merely wants directions to the men's room. Still, there is nothing like sitting at a table in a bookstore with a stack of your books in front of you to make you feel that you really *are* a writer. Now that you know some of the secrets of breaking into print yourself, maybe it'll be *your* turn to do just that someday soon.

Selected List of Writers' Organizations

American Society of Journalists and Authors, Inc.
1501 Broadway, Suite 1907
New York, N.Y. 10036
(Tel. 212-997-0947)

Founded in 1948, the ASJA has over 700 members engaged in the field of nonfiction writing. It provides them with a monthly newsletter, a referral service, a directory, a loan fund, and a code of ethics, makes annual awards, and holds regular regional gatherings and an annual conference.

Members must have been engaged in freelance writing, either part-time or full-time, on a regular basis for at least two years; staff-written material, fiction, drama, and poetry do not qualify a writer for membership in ASJA. Proof that your work has been published in book form, or in magazines or daily newspapers with substantial circulation, along with two letters of recommendation (at least one of which must be from an editor for whom you have written) and a nonrefundable $10 fee are required in order to apply for membership. If you are accepted, there is an initiation fee of $50; ASJA's annual dues are $120 per calendar year.

The Authors Guild, Inc.
330 West 42nd Street
New York, N.Y. 10036–3988
(Tel. 212-563-5904)

Founded in 1921, the Authors Guild has over 6500 members who, with the members of its sister organization, the Dramatists Guild, make up the

15,000-member Authors League of America. The Authors Guild exists to serve the professional interests of authors, and to that end provides regular symposia (the transcripts of which are published in the quarterly *Authors Guild Bulletin*), model trade book contracts, and publications like the 35-page pamphlet *Your Book Contract*. It engages in lobbying for matters of interest to writers such as copyright and tax, and files amicus briefs in cases which may affect those laws. The Authors Guild also provides access to group insurance for its members, and the Authors League provides an emergency loan fund for members who qualify.

Requirements for membership are the publication of either a book from an established American publisher within seven years prior to your application or three works of fiction or nonfiction in magazines of general circulation within eighteen months prior to your application. The membership committee can grant exceptions to those who do not meet these precisely defined requirements.

There is a sliding scale, based on income, for the annual dues: members earning less than $25,000 per year from writing pay $90, which can be paid in two installments; dues rise incrementally to $500 for members earning over $100,000 a year from writing endeavors.

Mystery Writers of America, Inc.
236 West 27th Street, Room 600
New York, N.Y. 10001
(Tel. 212-255-7005)

This organization exists to promote and protect the interests and welfare of mystery writers. It maintains a national office in New York City, has a permanent grievance committee, monitors concerns such as tax and legislation, and communicates with its members through its monthly publication, *The Third Degree*. It offers courses and workshops and holds an annual Edgar Allan Poe Awards dinner (at which the "Edgars" for best mysteries are awarded).

Active members must have published fiction or nonfiction in the crime, mystery, or suspense fields; allied professionals, such as agents and editors, qualify as associate members; writers of crime, mystery, or suspense works whose work has not yet been professionally published qualify as affiliate members; and writers qualifying for active membership who live outside the U.S. are designated as corresponding members.

The annual dues are $50 per year for all categories except for corresponding members based outside the United States, who pay $25.

National Writers Union
13 Astor Place
New York, N.Y. 10003
(Tel. 212-254-0279)

Founded in 1983, this union is devoted to working through "united action" to secure "just practices" for its members. It currently has approximately 2500 members, for whom it provides grievance procedures, collective bargaining, peer counseling with regard to contracts and agents, an agent database, a model magazine contract, and a code of professional ethics. The union also makes available group health insurance, a Visa card, and a quarterly publication, *American Writer.*

To qualify for membership, you must have published a book, a play, three articles, five poems, one short story, or an equivalent amount of other copy; however, if you have written an equal amount of unpublished material and are actively writing and attempting to publish your work, you may also qualify.

Annual dues are $50 if you earn under $5000 per year from writing, $85 if you earn between $5000 and $25,000, and $120 for those earning over $25,000. The dues may be paid in two installments.

PEN American Center
568 Broadway
New York, N.Y. 10012
(Tel. 212-334-1660)

PEN American Center in New York is the largest of the ninety-two centers which comprise International PEN, which was founded in 1921 in London "to foster understanding among men and women of letters in all countries." PEN American Center has branch offices in Boston, Houston, Chicago, and San Francisco, in addition to the PEN/Faulkner Foundation, located in Washington, D.C., which administers the PEN/Faulkner Award for Fiction.

The 2400 U.S. members of PEN make up almost a quarter of the international PEN membership. PEN sponsors public literary events, conferences, international congresses, and literary awards, as well as international human rights campaigns on behalf of writers, editors, and journalists who are censored or imprisoned. It also provides financial assistance to writers in need. PEN members can obtain group medical insurance and receive the quarterly *PEN Newsletter.*

To qualify for membership, an applicant must have published two or more books of a literary character, or one book generally acclaimed to be of exceptional distinction; editors, translators, and playwrights may also qualify if they have demonstrated "excellence in their profession." In addition to proof of publication, there is a requirement of two references, preferably PEN members; those who do not qualify as PEN members can join Friends of PEN, an affiliated group with its own benefits including invitations to PEN events.

The annual dues for PEN membership are $60.

Poets & Writers, Inc.
72 Spring Street, Room 301
New York, N.Y. 10012
(Tel. 212-226-3586)

Poets & Writers, Inc., is not a membership organization. It is, essentially, an information service, providing lists of writers, writers' conferences, and resources. Anyone may use its services or purchase its publications, which include its directory of poets and writers and the bimonthly *Poets & Writers Magazine.*

However, if you want to be included in its directory or on its lists, your poetry or fiction must have appeared in at least three publications, or you must have published a novel or a collection of short stories or poetry; a performance poet whose work has been performed on at least three occasions may also qualify. There is a onetime application fee of $5.

Poets & Writers, Inc., also sponsors workshop programs in which writers are paid to read from their works in New York and California. It also sponsors a national Writers Exchange program in which emerging writers selected on a competitive basis have an opportunity to meet with publishers, editors, and established authors.

Romance Writers of America
13700 Veterans Memorial Drive, Suite 315
Houston, Tex. 77014
(Tel. 713-440-6885)

Members of the Romance Writers of America can avail themselves of reduced rates for the annual RWA conference and receive the bimonthly *Romance Writers' Report,* which contains book reviews, interviews, and market information. The RWA and its many local chapters sponsor many contests and, in addition, the RWA's Professional Relations Committee will arbitrate members' disputes with editors, agents, and other writers.

To qualify for membership, you need only have an interest in romance writing; however, members must abide by RWA ethics and standards.

The RWA's application or reinstatement fee is $10, and its annual dues are $45. There is a $10 surcharge for members outside the United States.

Science Fiction Writers of America
Post Office Box 4236
West Columbia, S.C. 29171
(Tel. 803-791-5942)

Founded in 1965, SFWA has over 1000 members who write or edit in the broadly defined field of science fiction (which includes fantasy, horror, and speculative fiction, as well as alternate histories and alternate pasts).

SFWA members can avail themselves of a circulating book plan to keep up-to-date on the latest publications in this genre and a grievance committee which will act against publisher abuses. They can list themselves with a speakers bureau, exchange letters in the bimonthly *Forum,* and participate in the selection process for the annual Nebula awards. They also receive the quarterly *Bulletin of the Science Fiction Writers of America,* which contains market information, interviews and memorials, articles on writing, and my irregular column on "Writing and the Law."

Professional members must have published three short stories or one full-length book, either individually or in collaboration, or have three sales of poetry totaling 500 words or 100 lines. One professional sale is sufficient for affiliate membership, which is also open to allied professionals such as agents, editors, and publishers. All sales must be in professional publications, and must fall within the science fiction genre.

There is a onetime installation fee of $10, and annual dues are currently $56 for active members and $39 for affiliates. However, dues are subject to increase with inflation; members who can afford it can avoid such increases by purchasing a life membership for approximately ten times the current annual dues.

Society of American Travel Writers
1155 Connecticut Avenue, Suite 500
Washington, D.C. 20036
(Tel. 202-429-6639)

This elite organization was founded in 1956, and currently numbers approximately 850 members in five regional chapters. Membership is by invitation only. Applicants must be salaried or have steady involvement in the field of travel writing, must be "well-regarded in the field," and must be sponsored by two current members of the organization.

Because the SATW's stated purpose is the promotion of unbiased, objective reporting on travel topics, its members are required to abide by a code of ethics and professional standards that may restrict the invitations and services they can accept. This is necessary because, as a result of their listing in the SATW directory, they receive frequent promotional offers of travel, meals, and accommodations.

The SATW provides its members with a job referral service, a registry of press trips, a travel photo sourcebook, and insurance packages. Scholarships and awards are also available, *The Travel Writer* is published ten times a year, and there is an annual convention at which the Phoenix Awards are made.

The SATW requires a $35 fee with applications for membership. Once accepted, active members pay a $200 initiation fee, associate members (writers engaged in public relations within the travel industry who satisfy the membership committee that they are "well-regarded in the field") $400. The annual SATW dues are $100 for active members and $200 for associate members.

Western Writers of America
Fairgrounds
1753 Victoria
Sheridan, Wyo. 82801
(Tel. 301-672-2079)

The approximately 580 members of the Western Writers of America pay annual dues of $60 for an affiliation that includes *The Roundup Quarterly* and newsletter (also called *The Roundup*); the right to attend the WWA's annual convention; and a voice in the annual Spur Awards.

Requirements for membership in WWA are strict: three or more books, at least one of which pertains to the American West, published by a risk publisher; thirty or more short stories or articles (or a combination of the two) in nationally distributed periodicals, at least five of which must be about the West; ten or more original teleplays that have been produced and presented, at least five of which are western in character; or three or more produced and presented screenplays, at least one of which is a western. The criteria for associate members are only slightly less rigid; even for associate membership, publication is required.

Writers Guild of America East
555 West 57th Street
New York, N.Y. 10019
(Tel. 212-245-6180)

Writers Guild of America West
8955 Beverly Boulevard
Los Angeles, Calif. 90048
(Tel. 213-550-1000)

The WGA is a labor union representing those who write for motion pictures, television, and radio. There are two corporations, one on each coast, but membership in either of these organizations carries the same benefits and privileges. The WGA industry-wide agreements cover minimum fees, screen credits, arbitration of disputes, rights in material, and pension and health funds. To write for any studio, network, or producer that has signed the WGA agreements, you must join the union following your first qualifying sale.

There is an initiation fee of $1000 for new members once they have qualified by having a minimum number of sales (the number varies depending on the length of the material and the medium for which it was written) to WGA-signatory producers. Basic dues are $50 per year, paid in quarterly installments, plus an assessment of 1.75 percent of earnings from writing sales in the three media in which the WGA has jurisdiction.

WGA also provides a script and treatment registration service and a list of agents who have agreed to abide by the WGA representation agreements. These two services are available to nonmembers, but at a slightly higher price than members pay.

A Guide to Writers' Jargon

Advance. Money paid up front to a writer against royalties before they are actually earned. The advance must be *earned out* before any royalties will be paid. (See chapters 6 and 13.)

All rights. All the rights that an author has in a work; when you make an all-rights assignment, you are in essence selling your copyright. (See chapters 6 and 11.)

Bio. A short note about the author which accompanies a published work; also, a biographical statement submitted to a publisher when seeking an assignment or contract.

Byline. The listing of an author's name that appears on a published work.

Clip. A copy or photocopy of a published piece, usually submitted as proof that you have been published or as a sample of your writing style.

Contributor's copies. Free copies of a publication in which your work appears.

Copyedit. To edit a work for consistency or style. (See chapter 18.)

Copyright. The "bundle of rights" that an author has in his or her work. (See chapter 11.)

Derivative work. A work based on another work; derivative works include expanded versions of the original work, interpretations for other media (such as movie versions of a novel), and other works based on characters or settings in the original work (such as prequels, sequels, or other stories in the same series).

Header. A line across the top of each manuscript page that includes the author's name, a "slug" (q.v.) indicating the subject of the article, and the page number. (See chapter 7.)

Kill fee. A fee paid for an assigned article when, after it has been submitted, the publication declines to publish it. (See chapter 8.)

Lead. The first sentence or first paragraph of a work. (See chapters 15 and 16.)

On acceptance. Payment made when a manuscript is accepted by the publisher.

On assignment. Writing an article on contracted terms to a publisher's specifications. (See chapter 8.)

On signing. An advance for a book paid when the contract is signed.

On spec. Short for "on speculation"; writing something for a specific market with no guarantee that it will be accepted by the publisher.

Partial. An incomplete novel, submitted to a publisher in the hope of obtaining a contract to complete it. (See chapter 9.)

Proposal. An outline for a nonfiction book which is submitted to a publisher, with accompanying materials, in the hope of obtaining a contract to complete the book. (See chapter 9.)

Proofread. To edit a work for spelling and punctuation errors. (See chapter 18.)

Pseudonym. A *nom de plume,* or pen name, used instead of your real name in your byline.

Query. A letter written to an editor in the hope of eliciting an assignment. (See chapter 8.)

Reprint rights. The right to publish a work after its first publication. (See chapters 6, 11, and 13.)

Risk publisher. A publisher who pays you, and hence absorbs the risk involved in the publication of your work. (See chapter 9.)

Royalty. The percentage of each book's sale that is paid to the author. (See chapters 6 and 13.)

SASE. Self-addressed stamped envelope. This should accompany all queries and unsolicited submissions if you want to ensure a response.

Serial rights. The right to publish a work in one or more periodicals.

Sidebar. A shorter article, list, or chart that accompanies a published article; an author can often earn extra money for a sidebar.

Slug. A catchword or phrase used in the header to identify an article.

Sub or *subsidiary rights.* Derivative rights in a work; these rights are usually allocated between author and publisher by contract. (See chapter 13.)

Subsidy press. A publisher you pay to publish your book, hence subsidizing the publication. Sometimes also known as a "vanity press." (See chapter 9.)

Syndication. The sale of simultaneous publication rights to noncompeting publications. (See chapter 6.)

Tear sheet. A copy of a published article, used as a sample of an author's work.

Vanity press. A publisher you pay to publish your book, thus feeding your vanity. Sometimes also known as a "subsidy press." (See chapter 9.)

Work for hire (also termed "work made for hire"). A legal device whereby the hiring or commissioning party is deemed to own all the rights in a work. (See chapter 11.)

Selected Bibliography

BOOKS

Burack, Sylvia K., ed. *The Writer's Handbook*. Boston: The Writer, 1989.

Brohaugh, William. *Professional Etiquette for Writers*. Cincinnati: Writer's Digest Books, 1986.

Buchman, Dian Dincin, and Groves, Seli. *The Writer's Digest Guide to Manuscript Formats*. Cincinnati: Writer's Digest Books, 1987.

Evans, Glen, ed. *The Complete Guide to Writing Nonfiction*. New York: Harper and Row, 1983.

Grants and Awards Available to American Writers. New York: PEN American Center, 1990. (This is the 16th edition, dealing with 1990 and 1991. For further information, contact PEN American Center, 568 Broadway, New York, N.Y. 10012.)

The Guide to Writers' Conferences. Coral Gables, Fla.: Shaw Associates, 1989. (A new edition of this book is published annually; it may not be available in all bookstores. For information, contact the publisher at 625 Biltmore Way, Coral Gables, Fla. 33134.)

Kozak, Ellen M. *Every Writer's Guide to Copyright and Publishing Law*. New York: Henry Holt, 1990.

Larson, Michael. *How to Write a Book Proposal*. Cincinnati: Writer's Digest Books, 1985.

Leiper, Esther M. *How to Enter Poetry Contests to Win*. Alexandria, Minn.: Inkling Publications, 1984.

Neff, Glenda Tennant, ed. *Writer's Market.* Cincinnati: Writer's Digest Books, 1989. (A new edition of this book is published annually.)

Root, Wells. *Writing the Script: A Practical Guide for Films and Television.* New York: Holt, Rinehart and Winston, 1979.

Straczynski, J. Michael. *The Complete Book of Scriptwriting.* Cincinnati: Writer's Digest Books, 1982.

PERIODICALS

Freelance Writer's Report, Florida Freelance Writers Association (FFWA), Cassell Communications, Inc., Post Office Box 9844, Ft. Lauderdale, Fla. 33310 (a monthly market report available by subscription).

Writer's Digest, F & W Publications, Cincinnati (available at newsstands or by subscription).

Index